DATE DUE

AP 27 '09			

POLITICAL PROTEST
AND
STREET ART

Recent Titles in
Contributions to the Study of Mass Media and Communications

POLITICAL PROTEST AND STREET ART

Popular Tools for Democratization in Hispanic Countries

LYMAN G. CHAFFEE

Contributions to the Study of Mass Media and Communications,
Number 40

Bernard K. Johnpoll, *Series Adviser*

Greenwood Press
WESTPORT, CONNECTICUT • LONDON

Library of Congress Cataloging-in-Publication Data

Chaffee, Lyman G.
    Political protest and street art : popular tools for
democratization in Hispanic countries / Lyman G. Chaffee.
        p.   cm. — (Contributions to the study of mass media and
communications, ISSN 0732-4456 ; no. 40)
    Includes bibliographical references and index.
    ISBN 0-313-28808-9 (alk. paper)
    1. Street art—Spain—History—20th century.   2. Street art—South
America—History—20th century.   3. Politics in art.   I. Title.
II. Series.
    N8236.P5C53   1993
    751.7'3'09460904—dc20   92-45084

British Library Cataloguing in Publication Data is available.

Library of Congress Catalog Card Number: 92-45084
ISBN: 0-313-28808-9
ISSN: 0732-4456

First published in 1993

Greenwood Press, 88 Post Road West, Westport, CT 06881
An imprint of Greenwood Publishing Group, Inc.

Printed in the United States of America

The paper used in this book complies with the
Permanent Paper Standard issued by the National
Information Standards Organization (Z39.48-1984).

10 9 8 7 6 5 4 3 2 1

Copyright Acknowledgments

The author and publisher are grateful for permission to use excerpts from the following:

Lyman G. Chaffee, "Political Graffiti and Wall Painting in Greater Buenos Aires: An Alternative Communication System," *Studies in Latin American Popular Culture* 8 (1989):37–60; and Lyman G. Chaffee, "Poster Art and Political Propaganda in Argentina," *Studies in Latin American Popular Culture* 6 (1986):78–89.

Lyman G. Chaffee, "Public Art and Political Propaganda: Argentine Protest, 1986," *Ibero Americana* 18 (2) (1988):79–100.

Lyman G. Chaffee, "Social Conflict and Alternative Mass Communications: Public Art and Politics in the Service of Spanish-Basque Nationalism," *European Journal of Political Research* 16 (5) (September 1988):545–572. Reprinted by permission of Kluwer Academic Publishers.

To my parents,
Elene Chaffee-Loebbecke
and the late Wilber A. Chaffee

Contents

Acknowledgments

This research grew out of an interest that developed through educational and field research trips to South America and Spain over the past thirty years: study-abroad programs, dissertation research, summer field research each year, sabbatical leaves, and a year at the University of Madrid. Throughout these years, first as a student at the University of Madrid during the Franco period, and later while doing dissertation research in Argentina during the Onganía dictatorship, I became fascinated by the political street art propaganda placed on public walls. I began to record these images mentally and by taking notes and photographs. This study developed from those experiences.

First, I would like to acknowledge an intellectual debt to Alberto Ciria. When I was a graduate student, he helped to direct my interest toward Argentina, where the work on this project began. His writings on Argentine popular culture have been an inspiration. A second debt goes to Harold Gresham, who first encouraged me to study in Spain many years ago. My brother Wilber, who shares my interest in Latin America, provided intellectual stimulation through many conversations. He kindly read and provided comments on the manuscript. George Heneghan read sections of the manuscript. Wayne Martin read the whole text and provided over the years an intellectual exchange based on a shared interest in Spanish politics and culture. A debt is owed to Anne Fitzgerald for editorial work and comments on the manuscript. My family over the years encouraged me in my intellectual interests regarding international study and tolerated my long periods of absence.

Elizabeth Mahan gave much needed early encouragement and commentary to the project. Donald Castro organized a number of professional panels on popular culture that provided me with an opportunity to present segments of this project professionally. I am grateful to Charles Tatum and Harold Hinds, co-editors of *Studies in Latin American Popular Culture,* for providing a forum for Latin American popular culture. They encouraged this research by publishing several of my articles on this subject. Partial funding came from the California State University Dominguez Hills Foundation, from Faculty Development Funds, and from the School of Social and Behavioral Sciences. The Office of International Programs of California State University provided the opportunity to spend a year at the University of Madrid, 1987–1988.

Abbreviations

AAA	Alianza de Acción Anticomunista (Anti-Communist Action Alliance)
AHI	Agrupación Herreña Independiente (Herreña Independent Group)
AIC	Agrupaciones de Independientes Canarios (Canaries Independent Group)
AIT	Asociación Internacional de Trabajadores (International Workers' Association)
ANC	African National Congress
AP	Alianza Popular (Popular Alliance)
ARENA	Aliança Renovadora Nacional (National Renovating Alliance)
ASK	Comites Abertzales Socialistas (Patriotic Socialist Committees)
BB AA	Bases Autónomas (Autonomous Bases)
BNG	Bloque Nacionalista Galego (Galician Nationalist Bloc)
CAV	Comunidad Autónoma Vasca (Basque Autonomous Community)
CEB	Ecclesial Base Communities
CEDA	Confederación Española de Derechas Autónomas (Spanish Confederation of the Autonomous Right)
CEDADE	Círculo Español de Amigos de Europa (Circle of Spanish Friends of Europe)
CG	Coalición Galega (Galician Coalition)
CGT	Central Geral dos Trabalhadores (General Confederation of Labor)
CGT	Confederación General del Trabajo (General Confederation of Labor)
CiU	Convergencia i Unió (Convergence and Union)
CNOP	Coordenadora Nacional de Organizacios pola Paz (National Coordinating Organizations for Peace)

CNT	Confederación Nacional del Trabajo (National Confederation of Labor)
CONTAG	Confederação dos Trabalhadores de Agricultura (Confederation of Agricultural Workers)
CP	Coalición Popular (Popular Coalition)
CSC	Corriente Sindical Clasista (Classist Union)
CSCA	Comité de Solidaridad Centro América (Central American Solidarity Committee)
CSPC	Comités de Solidaritat amb els Patriotes Catalans (Committees for Solidarity with Catalán Patriots)
CUT	Central Unica dos Trabalhadores (Unitary Confederation of Workers)
EA	Eusko Alkartasuna (Basque Solidarity)
EAB	Emakume Aberatzale Batzar (Women's Patriotic Association)
EC	European Community
EE	Euskadiko Ezkerra (Basque Left)
EGI	Euzko Gastedi del Interior (Basque Youth)
EGPGC	Exército Guerrilleiro do Pobo Galego Ceibe (Armed Soldiers of the Galician Celtic People)
EIA	Euskal Iraultzale Alderdia (Basque Revolutionary Party)
ERC	Esquerra Republicana de Catalunya (Catalán Republican Left)
ERP	Ejército Revolucionario del Pueblo (People's Revolutionary Army)
ETA	Euzkadi ta Askatasuna (Basque Homeland and Liberty)
EU	Extremadura Unida (Extremadura United)
FAI	Federación Anarquista Ibérica (Iberian Anarchist Federation)
FAP	Fuerzas Armadas Peronistas (Peronist Armed Forces)
FAR	Fuerzas Armadas Revolucionarias (Revolutionary Armed Forces)
FIJI	Federación Ibérica de Juventudes (Iberian Federation of Libertarian Youth)
FMLN	Frente Farabundo Marti para la Liberación Nacional (Farabundo Martí National Liberation Front)
FN	Frente Nacional (National Front)
FNV	Frente Nacional Vasco (Basque National Front)
FPG	Frente Popular Galega (Galician Popular Front)
GAL	Grupos Antiterroristas de Liberación (Anti-Terrorist Groups of Liberation)
GAS	Grupo Armenio Suicioa (Armenian Suicide Group)
GRAPO	Grupos de Resistencia Antifascista Primero de Octubre (Anti-Fascist Resistance Groups October 1)
HAMAS	Islamic Resistance Movement
HB	Herri Batasuna (Popular Unity)
IC	Iniciativa per Catalunya (Initiative for Catalonia)

IMF	International Monetary Fund
IU	Izquierda Unida (United Left)
IU-CA	Izquierda Unida-Convocatoria por Andalucía (United Left-Convocation for Andalusia)
JONS	Juntas de Ofensiva Nacional-Sindicalista (National Syndicalist of Junta Offensives)
JUGA	Juntas Galegas pola Amnistia (Galician Juntas for Amnesty)
KAS	Koordinadora Abertzale Sozialista (Patriotic Socialist Coordinating Council)
LAB	Langile Abertzale Batzordea (Patriotic Workers' Councils)
LAK	Langile Abertzale Komiteak (Patriotic Workers' Committee)
LCR-LKI	Liga Comunista Revolucionaria-Langileria Komunista Iraultzailea (Revolutionary Communist League)
MAS	Movimiento al Socialismo (Movement to Socialism)
MCA	Movimiento Comunista Andalucía (Andalucian Communist Movement)
MCC	Movimiento Comunista de Catalonia (Catalán Communist Movement)
MCE-EMK	Movimiento Comunista de España-Euskadiko Mugimendua Komunista (Spanish Communist Movement)
MCG	Movimento Comunista Galego (Galician Communist Movement)
MDB	Movimiento Democrático Brasileiro (Brazilian Democratic Movement)
MDT	Moviment de Defensa de la Terra (Movement in Defense of the Homeland)
MDT-IPC	Moviment de Defensa de la Terra-Independentistes del Paisos Catalans (Movement in Defense of the Homeland-Independents of the Catalán Country)
MDT-PSAN	Moviment de Defensa de la Terra-Partit Socialista d'Alliberament Nacional (Movement in Defense of the Homeland-Socialist Party of National Liberation)
MOC	Movimiento de Objetores de Conciencia (Conscientious Objectors Movement)
MPT	Movimiento Todos por la Patria (All for the Homeland Movement)
NATO	North Atlantic Treaty Organization
NPA	New People's Army
OJL	Organizacão da Juventud pela Liberdade (Organization of Youth for Liberty)
PA	Partido Andalucista (Andalusian Party)
PANCAL	Partido Nacionalista de Castilla y León (Nationalist Party of Castile and León
PAR	Partido Aragones Regional (Aragonese Regional Party)
PC	Partido Castellano (Castilian Party)

PCA	Partido Comunista de Andalucía (Andalusian Communist Party)
PCB	Partido Comunista Brasileiro (Brazilian Communist Party)
PCC	Partit dels Comunistes de Catalunya (Catalunya Communist Party)
PC do B	Partido Comunista do Brasil (Communist Party of Brazil)
PCE	Partido Comunista de España (Spanish Communist Party)
PCLN	Partido Comunista de Liberación Nacional (Spanish Party of National Liberation)
PCPA	Partido Comunista del Pueblo Andaluz (Andaluz People's Communist Party)
PCPE	Partido Comunista de los Pueblos de España (Spanish People's Communist Party)
PCPG	Partido Comunista del Pueblo Gallego (Galician People's Communist Party)
PDC	Partido Democrático Cristão (Christian Democratic Party)
PDS	Partido Democratica Social (Democratic Social Party)
PDT	Partido Democrático Trabalhista (Democratic Labor Party)
PI	Partido Intransigente (Intransigent Party)
PL	Partido Liberal (Liberal Party)
PLO	Palestine Liberation Organization
PMDB	Partido Movimento Democrático Brasileiro (Brazilian Democratic Movement Party)
PND	Partido Nacionalista Democrático (Democratic Nationalist Party)
PNG	Partido Nacionalista Galego (Galician Nationalist Party)
PNV-EAJ	Partido Nacionalista Vasco-Eusko Alderdi Jeltzalea (Basque Nationalist Party)
PO	Partido Obrero (Workers' Party)
POUM	Partido Obrero de Unificación Marxista (Workers' Party of Marxist Unity)
PP	Partido Popular (Popular Party)
PPD	Partido por la Democracia (Party for Democracy)
PRC	Partido Regionalista Cantabria (Cantabria Regionalist Party)
PREPAL	Partido Regionalista del País Leones (Regional Party of León Country)
PRIM	Partido Regionalista Independiente de Madrid (Independent Regionalist Party of Madrid)
PRN	Partido de Reconstrução Nacional (National Reconstruction Party)
PRP	Partido Riojano Progresista (Riojan Progressive Party)
PSB	Partido Socialista Brasileiro (Brazilian Socialist Party)
PSDB	Partido Social Democrático Brasileiro (Brazilian Social Democratic Party)
PSG-EG	Partido Socialista Galego-Esquerda Galega (Galician Socialist Party)
PSOE	Partido Socialista Obrero Español (Spanish Socialist Workers' Party)

PST	Partido Socialista de los Trabajadores (Workers' Socialist Party)
PSUC	Partit Socialista Unificat de Catalunya (Catalán United Socialist Party)
PT	Partido dos Trabalhadores (Workers' Party)
PTB	Partido Trabalhista Brasileiro (Brazilian Labor Party)
PTE	Partido de los Trabajadores de España (Spanish Workers' Party)
SEU	Sindicato Español Universitario (University Student's Union)
TL	Terra Lliure (Free Homeland)
UC	Unión Coruñesa (Corunese Union)
UCD	Unión de Centro Democrático (Democratic Center Union)
UCE	Unificacíon Comunista de España (Spanish Communist Unification)
UCR	Unión Cívica Radical (Radical Civic Union)
UD	Unión Democrático (Democratic Union)
UDN	União Democrática Nacional (National Democratic Union)
UDR	União Democrática Ruralista (Rural Democratic Union)
UGT	Unión General de Trabajadores (General Workers' Union)
UJS	União da Juventud Socialista (Union of Socialist Youth)
UM	Unión Mallorquina (Mallorca Union)
UPM	Union del Pueblo Melillense (Union of Melilla Pueple)
UPN	Unión del Pueblo Navarro (Union of Navarran People)
UPV	Unitat del Poble Valencia (Union of Valencian People)
UV	Unió Valenciana (Valencia Union)

Part I

A COMPARATIVE ASSESSMENT

1

Street Art as Political Communication: An Overview

Communication is multifaceted; information can be transmitted through a variety of forms. Societies evolve communication systems that allow governments, organizations, and individuals to present their views, demands, needs, and ideas. Politically speaking, the context for communication depends upon historical and cultural circumstances and the type of political system.

This book is about the transmission of one form of low-technology, mass communication in an age of high technology. Today, the idea of mass communication is most often associated with high technology as exemplified in sophisticated electronic media. Through this communication, technology is supreme, and a mass culture results. This presupposes that the culture of mass communication is imposed from above by experts and technicians hired by capitalist interests or by the state with the control and flow of information from above down to the masses. The idea of mass communication should not be limited to major high technology and professionalism. There are other significant processes and cultural settings involved in the flow of political information that often, though not exclusively, originate from below by grass-roots groups. This is politicized street art or graphics.[1]

A major thesis of this study of street art is that in many countries—particularly in the Hispanic world, where street art is a traditional means of communication—it is utilized by a cross section of collectives and the state to inform and persuade. Because street art is universal in its reach, it should be viewed as a mass communication medium in a general sense. Yet despite its prevalence and importance, street art is often ignored and seldom researched as a mass communication. As one of numerous information sources, it should be viewed as one dimension of the multimedia, multiformat communication system. It gives expression to groups that otherwise could not comment upon or support current or perceived social problems. In the process it provides a popular record.

The term *street art* is utilized throughout this study as an organizing principle and for the purpose of defining and examining a particular form of expression. It is not given an all-inclusive definition, nor is the purpose to define art or argue whether such forms of graffiti are art. Neither does the study assess the aesthetic qualities of street art. The purpose is to focus upon those forms of street art most commonly and systematically employed by collectives and state interests as a communication device for informing and persuading. Included in this concept of street art are what I consider the most common forms utilized for political communication—posters, wallpaintings, graffiti, and murals. Additional auxiliary forms that could be incorporated would be political stickers, T-shirts, lapel buttons, billboards, placards, and banners, some of which are more individual than collective expressions. The emphasis in these pages is on the collective expressions. However, when auxiliary forms are illustrative of the sociopolitical struggle, these are referenced. Furthermore, the term *street art* is used in a collective sense, to group the various forms of street art as one medium of political expression.

A second point is that street art can shape and move human emotions and gauge political sentiments. Language and visual symbols help shape perception. Clichés, slogans, and symbols—the substance of political rhetoric—help mobilize people. Those who dominate political clichés maintain the edge. The concept of establishing political space by dominating clichés and symbols was used by the prodemocratic student movement in China in 1989. The regime had dominated the cliché, people's democracy. Student reformers seized this democratic cliché and used it to mobilize the citizenry and delegitimize the system. Street art's importance can be seen in repressive regimes where authoritarian systems attempt to reduce public space, including opposition street graphics. Street art breaks the conspiracy of silence. Like the press, one role of street art is to form social consciousness. In authoritarian systems where outlets for free expression are limited, it is one of the few gauges of political sentiment. In more open systems, street art enables various entities to lobby for their interests. Street art, in essence, connotes a decentralized, democratic form in which there is universal access, and the real control over messages comes from the social producers. It is a barometer that registers the spectrum of thinking, especially during democratic openings.

This study looks at the broad spectrum of social and political forces, however marginal some may be. It encompasses both a grass-roots and a state perspective, creating a popular social history. This is helpful in understanding the conflicts between the state and civil society and between collectives within society. Thus, in the unending process of social conflict and state formation, street art can be a tool for analyzing and describing that process. In essence, two dimensions make up this study: The first is the focus on the producer side, the articulated collective and state interests. Why, it may be asked, do certain groups, political parties, and even governments spend so much energy on this form of communication? What are the political demands raised, the ideas expressed, the interests represented, and the political discourse and conflicts revealed? As is revealed, the practitioners of this form of political expression cut across the ideological spectrum from left to right and include dominant and dominated groups. Even the most marginal groups are considered, for they reveal subcultures. Who is to say whether a particular marginal group or party is or will be significant or insignificant? Yesterday's marginal groups may be tomorrow's influential ones. This was dramatically illustrated in the sweeping political changes of the 1980s.

The second dimension is street art as a source for popular history and conflict. Here the case studies combine the use of street art by political interests with the process of how it reflects popular history. This approach is applied through case studies written from a popular history perspective.

FRAMING THE COMPARATIVE STUDY

This study assesses the relevance of the genre of street art as political expression in the Hispanic world by using a comparative historical, sociopolitical approach. Historical description of events and issues illustrate the context for the ideological and sociopolitical conflicts reflected in the street art, although there is not a continuous or systematic historical account.[7] Historically, the time frame is contemporary, with an emphasis on the most recent political concerns and conflicts reflected in the street art during the decade of the 1980s. While the focus is contemporary, the research reveals the continuity of this means of expression in the twentieth century, and demonstrates how historical memory is imprinted in the street art as visual popular history. Thus, ideological and political struggles prior to the 1980s are assessed to illustrate particular political systems. The sociopolitical context identifies and explains the multifarious groups, parties, and regimes involved in the process of the political struggle—their ideas, demands, visions, and alternative views—and describes how street art characterizes the social conflicts.

This work investigates how street art is exemplified in four Hispanic case studies—Spain, the Basque Country (Euskadi), Argentina, and Brazil. There is nothing exclusive about restricting this comparative analysis to these Hispanic countries, for the use of street art is universal. The Basque case is considered separately from Spain, because the former exemplifies a specific ethnic identity with unique sociopolitical and culture characteristics. These are forcefully reflected in the street art of the region. The Basque conflict stems from the cultural-political struggle occurring between Spain and its Basque region. This conflict has characteristics of a classic colonial struggle against a dominant state with all the implications of nationalism and cultural-political identity. The Basque's intense use of street art as a medium of expression and its symbolic sociopolitical and cultural resistance to Spanish hegemony are the justifications for considering the Basque case separately.

Each case entails recent experience with authoritarian rule, longer in duration in some cases than in others, although at the time of this writing none of the countries was under authoritarian rule. Each has experienced a democratic opening with accompanying elections. Beginning with the transition at Francisco Franco's death in 1975, Spain emerged from forty years of authoritarian rule to establish a vibrant democracy. Brazil began a formal democratic reopening in 1985 after twenty-one years of military rule, and Argentina began anew in 1983 one of its many periodical swings between democratic and authoritarian regimes. The Basque case is tied historically and politically to Spain.

The book's organization is as follows: An introductory chapter discusses general characteristics of street art as communication, followed by explanatory categories on what motivates one to utilize this medium. In this chapter, examples demonstrate the universality of this mass communication. The second chapter takes up the question of how this communication medium is effective. This is followed by the four case studies, each assessed separately. The concluding chapter assesses street art's continued utility.

The materials for this study came from primary field research data I have collected over the past twenty-five years. I have spent considerable time in each country since the 1960s and concentrated intensely on this subject during the 1980s. Secondary sources, including major political and historical works, supplement the primary field research data, providing the historical context and use of street art. In addition, I have collected numerous examples of how the print and electronic media have focused on issues articulated through street art.

FACTORS IN VISUAL IMPACT

Color and Design

Color and design affect visual impact. Collectives are very conscious of this fact in conveying their messages. Just as commercial advertisers are conscious of the use of color as a means of manipulating emotions, so are political action groups. The warm, vibrant colors—reds, oranges, yellows—generate a feeling of excitement. Reds and black are passionate colors, conveying emotions of revolution, death, and violence. The cool colors—blues and greens—indicate calm, reassurance, and the environment. White is symbolic of peace and purity. Variations in shade and intensity can be manipulated to evoke the somber, the amusing, the reassuring, or violent and shocking messages.[3] Within this context, political collectives adopt logos and colors to identify themselves and convey the emotional images they wish to impart. Nationalistic groups wrap themselves in national colors; revolutionary groups adopt combinations of reds, yellows, and blacks. Green parties attach themselves to calming, ecological hues, while human rights groups utilize white. Colors parallel image and message.

In addition to color, groups can intensify their messages through the shape and size of a design. Furthermore, with wallpaintings and murals producers ensure their messages stand out through background preparation utilizing white-wash and contrasting colors. A nonprepared background suffers visually. Impact is achieved also through redundancy. Political groups duplicate their messages by using many forms of expression. Clarity in design is critical. Making a message simple and easy to grasp is paramount. It must be brief, clear, and visible.

Positioning

Positioning, placing one's message in the most heavily trafficked or targeted areas, is important in considering visual impact.[4] Groups seem to have an innate understanding of how to maximize visibility to the greatest number of people. Key walls, buildings, fences, roads, highways, and embankments in cities or neighborhoods are sought after for maximum viewing. These coveted locations are usually on main streets and highways, along plazas and transportation depots, within the core business district, at educational facilities (especially universities), in working-class districts, and in manufacturing centers. In fact, there are few places that are off limits. In all cases in this study, posters and graffiti were plastered on sides of government buildings, on banks and commercial buildings, even on churches and national monuments. These characteristics, of course, pertain to open democratic systems; self-imposed restrictions are far greater under authoritarian regimes.

Street Art as Form

The poster's greatest asset is its mass duplication and, thus, visibility. One can disseminate a message by massively papering a city or town overnight. Posters are designed to be ephemeral, for quick consumption and short duration, not to constitute artistic treasures to be preserved. Murals are more complex in visual impact. Duration can extend from several days to several years, depending upon the political environment. For the most part, political murals are designed to be ephemeral, not permanent, unless produced under state sponsorship. They are produced quickly, inexpensively, and for an immediate purpose; they are meant not to decorate, or to effect artistic grandeur, but to inform and educate.

Political graffiti tend to be furtively placed in quick fashion with little artistic consideration. They are usually applied with aerosol spray paint, and the background surface is seldom prepared. Wallpainting, on the other hand, is not usually done with aerosol paint, and in most instances background preparation takes place. The wall or fence on which the message is to be placed is white-washed to provide the proper visual contrast. Wallpainting is executed in a much more deliberate form than graffiti; blocked-off lettering painted in a combination of color schemes is often used. In wallpainting, color is employed to reinforce and intensify the message. This is less often the case with graffiti.

CHARACTERISTICS OF STREET ART AS A MASS MEDIUM

What characterizes this mass medium? First, the process is *primarily collective*. Groups employ this communication channel to identify problems, question values, make claims, and suggest alternatives.[5] The process takes planning and organization. Based on the cases studied, about 80 percent of the street art had identifiable sponsorship. There was seldom a mystery as to sponsorship. This was characteristic of the street art under democratic regimes. Under authoritarian regimes where political space is reduced, the opposition displayed graffiti with greater anonymity due to fear of state retaliation. For instance, in Paraguay under Alfredo Stroessner, street art that was not government sponsored was mostly anonymous. However, in Chile, with its myriad leftist sectarian groups, there was a greater tendency toward group identification in street art, for groups sought recognition as the vanguard, and identification via street art was an important ingredient of that process. This was true for the ETA (Euzkadi ta Askatasuna) movement under Franco and for the Montoneros and the ERP (Ejército Revolucionario del Pueblo) in Argentina during the Juan Carlos Onganía military period of the early 1970s. Street art is not always group based. Individual expression often occurs during the catharsis following the demise of authoritarian regimes.

A second characteristic of street art is that it is a *partisan, nonneutral politicized medium*. It serves as an advocacy and reporting forum. Its social function runs from identification to announcement of events, to social commentary, to articulation of full political agendas, to presentation of visions. Thus, it is not normally presented as consensual.[6] In contrast to print and electronic journalism, in street art there is no compelling sense of aiming to be neutral or professional. However, street art does have a parallel with the print media. It often serves an opposition role—criticizing, probing, and commenting. Being partisan, street art makes no attempt to be neutral, value free, or impartial or to weigh the facts. Its purpose is to advance a cause or an idea. There are politically oriented murals commissioned for their aesthetic value; however, street art is generally a channel for partisan advocacy.

A third feature of street art is its *competitive, nonmonopolistic, democratic* character. It is accessible to all producers regardless of ideological perspective. It can be officially sanctioned, simply tolerated, or painted on the run as graffiti. By its nature, street art is an arena for the transitory display of ideas and images, a place where the ideas of minority and marginal groups can be expressed. There is greater ideological variation and visual representation in this medium than in most other media, even under authoritarian regimes. The greater the variety of groups represented in street art, the greater the spectrum of views that are articulated and seen. Since this medium is cost-effective, any collective can use it. Producers run the gamut from extreme right to extreme left. They include mainstream groups and parties as well as protest movements, violent groups, and newly emerging groups seeking to acquire political space. Such mainstream parties as the governing populist Peronist party of Argentina, the Socialist party of Spain, and the Colorado party of Paraguay utilize this medium as do the Basque nationalist parties and the terrorist organization ETA.

Fourth, street art is characterized by *direct expressive thought,* using an economy of words and ideas, and rhetorically simple discourse. Seldom are the messages ambiguous or obscure, as political cartoons tend to be. Street art is structured to simplify the message, synthesize thoughts and ideas, and project concise messages and clichés. The latter sets the tone for political debate by condensing an experience or ideology. Political groups need organizing concepts; they reduce sociopolitical reality to a small number of words, slogans, phrases, and labels for the public's comprehension. Those individuals and/or collectives that most effectively shape public understanding and determine the political discourse set the political agenda.[7]

Fifth, street art is a *highly adaptable medium;* its form changes to meet the conditions of the political system. In open, pluralistic societies, collectives vying for political space often utilize all forms to record their historical memory. However, in noncompetitive, authoritarian systems where government dominates public space, graffiti becomes the primary medium, posters, wallpaintings, and murals are more risky. Until the twilight of the Augusto Pinochet regime, the painting of murals ceased because of the high political risks. Leaflets supplemented the underground graffiti. At times they were displayed as wallposters. Themes also adapt to reflect pressing national problems. In an authoritarian system, political matters take precedent over social, cultural, and economic questions. The opposition's push is to resolve political questions first; their themes record a regime's sins. In a competitive system, once the transition questions are resolved, the street art begins to reflect an array of pressing problems—political, social, economic, or cultural in nature. These are recorded in posters, graffiti, wallpaintings, and murals.

MOTIVATING FACTORS/EXPLANATORY CATEGORIES

The following discussion is a suggestive assessment of the reasons motivating producers to utilize street art as communication. This section seeks to pursue why individuals, collectives, and governments use this less sophisticated, low-technology mode of communication as a form of expression. What compels them to place so much energy and importance on this medium? The reasons vary. In this section, I develop a number of suggestive categories for discussing this phenomenon. The categories are for explanatory purposes and are not necessarily mutually exclusive. Thus, the particular examples cited might well be placed in several explanatory categories.

The Catharsis/Protest Explanation

Military regimes have been an endemic problem in the Hispanic world. In Latin America, swings between authoritarian and democratic regimes are normal. Common to each case study is recent experience with authoritarian regimes and democratic openings. In regimes of particularly long or harsh authoritarian rule, an emotional catharsis often takes place immediately following its demise. The emotional rage and frustrations from repressive control and the inability to freely express oneself or to air one's grievances often produce an outpouring of slogans and sentiments from a broad spectrum of society. This creates a therapeutic catharsis that may last from weeks to several years in which both groups and individuals randomly indulge in expressive excess after years of suffering silence. It serves not only as a symbolic act of protest and defiance against fallen regimes but also to symbolize the regenerated values of democracy. This catharsis commemorates a political transformation and in the process creates a historical memory of events, happenings, emotions, and thinking. Graffiti is generally the preferred form of expression due to the ease with which it can be produced. In addition, individual expression blossoms after repression.

The cathartic process of visually imprinted street art greeted the sweeping revolutionary changes in Eastern Europe and in the Soviet Union in 1989. The streets of Prague were papered with both serious and funny slogans, the result of forty years of pent-up feelings.[8] In Romania, a similar process was readily visible; every fence and stairwell was utilized to air grievances from the revolution up to the national elections of May 1990.[9] A prolific outpouring of graffiti greeted the demise of the Spanish and Portuguese dictatorships in the mid-1970s. In Chile, the end of the Pinochet regime saw a resurgence in defiant murals, one of the most important symbols of the left. The Argentines, following the demise of military regimes in 1973 and in 1983, utilized graffiti and other street art as defiant gestures to military rule. In Paraguay, Brazil, and Uruguay, democratic transformations had an accompanying outburst of street art. The streets of Haiti exploded with graffiti after the fall of the Duvalier regime in 1986; a series of articles in the *Los Angeles Times* three months before had commented that the Haitian people were so apathetic that not even resistance graffiti were evident.[10]

The Street Culture/Receiver Explanation

There is a practical consideration on how best to reach and engage the public. An interesting study conducted in Spain corroborated that the Spanish are basically a street people. They spend their leisure time out of their homes, on the street. This study also found that 45 percent of the Spanish population never read print media.[11] If this premise were to be extended to Latin America and other places where there is a vibrant street culture, where the masses are out on the streets and in the parks and plazas where they engage friends and neighbors in conversion and social mingling, then a rational argument would suggest that one way to reach the populace is through street art. It would be logical that an important way to communicate politically with the masses is through street graphics. Furthermore, the street culture tradition is linked to political styles. The populist style in Latin American politics, applicable to Spain as well, dictates that politicians must engage people directly on the streets and in plazas. The phenomenon of reaching an audience via street graphics is not confined to the Latin world. Even in the United States, gangs and "taggers" employ graffiti to communicate and exchange messages. It is also seen in commercial advertising. The billboard industry claims exposure to an advertiser's message reaches 79 percent of the population in a city, that people see a billboard's message much more often than the same message on television, and that they can target an audience, something the electronic industry is less designed to do.[12]

The Cultural, Ethnic-Linguistic Identity Explanation

Ethnic and ethnic-linguistic identification and symbols often find strong expression through street art. It provides a vehicle for creating interest among subcultures striving for political recognition and rights under dominant cultures. Language and linguistic symbols can provide individuals with cues for new and meaningful identifications, redefining political discourse in relation to the dominant culture and helping create a force for micro-nationalism.[13] A vivid example presented in the case studies is the radical Basque nationalists spearheaded by ETA-HB (Herri Batasuna). They have been prolific producers of street art designed as a cultural-political expression of collective consciousness and are patterned to stimulate and diffuse the linguistic presence of the Basque language. The daily visibility of the Basque language through street art is one factor that helps create a reality for an indigenous language. The Basque experience stimulated other regional ethnic groups in Spain to combine street art and linguistic symbols. This phenomenon is especially strong among the Catalans and the Galicians. In each of these historical regions, nationalists have broadened interest in regional languages by writing slogans in the vernacular on town, city, and highway walls.

In Mexico, the revolutionary movement of 1920 forged a hybrid national identity between Hispanic and indigenous cultures. This found expression in the street art of the muralists. The muralists used the figure of the native Indian to symbolize the new Mexico. In addition, as part of the new identity, they used native names and words from the indigenous linguistic heritage to distinguish Mexican identity from the dominant Spanish culture. In Northern Ireland after World War II, one symbol of revived Irish nationalism was the rediscovery of language made more visual and conscious through graffiti and murals.[14] The nascent nationalistic movement in Wales headed by the Welsh Language

Society has pushed linguistic identity through a variety of means, one was graffiti written in the Welsh language throughout the countryside.[15] And in Korea during the decades of Japanese occupation, graffiti helped to keep alive the Korean language, the use of which was prohibited by the Japanese.[16]

The Marginalized Group, Alternative Media Explanation

Lacking access to the conventional media or the financial means to engage in high-technology propaganda, marginalized collectives are motivated to seek alternative means for achieving sociopolitical recognition and expression. In western democracies, many nascent grass-roots movements do not have access to the major media. For example, the Green movement in Europe had to develop its own alternative media system as have various gender movements. In patriarchal Spain, feminists, especially the Assembly of Women, have taken their message to the public through an aggressive street graphics campaign.

Even mainstream groups can be marginalized from the dominant media outlets. They may constitute a strong oppositional force but lack access to the mass media system dominated by the establishment. For example, nationalists in Northern Ireland, denied access to mass communication by the dominant unionist culture, used the one medium that was readily available—community walls. Graffiti writing slowly evolved into a vehicle of politicized murals to support their nationalist cause.[17] In the Republic of Ireland, where abortion counseling was illegal, women needing a crucial telephone number found it scribbled on public rest room walls.[18] The leftist Salvador Allende movement in Chile, which won the 1970 elections, had to contend with a dominant mass media that was emotionally oppositional. This was a factor motivating the expanded development of street art under Allende. The Peronist movement, the largest political force in Argentina, became a powerful communicator via street art, motivated by the inaccessibility of the major media. Argentine human rights groups in the early 1990s lobbied against a national pardon for human rights violators, relying on street graphics when denied access to the dominant media that refused to run issue ads for their campaign.

Impacting the Dominant Media Explanation

Often political participants cater to the major media for access in an indirect way. They intentionally utilize street art to attract the major media to give greater dissemination of their messages. Demonstrators and protesters carry placards, paste posters, write graffiti, and construct banners and satirical figures to purposely attract the attention of the public and the major media. Often, the major media in Spain and Latin America illustrate an event with photos of posters, placards, or graffiti that directly relate to a story on protests or demonstrations or other political events because they consider it news. This is pro forma for leading dailies such as *El País* and *Clarín;* even in the United States the print and electronic media transmit street art as news. For instance, three articles in the November 24, 1987, issue of *El País* referred to graffiti commentary in three different countries under political stress.[19] When infamous Nazi Rudolf Hess died in August 1987, overnight Spanish fascists pasted major cities with posters and graffiti commemorating Hess as a hero. This street art received major coverage and commentary in the media. Likewise, in Asunción, Paraguay, in 1986 Nazi posters featuring anti-Semitic messages and commemoration of Hitler attracted major media coverage. In February 1991, the *Los Angeles Times* carried three different references to street art as commentaries on three different stories. The first, featuring a colorful mural in Teheran, Iran, was placed on page one of the world section in full color. The paper captioned the mural as summing up the sentiments of Iranian foreign policy. The second article related the dilemmas of Arabs in Europe during the Persian Gulf War; it featured antiwar posters in France. The third, also depicting the Persian Gulf War, related how Washington, D.C., sidewalks were "spackled with spray-painted antiwar slogans."[20]

The appeal and impact of this communication process is both national and international. For example, in non-English-speaking countries many placards, wallposters, and graffiti are written in English to attract the international media and generate worldwide exposure through wire services and networks. Throughout Latin American, the ubiquitous anti-American sentiment is impressed in a variety of ways, often with the graffito "Yankee go home," written in English. In a story on post-Noriega Panama, ABC's "World News Tonight" flashed to a "Yankee go home" graffito when asking a rhetorical question about long-term United States presence in Panama.[21] Protesters in Italy carried Ronald Reagan Wanted posters, which were featured in color to highlight a *Newsweek* article on United States military policy in Europe.[22] *Business Week* illustrated an article on terrorism in Europe against American firms with a "US Go Home" graffito written on the facade of an American corporation in Lyons, France.[23] After the fall of the Communist regime in Prague, a gigantic "IT'S OVER, CZECHS ARE FREE" graffito was picked up by the international press and flashed over United States television networks and trumpeted in the press.[24] It was also carried in each of the Argentine dailies, even though it was written in English. When President George Bush made an official visit to Poland in 1989, English placards with anti-Soviet, anticommunist slogans were quickly transmitted via United States media.[25] During the prodemocratic movement in China in 1989, participants wrote hand-held posters in English for international consumption.[26] Burma's first national elections in years inspired posters written in English and Burmese, urging boycott of the "democratic" elections. They were picked up to highlight a *Los Angeles Times* article on the subject.[27] Likewise, handwritten banners carried by demonstrators in the African country of Gabon accusing President Omar Bongo of murder and demanding his resignation were spotlighted on the second page of the *Los Angeles Times*.[28] A 1989 report by the *MacNeil/Lehrer News Hour* on violence and drugs in Washington, D.C., began with a shot of a large ghetto wallpainting that read, "Say no to drugs." [29] Thus, like political demonstrations and protests, street art is reported as front-page news in national and regional dailies. Weeklies and television also carry it as news.

The Electoral Campaign Explanation

Unlike the United States, European and Latin American electoral campaigning is not dominated by television but remains a street affair. This is fostered by laws that prohibit paid campaign advertisements on radio and television. [30] Some countries allot free time for political messages to major parties and contenders. Limited by legal restraints, candidates and parties must rely on traditional forms of electioneering, resulting in street art. Additionally, many countries have multiparty systems with a plethora of minor parties lacking the financial resources to engage in electronic campaigning. Furthermore, in many Latin American countries the prevailing cultural norms favor street campaigning with rallies in the plazas and the visual features of street propaganda that accompany it. In a *New York Times* article on Colombian elections, politicians and citizens spoke of the indispensable requirement of direct contact with people in the tradition of the public square as the center of political debate. [31]

The Announcements, Special-Events Explanation

In countries with street art, political events often are announced via this medium. In each case in this study, it was common for unions to announce strikes and demonstrations through posters, wallpaintings, and graffiti. The powerful Argentine Confederación General del Trabajo (CGT) especially liked this medium. They declared each of the thirteen general strikes against the Raúl Alfonsín government via this means. General strikes in post-Franco Spain on December 14, 1988, and in spring 1992 relied heavily on graffiti and street graphics. In the occupied territories of Palestine, graffiti announced general strikes and other resistance actions against the Israelis. In other situations, fallen leaders and charismatic figures are commemorated; street art also recounts stories of people or events significant to particular subcultures. Spanish fascists commemorate Franco's death on November 20 with rallies, posters, and graffiti slogans. In Argentina, Evita Perón is commemorated on July 26 with an abundance of posters and graffiti. The figure of Che Guevara in street art still appears among revolutionary Marxist groups on the anniversary of his death. In other situations, such as in Lebanon, the Beirut suburb of Chia pasted commemorative posters on the suicide bombing attack against the Israeli army. [32] The Armenian communities in Brazil and Argentina keep alive the memory of the 1915 genocide in Turkey. The Jewish community in Argentina also remembers its genocide, and the Madres de Plaza de Mayo annually memorialize the "disappeared," victims of the "dirty war."

The Collective, Grass-roots Explanation

Street art has an implied collective, grass-roots appeal. A perception by the viewer that it may carry grass-roots sentiments, or be an indicator of "who is active on the streets," exists. Its use is appealing especially to those who stress a collective consciousness and claim to speak for and represent the people. Marxist, socialist, or populist groups view this means of communication as symbolically significant for maintaining a popular image, a collective sense,[33] and direct contact with people on the street. This is in contrast to bureaucratic political parties and out of touch government officials. For example, the Argentine Peronist movement maintains a strong visibility through street art even though at this historical period it has financial means and access to the major media.

Seeking the grass-roots, popular image conveyed in street art has not been confined to the left. Right-wing groups that proclaimed a popular base participated in political discourse through street art as well. Fascist movements were especially prone to utilize it. Nazism projected a collective street sense in the 1930s, employing posters and billboards to convey a strong community presence. After the Civil War, Spanish Falangists were strong practitioners of street graphics.[34] Modern-day fascists are likewise prolific utilizers of street graphics. Military dictatorships in Latin America constantly repress oppositional street art. Periodically, they attempt to demonstrate "popular will" through street art. During the Falkland/Malvinas War in 1982, the Argentine military regime encouraged visual expressions of anti-British, pro-Argentine popular street art. The Pinochet government, which tried to clean the country of popular leftist visual expression, utilized government employees, police recruits, and citizen groups to blanket the walls of towns and cities with "Yes" and to paint over opposition "No" slogans, in an attempt to demonstrate grass-roots support during the 1988 plebiscite on a return to democracy.[35]

Often the major media focus on some street graphics as an indicator of grass-roots ferment. In spring 1987, before the outbreak of the Intifada, *Newsweek* illustrated an article about student unrest in the West Bank by highlighting handwritten placards, "Freedom and independence for Arab Palestinian People!" which the reporter characterized as representative of the collective grass-roots ferment.[36] In mid-1990, when Germany was moving swiftly toward reunification, the *Los Angeles Times* reported that political graffiti in the new East Germany was a rarity, but a graffito scrawled in red, "Russians Out," captured the public anger East Germans felt toward the Soviet military forces stationed on their soil.

The State Sponsored Explanation

Regimes and leaders want to advertise their accomplishments. Marxist and radical revolutionary regimes often attempted to transform national culture and identity by utilizing street art as one means of forging a new national class cultural identification. Castro's Cuba and the Sandinistas in Nicaragua are the most recent examples; billboards, murals, and posters recalled martyrs and informed the public of changes taking place. Street art in these cases served as a class consciousness-raising tool. In Nicaragua, muralists were given the task of teaching recent history beginning with Sandino, as revisionists teaching a new historical memory.[37] In Chile during the Allende regime government posters were used to inform, advocate, and push for sociopolitical reforms.

As mentioned above, sponsorship of street art was not restricted to the left. For instance, in Catalonia, Spain, the conservative nationalist regime of Jordi Pujol made posters a device for informing the public by announcing in 1980 via posters a government campaign to improve the roads.[38] Frequently, right-wing military dictatorships in Paraguay, Chile, Argentina, and Spain commandeered public space for street art to inform, socialize, mobilize, and create feelings of fear. In 1986, thousands of posters were used by the Romanian government to urge its citizens to not use their cars and walk or use public transportation.[39] Similarly, the Chinese government issued wanted posters for leaders of the prodemocratic movement; the West German government did the same for Red Brigades members. In rural areas, the Philippine government mass distributed gruesome posters showing decapitated bodies. They proclaimed the New People's Army (NPA) was responsible for the atrocities in an effort to reverse the Robin Hood image of the NPA and erode its mass base.[40] Fighting the guerrillas in El Salvador, the military made liberal use of street graphics to combat the insurrectionists. Posters advising, ''Your rights will be respected'' offered bounties to Frente Farabundo Martí para la Liberación Nacional (FMLN) guerrillas who turned in their weapons.

The Underground Media Explanation

This phenomenon is particularly germane to repressive authoritarianism where political space is reduced.[41] Underground media is distinguished from alternative media to emphasize the utilization of street art in open pluralistic systems with informal censorship and its use in closed nonpluralistic authoritarian states. Street art in authoritarian regimes is one way to break the complicity of silence; to mobilize against demobilization attempts; to inspire and motivate; and to manifest through pamphlets, leaflets, street art, and other means that there is an organized opposition to the government. In essence, this forum circulates a critique of dictatorial regimes and keeps the resistance alive. Graffiti is most commonly employed, although in some instances wallpaintings, posters, and crude murals are also utilized. For example, the Kuwaiti underground used small posters as well as graffiti to circulate information and fuel opposition against the Iraqi occupation. Some of ETA's first forms of resistance were anti-Franco, pro-Basque slogans circulated through graffiti. As the walls came alive with slogans, people asked questions and a community dialogue began. This forced people to think about and react to a new reference. By visually manifesting a presence, the underground indicates to the regime and to the populace that there is an active opposition movement.

The Psychopolitical Explanation

The psychopolitical explanation involves the perception of who controls the street. In Latin America and Spain, painting the streets, postering the cities, and holding demonstrations and rallies are perceived as creating a feeling of who controls the tenor or tone of the street. Newspapers, the electronic media, and political groups refer to the phenomenon of *que opina la calle* (what does the street think). There is a perspective that influence is dependent upon manifesting a psychopolitical hold over street opinion. Elections are viewed as time bound, a limited expression that taps public opinion periodically.

Expressions of the belief in the psychopolitical relevance of taking control of the streets is evidenced in the following examples. In October 1945, Argentine workers took control of the streets with a massive demonstration, horrifying the establishment by writing political graffiti in chalk everywhere they went.[42] These activities exemplified the workers' new political and cultural expression that seized the nation with the nascent Peronist movement. In similar fashion, the Madres de Plaza de Mayo in the recent postmilitary period made silhouetted profile posters of the disappeared and pasted them the first day of the democratic opening. This set a new tone by emotionally calling for justice for those who committed human rights abuses. Street tone was also evident in Chile. In preparation for the 1989 national elections, Ricardo Lagos of the Partido por la Democracia (PPD) told the party youth section that they were going to paint the walls, put up posters, and win the battle of the streets.[43] In an article about the 1988 referendum in Chile, one political leader related how the walls were quiet but they were going to break the silence.[44] During the massive demonstrations against Pinochet surrounding the 1988 referendum and 1989 elections, the anti-Pinochet forces painted murals and papered the walls, manifesting that a resurgent democratic movement now set the tone in the streets. Conversely, the Pinochet regime had made it a policy to cleanse the country of the opposition street art that characterized the Allende years, 1970–1973, a gesture to manifest the change in the ideological tone of the streets from Marxist to militarist.

The Territorial Demarcation Explanation

Collectives and states utilize street art to symbolically demarcate a particular area as controlled or liberated, or as rightly belonging to a specific group, ethnic population, or nation. This category is separate from the preceding one to designate another level of control, one oriented toward perceived physical control of territory. The Intifada is a case in point. The abundant Palestinian graffiti scrawled throughout the occupied territories symbolized that the territories belonged to the Palestinians and could not be controlled by the Israelis. Lebanon's warring factions marked off their territories symbolically using posters and murals.[45] Syrian forces in 1987 stripped the posters and painted over the murals in an attempt to end the reign of the warring militias.[46] In Latin America, guerrilla movements create liberated zones, often demarcated with graffiti to indicate their jurisdiction over a specific area. The Sandinista rebellion made liberal use of graffiti to demarcate liberated territories and demonstrate to the Somoza regime that the government's jurisdiction was tenuous. Likewise the FMLN in El Salvador controlled much of rural Morázon province, and the walls there were marked off with FMLN graffiti.

In Peru, Sendero Luminoso guerrillas dominate nearly one-third of the country. The Sendero's graffiti are liberally splashed over public space to give credence to their claim.[47] The University of San Marcos in Lima, Peru, became a liberated zone for radical Marxists. It was demarcated with murals, graffiti, and elaborate wallpaintings until a government raid on the campus in the late 1980s retook the space. In the Nogales and La Victoria slums of Santiago, Chile, radical left groups painted murals and wallpaintings to demonstrate they, not Pinochet, controlled the political space in their neighborhoods.[48] During the Spanish Civil War, conquering Franco Nationalists laid waste to Republican villages, demarcating them with such graffiti as "Your women will give birth to fascists," or "Viva Franco," scribbled on the walls as symbols of a conquering force. Tourists arriving in Spain via France are greeted with graffiti and wallpainting informing them that "Catalonia is not Spain." The Catalonia government used this theme during the 1992 Olympics in advertisements in the Western press. And in Canada, French nationalists constantly remind citizens via linguistic graffiti monikers that Quebec is French. In the United States, street gangs lay their territorial claims by using graffiti monikers.

The Political Intimidation Explanation

Just like leaflets and other media, posters and graffiti can be utilized to intimidate by making threats to particular individuals or collectives. These tactics are employed in campaigns of psychological violence. Historical experience teaches that credibility must be attached to such threats. Tamil guerrillas in Sri Lanka, who have raided, pillaged, and killed villagers, left signs written in red paint warning Muslims not to work for the government.[49] The human rights organization Madres de Plaza de Mayo has been threatened continually with graffiti such as "Bolches out" and "Camps will return," slogans aimed at creating an intimidating environment.[50] Guido Peeters, a Belgian priest working in Chile, known for his outspoken condemnation of human rights abuses, was threatened by Chile's Anti-Communist Action Alliance via graffiti slogans written on parish walls. He was later kidnapped and tortured.[51] In Honduras, it was common for the right-wing death squad, the Anti-Communist Action

Alliance (AAA), to mark particular human rights organizations and individuals for execution through public posters and graffiti. Two human rights workers were assassinated in January 1988 after posters were placed warning of retribution for their activities, and Ramón Briceño, affiliated with the economics department at the National University, was assassinated three days after an AAA signed graffiti, "Briceño, you are dead," appeared on the wall of the economics department.[52] The United Nations transferred its offices in 1989 from El Salvador to Guatemala for "lack of guarantees" after "UN-FMLN-Traitors" graffiti was scrawled on its office walls.[53] In northern Mexico, two investigative reporters were killed after posters appeared one night singling them out.[54] Argentine and Brazilian militants within the Armenian communities issued graffiti for revenge against Turks for the 1915 genocide. And ETA has long practiced selective assassination of traitors, utilizing graffiti to warn targeted individuals and the community. These included suspected *chivatos* (or community spies) and ex-ETA combatants who abandon the armed struggle and opt for community reinsertion.[55] The most renowned was María Dolores "Yoyes" González, who was warned through graffiti that she was a marked woman. Also targeted are suspected drug traffickers who corrupt Basque youth.

The Literacy Campaign Explanation

Some analysts think street art can induce reading and become a supportive device in the war against illiteracy. It is argued that individuals learn to read images and words, and that large wallpainting letterings tend to obtain the force of images. In Chile under Allende, murals with slogans were thought to have the value of encouraging semiliterates to acquire reading habits and to further stimulate their interest in literacy. In revolutionary Mexico in the 1920s, the ministry of education sponsored murals to aid the literacy campaign. In Cuba, billboards and posters served the same purpose. Murals and posters in Nicaragua and wallpaintings with slogans in the Indian states of Kerala and Bengal were employed to increase literacy.[56] During the Palestinian Intifada, concerned officials who lamented the Israeli closing of schools in the occupied territories stated that youth were learning to read the graffiti.[57] In Europe, the nationalist minorities have used street art to stimulate interest in literacy of repressed languages. This has been true for the Basques, the Catalans, and the Galicians in Spain, for the Irish nationalists in Northern Ireland, and is occurring in Wales.

The Commercial Advertising Neutralization Explanation

David Kunzle's studies on Sandinista Nicaragua and Allende's Chile stress that one motive for utilizing street art was to neutralize and compete with street commercial advertising. This somewhat parallels the theme of who controls the ideological discourse of the streets, the capitalists or the socialists. Chilean murals, viewed as creative neighborhood projects rooted in national symbols, were seen as neutralizing a transnational capitalist culture. Kunzle argues that in Nicaragua revolutionary billboards competed effectively with commercial ones both on a numerical and visual level.[58] In Cuba, where pluralism is not tolerated, competition is not an issue.

Street Art As Political Inspiration Explanation

Street art can be a means to inspire people, to energize them, to raise spirits and generate morale. This is most pronounced at times of crisis, war, or revolution. Wars motivate governments and citizens to turn to street art in an attempt to inspire the citizenry. The Argentine military regime from 1976 to 1983, which had sought to repress street art, turned to its use. They encouraged citizens to participate in the Malvinas War effort by producing street art to inspire people. The long war between Iran and Iraq had accompanying street art to inspire the war effort. Following revolutions in Marxist states, street art was morale driven. It was employed to raise people's vision that goes along with revolutionary fervor. Street art produced by the radical Basque nationalist party Herri Batasuna is often triumphal, stating that radical Basque nationalism is the vision of the future. Bill Rolston, in a study on political wall murals by Nationalists in Northern Ireland, argues that murals were an inspirational factor in the revival of the subordinate Nationalist culture that had chafed under the hegemonic Unionist culture. It gave Nationalists a reawakened identity.[59] In June 1990, East German excavators uncovered Hitler's World War II bunker. It was replete with murals glorifying the Nazis, all aimed at keeping morale high.[60] When locked together in one Peruvian prison, prisoners of the Peruvian guerrilla movement Sendero Luminoso wrote graffiti slogans on the cell walls as a means of keeping spirits high.[61] In the Warsaw ghetto during World War II, one survivor explained that graffiti by the resistance kept his spirit alive because it indicated there was an active resistance and all was not lost.[62]

NOTES

1. See Rosalind Bresnahan, "Mass Communication, Mass Organizations and Social Participation in Revolutionary Cuba and Nicaragua," in *The Critical Communication Review, Volume III: Popular Culture and Media Events,* Vincent Mosco and Janet Wasko, eds. (Norwood, NJ: Ablex Publishing Corporation, 1983). Bresnahan argues that there can be a different concept than the traditional one for defining mass communication. He argues that mass communication in Cuba and Nicaragua should be seen as the social interaction of the dissemination of messages carried out by the mass organizations.

2. Carlos H. Waisman, *Reversal of Development in Argentina* (Princeton, NJ: Princeton University Press, 1987), Preface.

3. Sally Henderson and Robert Landau, *Billboard Art* (San Francisco: Chronicle Books, 1980), p. 61.

4. *Los Angeles Times,* August 3, 1989.

5. For thoughts on communication utilization see Emile McAnany et al., eds., *Communication and Social Structure: Critical Studies in Mass Media Research* (New York: Praeger, 1981).

6. See Cynthia McClintock, "The Media and Re-Democratization in Peru," *Studies in Latin American Popular Culture* 6 (1987).

7. David Green, *Shaping Political Consciousness: The Language of Politics in America from McKinley to Reagan* (Ithaca, NY: Cornell University Press, 1987), Preface.

8. *Los Angeles Times,* January 8, 1990.

9. *Los Angeles Times,* May 18, 1990.

10. *Los Angeles Times,* February 10–17, 1986.

11. *El País,* November 3, 1989.

12. *Los Angeles Times,* August 3, 1989.

13. See Melvin L. DeFleur and Sandra Ball-Rokeach, *Theories of Mass Communication,* 5th ed. (New York: Longman, 1989).

14. See Bill Rolston, "Politics, Painting and Popular Culture: The Political Wall Murals of Northern Ireland," *Media, Culture and Society* 9 (1987).

15. *International Herald Tribune,* March 12, 1988.

16. Thanks goes to an anonymous reader for this information.

17. Rolston, "Politics, Painting and Popular Culture," p. 15.

18. *International Herald Tribune,* September 16, 1988.

19. For example, *El País,* November 24, 1987.

20. *Los Angeles Times,* February 5, 1991.

21. ABC's "World News Tonight," January 4, 1990

22. *Newsweek,* June 16, 1986.

23. *Business Week,* May 12, 1986.

24. *Clarín,* November 30, 1989, *La Nación,* November 30, 1989, and ABC's "World News Tonight," January 16, 1990.

25. See *Newsweek,* July 24, 1989.

26. *Los Angeles Times,* December 24, 1989.

27. *Los Angeles Times,* May 18, 1990.

28. *Los Angeles Times,* May 28, 1990.

29. PBS, *MacNeil/Lehrer Report,* March 20, 1989.

30. Anthony Smith, "Mass Communication," in *Democracy at the Polls,* David Butler et al., eds. (Washington DC: American Enterprise Institute, 1981), pp. 174–75.

31. See *New York Times,* September 24, 1989.

32. *US News and World Report,* July 1, 1985.

33. See Jean Franco, *The Modern Culture of Latin America: Society and the Artist* (New York: Praeger, 1967).

34. See Stanley Payne, *Falange: A History of Spanish Fascism* (Stanford: Stanford University Press, 1961).

35. See *La Epoca,* September–October 1988.

36. *Newsweek,* April 6, 1987.

37. See Kunzle, "Nationalist, Internationalist and Anti-Imperialist Themes in the Public Revolutionary Art of Cuba, Chile and Nicaragua," *Studies in Latin American Popular Culture* 3 (1984).

38. *El País,* March 3, 1987.

39. *Los Angeles Times,* November 29, 1986.

40. *Los Angeles Times,* November 5, 1989.

41. Underground media can also occur when violent revolutionary groups bent upon overthrowing regimes organize in open democratic regimes.

42. Daniel James, *Resistance and Integration: Peronism and the Argentine Working Class, 1946–1976* (New York: Cambridge University Press, 1988), pp. 77–81.

43. *La Epoca,* July 9, 1989.

44. Alfred Stepan, "The Last Days of Pinochet," *New York Review of Books,* June 2, 1988.

45. *Los Angeles Times,* March 29, 1987.

46. *Los Angeles Times,* March 8, 1987.

47. *Latinamerica Press,* June 8, 1989, and May 17, 1990.

48. See Ariel Chabalgoity, Sengo Pérez, and Roger Rodríguez, *Chile: La Derrota del Miedo* (Buenos Aires: Puntosur Editores, 1988).

49. *Los Angeles Times,* June 23, 1990.

50. Camps was an infamous symbol of repression during the Argentine dirty war.

51. *Latinamerica Press,* March 5, 1987.

52. *Latinamerica Press,* February 2, 1989.

53. *Buenos Aires Herald,* December 5, 1989.

54. *New York Times,* July 23, 1986.

55. See Joseph Zuliaka, *Basque Violence: Metaphor and Sacrament* (Reno: University of Nevada Press, 1988).

56. See Kunzle, "Nationalist, Internationalist and Anti-Imperialist Themes."

57. *Los Angeles Times,* May 17, 1989.

58. Kunzle, "Nationalist, Internationalist and Anti-Imperialist Themes."

59. See Rolston, "Politics, Painting, and Popular Culture."

60. *Los Angeles Times,* June 11, 1990.

61. *Nuestro Tiempo Argentino,* July 6, 1986.

62. This information on the Warsaw ghetto was from an article several years ago. I did not note the citation.

2

Street Art: How It Is Effective

This chapter considers how political street art is effective. Evaluating that factor is difficult. What constitutes effectiveness can have different interpretations. Critical theorists in the field of communication who have focused on the Third World, such as the pioneering work of Armand Mattelart, believed the penetration of transnational media had an adverse effect. It induced a passivity to capitalist consumption values, eroded indigenous cultures and values, and created a subservient relationship to the dominant culture of the central core.[1] But questions are: How passive are the masses? From which sources do they receive their political information? How hegemonic is the dominant media?

The political events in China and the revolutionary changes in Eastern Europe and the Soviet Union, where state-controlled media were monopolistic, provide evidence that the dominant media cannot pacify the citizenry over the long term. People who want to be informed, independent, and intelligent thinkers can; those who do not care, will not. Individuals act within social structures, and political information is passed along in one manner or another. People receive political information and convey it according to their preferences. They consume political information on the basis of what is available.[2] In countries using street art, the messages conveyed augment the existing availability of information and ideas.

Is street art an effective means of communication? Do citizens and the state recognize it as such? In the cases presented in this study, the producers and the governing elites who respond to street art believed it was effective. If not, producers would not rely on this form of mass communication, nor would authoritarian states have responded the way they did in suppressing it. In Portugal, left-wing activists bitterly fought a law that would ban politicized street wall art. Citing Article 37 of the constitution, their representatives in Parliament argued "everyone has the right to express his thoughts and to inform through words, image or any other media . . . without impediment or discrimination." They stated the new law allowing cities to eliminate this expression was a ploy to deprive the poorer and marginal political groups of an inexpensive and effective means of mass communication and was an "unconstitutional attempt by the government to strengthen its information monopoly." Moreover, the left contended that the right would ignore the proliferation of commercial advertisements and use the law to ban political expressions with which it disagreed. The left agreed regulation was needed but said it should be directed toward the commercial sector.[3] This debate summed up several factors: that street art was perceived as an effective means of communication, that it was an expression where the issue of dominant media versus alternative media was at stake, and that it competed with commercial propaganda.

If groups in democratic and authoritarian systems utilize political art, they must believe it serves a useful function and produces an impact. From random conversations with political activists who paste posters or paint murals in the streets, and from casual conversations with political militants, it appears that they thought it was an effective and necessary practice, since in certain circumstances it is the only available channel for informing the citizenry. People do read signs. In many Latin American countries, as well as on the Iberian Peninsula, commercial advertisers entice consumers with public posters. Additionally, the state uses them to inform the public about state-sponsored cultural events, among other things. They target individuals to whom the event or product might appeal the most. For example, on a regular basis municipal governments in Brazil, Spain, and Argentina post posters about a variety of topics, most often cultural events. If commercial advertisers and the state see this medium as effective, there is no reason for political activists to behave differently. It is logical to assume that certain messages, information, or slogans attract the targeted audience: an audience defined as those interested in sociopolitical and economic issues, the curious, or those sympathetic to a particular point of view.[4]

How one defines and approaches effectiveness will, of course, impact the argument. This approach is based upon citing examples to demonstrate how street art is effective. The examples cited are universal, collected from primary and secondary sources. Especially relevant are those that received recent intense electronic and print media attention, the Intifada, the Chinese prodemocratic movement, and the revolutionary changes in Eastern Europe and the Soviet Union. The examples are not from one particular regime type, but rather include dictatorial, authoritarian, and democratic regimes. Examples should demonstrate that definite kinds of information and symbols carry unequivocal images which can evoke various emotions such as fear, tranquility, encouragement, alienation, and rage.

One difficulty in evaluating effectiveness is time, which complicates generalizations about effectiveness. Effectiveness is difficult to determine as time frames blur and obscure long-term implications. Street art must be seen as part of a process, not as a single event, slogan, or expression analyzed in isolation.

It should be viewed as a series of events with possible long-term implications and as an indicator of political discourse and group conflict in a society. Furthermore, ideas are disseminated through a variety of means; street art is but one medium. This creates difficulty in sorting and evaluating the most influential factors over time.

One way to begin this discussion is to state that street art reflects the thinking of those collectives, individuals, and states that produce it. From this perspective, street art allows collectives to have a public voice and to record their feelings, their views, or their ideas of the moment. For some collectives, particularly those of repressed people, it may be the only possible means to record their feelings. From a grass-roots perspective, the significance is that it can be a gauge of political sentiment, just as government-sponsored street art is an indicator of state opinion. Thus, these expressions offer a snapshot or historical summary of the social and political struggles of the moment. For example, the Moscow Museum of Revolution opened an exhibit in fall 1990 titled "The Way to Political Pluralism." It contained street graphics and other symbols of the turbulent five years of perestroika. The purpose of the exhibit was to summarize and clarify the struggles and forces battling for power during perestroika. It provided a retrospective summary of the popular history of the era.[5] Thus, street art communicates something: people use it, know about it, and are aware of it, and that in itself makes it effective. If the desired outcome is to draw attention to an issue, event, group recognition, or election process, street art is effective if citizens or the government acknowledge it in some way.

Targeting is another aspect of effectiveness. Some groups aim to politicize general issues, while others may target a selected audience. Producers can post or paint to reach and appeal to diverse ethnic, class, or cultural groups on a selective basis, trying to attract the critical audience. The objective may be to recruit a small vanguard of militants or a broader following to form a critical mass for the functioning of an organization. Recruitment of a cadre of militants was the reason universities, particularly in Latin America and Spain, were targeted by groups with their street art and why campuses were graveyards of politicized street art. For decades, the working-class districts were targeted by leftists, unionists, Marxists, anarchists, and fascists, all seeking to speak for and represent workers. In Spain, a deluge of electoral street propaganda is targeted at the 4–5 percent undecided vote, a critical sector that can swing an election.[6] Moreover, regional parties target regional sentiments. Whatever the main reason for targeting an audience, effectiveness is not easy to gauge. If a group or party is targeting a specific audience, it may not make any difference if the general public is alienated by abusive wall art slogans; if the graphics recruit, it is successful.

MARGINAL GROUPS IN THE HISTORICAL PROCESS

Marginalized groups articulate subculture sentiments that should not be discounted, for tomorrow their ideas could be influential. Certain groups may be in decline, fighting to survive, while others may be in a formative stage, attempting to establish an identity and carve out a political space. Whatever the case, without a means of popular communication, organizations are deprived of their social identification. For some observers, an organization's particular ideas and demands as expressed through street art may seem irrelevant. However, several examples of new groups vividly illustrate their impact and importance: the growth of the radical Basque ETA-HB movement; the regional movement in Spain; the prodemocratic student movement in China; the phenomenal rise of the semifascist Le Pen movement in France; the dramatic grass-roots movements in the Soviet Union and Eastern Europe against the state; the unforeseen blitzkrieg of the Cambio 90 political phenomenon in Peru, where a political unknown, Alberto Fujimori, was elected president on a shoestring campaign; and the extraordinary evolution of the human-rights movement in Latin America, exemplified in the Madres de Plaza de Mayo, who defied Argentina's military establishment and created a new moral consciousness movement. These marginal groups and movements acted to challenge the structures of the state and civil society and to redefine what the state should be.

For others, it has been a rear-guard action to keep formerly influential groups and movements alive and in the public eye. For example, the anarchist movement, prolific producers of street art, garnered great support and political space throughout Europe, Latin America, and elsewhere during the first decades of the twentieth century but fell upon hard times. They lost their appeal and became small skeletal organizations. However, they continued their militant activism through street art and confrontational tactics. In Europe, in recent years, the diffuse anarchist movement has attracted many alienated youth and become a symbol of their identity. Through this process they gained new political space. In the twilight of Prime Minister Margaret Thatcher's government, a tiny anarchist group, Class War, claimed credit for organizing one of the most violent demonstrations in recent British history, the protest against the unpopular poll tax.[7] In Germany, anarchist youths have been blamed for much of the violence occurring in protest demonstrations in the mid-1980s. Spanish Nazi-fascists, particularly in Madrid, keep a high visual profile through street art, hoping to attract the discontented, just as the semifascist Le Pen movement did in France, or the ultraright in Germany, and the fascists in Italy.

There is always the possibility of regaining political space regardless of a seemingly hopeless situation for marginalized groups. Visual street art campaigns help keep marginal organizations before the public eye, hopefully attracting that viewer seeking a particular sociopolitical identity. Furthermore, the argument could be made that marginalized collectives which utilize street art, such as some Marxist groups, while not attracting much formal support, are a contributing factor in politicizing a particular issue or in undermining the legitimacy of Third World regimes. In those countries with a repressed or an alienated working class, Marxists may keep the idea of class struggle alive. Fascists, for example, play a similar role. They contribute to an anti-Semitic atmosphere. Rudolf Hess posters pasted by the Spanish profascist groups had an immediate impact; the major print media featured the poster, providing these groups and their ideology with national coverage. Zubin Mehta and the Israel orchestra were touring Spain at the time. Mehta commented that he and orchestra members were greatly offended by the anti-Semitism message of the wallposters, indicating the posters were visually absorbed by the casual person on the street.[8] Further, it is evident that graffiti-splashed swastikas painted on synagogues and Jewish-owned businesses, institutions, and homes are effective. Their increased frequency symbolizes the revival of anti-Semitism and raises concerns. Statistics on hate crimes in the United States include graffiti vandalism. In California, charges of misdemeanor terrorism can be filed against individuals writing graffiti racial slurs. People pay attention to these signs of hate crimes. They are reported in the print media and on television, receive wide diffusion, and create alarm and fear.

GRASS-ROOTS ACTIVISM

Two non-Latin countries attest to street art effectiveness as a medium to challenge the dominant culture. Both witnessed prolonged protests and revolts in which street art—graffiti and wallposters—played a prominent role. The first is the Intifada in Palestine, which broke out in December 1987; the second is the student protests in the People's Republic of China. The Israelis have fought Palestinian nationalism since 1967 in the occupied territories; they have made it a policy not to tolerate visual signs of Palestinian nationalism. One effective method the Palestinians employed during the Intifada was graffiti. It was a way to circulate information and symbolize resistance. The Israelis tried to repress this, ordering Palestinians to paint over nationalistic graffiti.[9] The world press and television showed incidents of Israeli soldiers compelling Palestinians at gunpoint to paint over the graffiti.[10] Here a democratic government felt threatened by the visual images expressed through street art.

The Palestinian leadership believed in the efficacy of street art. The underground command of the Intifada called upon its followers to hoist or paint Palestinian flags and to scrawl graffiti on every available wall. In compliance, Palestinian youth carried out a campaign of painting the four-color national flag on building after building, symbolically marking the territory as Palestinian. Posters of former Israeli Prime Minister Yitzhak Shamir were pasted up and defaced with donkey ears, others bore crude depictions of him as a pig, and graffiti denounced him.[11] The Israelis were unsuccessful in stopping this display of nationalistic graffiti. As fast as it was covered over, new graffiti appeared.

When the United States government pushed a new peace initiative between Israel and the Palestine Liberation Organization (PLO) in March 1989, they presented three options to the PLO to lessen tensions. One was to desist in the distribution of inflammatory leaflets.[12] Clearly, the United States and Israel saw leaflets as an effective popular tool that encouraged the continuation of the Intifada. Leaflets are easily pasted up as wallposters. In essence, the Palestinians developed a mass-media system that included graffiti and leaflets to inform, issue warnings, and irritate the Israelis. In addition to being a form of nationalistic resistance, the underground media was a channel for information and leadership conflict within the resistance. A Palestine organization, HAMAS, challenged the PLO in the occupied territories for leadership. They used graffiti and leaflets to circulate information. The PLO responded with its own street art.[13] Certainly, in assessing street art during the Intifada, Israel's response testifies to its effectiveness.

The Chinese student democratic movement is another example of street art effectiveness. Wallposters came to symbolize the hopes of the young and reformers within China. Street art was a means to an end for the Chinese underground. It was the power to have a public voice, and to thrust their agenda into the national debate. For Chinese dissidents, wallposters served that end. Their complaints were aired via wallposters and became material for the country's political discourse, forcing the dominant culture to defend its system both nationally and internationally in the face of an upsurge from the underclass. Simply as a symbol wallposters were effective. This form of expression has symbolized the voice of a marginal movement in China since the late 1970s. It offers another case of a seemingly innocuous offbeat group drawing attention to their cause through a vehicle some analysts would say was an insignificant form of resistance. A decade earlier, the student dissident movement known as the Democratic Wall movement, which broke out in 1978–1979, erupted when activists pasted wallposters listing their grievances and making denunciations. This action quickly stimulated public debate. New Democratic Walls sprung up throughout China, starting a heated debate in Chinese society. Because of its disruptive consequences, the government cracked down and arrested the leaders; some were tried as counterrevolutionaries and given long prison terms.[14]

When the student democratic movement reemerged in 1986, wallposters again became the favored vehicle for expressing protest and mobilizing the opposition. The 1989 resistance greatly threatened the system because of its emotional intensity, level of support, and duration. Wallposters played a prominent role. Posters criticizing Chinese leaders were immediately torn down by police, while posters urging greater democracy were seen as less threatening.[15] As the movement went into its sixth week, the government tried to counteract the grassroots image of the dissidents by ordering building managers in Beijing to put up progovernment banners under such slogans as "Firmly take the socialist road" and "Maintain order in the capital."[16] During the prolonged April–June resistance, the Chinese leadership cited the wallposters as one factor responsible for "stirring up turmoil."[17] The evening news showed citizens pasting up posters or groups standing around reading them. It became a means of mass communication among students, a way to learn about individual grievances and what the student leadership was proposing.

These wallposters set the stage for the mass demonstrations finally crushed by the army. Through graffiti and wallposters, the army was proclaimed fascist. Burned out military vehicles debilitated by the resistance were inscribed with swastikas. With the repression that followed, the government communicated via posters requesting people to turn in any known participants in the pro-democratic movement. Furthermore, the government announced the executions of militants through wallposters; a red check at the bottom of the posters indicated the execution had been carried out.[18] The state thus understood the merit and effectiveness of this communication form. On the eve of the first anniversary of the prodemocratic movement in April 1990, it was reported that on the campus of Beijing University, near where wallposters had been put up, plain-clothes police were stationed to prevent any symbolic commemoration of the event. It seems the symbol of the wallposter itself, not even the message was a threat to the stability of the ruling regime. The regime's new regulations prohibited posters on campus.[19] ABC's "World News Tonight" reported in May 1990 a "Down with Deng Xiaoping" wallposter went up in Beijing and within minutes police converged to tear it down.[20]

The revolutionary changes in Eastern Europe produced their own manifestation of street art. In Czechoslovakia, the velvet revolution erupted as a political catharsis, producing thousands of individually expressed thoughts and slogans. These were not spray painted on walls and buildings but written on sheets of paper and carefully taped to buildings and walls.[21] People gave full vent to their rage, emotions, and ideas without censorship for the first time since 1968. It was effective. It gave the observer the ability to assess the gamut of thinking and emotions at this historical period, and in the process it recorded a popular memory. In Romania, there was no velvet revolution; it erupted violently. While fighting for control of downtown Bucharest, people expressed their uncensored feelings for the first time in decades. Bucharest residents scrawled slogans such as "Hitler, Stalin, Ceausescu," "Down with Ceausescu and his clan," and "Down with the tyrant."[22] Automobiles carried small handbills or photo posters of Nicolae Ceausescu with "CRIMINAL" written in large letters across them. As the revolt grew more bloody, old photo posters of Ceausescu were scrawled with "Killer, torturer," some written in English, while others splashed with red paint to indicate he had blood on his hands were taped on facades.[23] One popular poster read, "Ceausescu is a pig, packed for export." This slur referred to the severe export agricultural policy in which the country exported everything to pay off the debt, bringing hardship.[24]

A particular street art project by Romanian student activists became a crucial factor sparking the rebellion and mobilizing the rage against Ceausescu's regime. In Ceausescu's penultimate speech, he boasted that Soviet-style reform would come "When apple trees grow pears," defiant words of Marie Antoinette fame. Cinema and drama students at the University of Bucharest took the challenge. They hung all the pears they could find on the barren trees that lined the capital's main street. This political taunt so infuriated Ceausescu that he ordered the Securitate (secret police) to identify the perpetrators. As a result, students were attacked in their dormitories on Thursday, December 21; some were killed. The next day students organized by actor Ion Caramitru began the catcalls that disrupted the final Ceausescu speech, triggering his flight and the mass uprising. The exaggerated reaction to the pop art pear trees was destructive for Ceausescu; the students had effectively goaded the regime into action that produced a greater reaction and subsequently a greater level of rage, of consciousness, and the loss of fear of confronting the regime.[25]

Bill Rolston, writing on the conflict in Northern Ireland, argues that the Nationalists in the North started a mural movement as an alternative political support medium. Its efficacy in encouraging and stimulating community interests inspired the Nationalists. British soldiers reacted by paint-bombing the more offensive murals depicting soldiers negatively. The Unionists, argues Rolston, did not know how to respond to the messages that presented an alternative historical memory. Their culture had dominated the visual horizon until the Nationalist visual assault.[26]

REGIME RESPONSE

One sign of effectiveness is the ability to evoke responses. A way to assess effectiveness is to evaluate the responses regimes make to street art. If there is resistance-oriented street art, and if governments try to repress it, then it must be effective in some way. Why do regimes react? First, under authoritarian regimes, the underground production of street art connotes an activist, collective sense. In essence, it becomes a form of psychological warfare against the dominant culture and elite and reveals an emerging subterranean movement. This is threatening because it connotes a prelude to an organized opposition, or the existence of one. The repression of street art may not be directed at the message but at the symbol the act conveys. The act symbolizes a culture of resistance exists that dictators pretend to ignore. This denial of resistance and of alternative views was particularly evident in the old communist regimes, although less so in those of Latin America, where the civil society and the state are accustomed to authoritarian–democratic cycles and where the presumption exists that there are alternative perspectives.

The appearance of street art under authoritarian regimes is a symbolic contradiction, for its democratic form of expression is the antithesis to the system. Underground street art can break the censorship imposed on information by authoritarian states and pierce the complicity of silence with the regime. If regimes did not believe ideas have an effect, then they would not worry about suppressing them; but they do believe. Therefore, they either have to be tolerant or stamp them out. An additional factor in the effectiveness of the underground media stems from the lack of credibility of the state-controlled media. If the latter lack credibility, a vacuum results, creating political space for low-technology media. Whatever the factors, the response by regimes connotes that this channel cannot be used as a vehicle to express opinions contrary to the regime's.

The ferocity with which some regimes respond attests to the effectiveness of political street art. The Chinese meted out long-term sentences to leaders of the democratic movement. New regulations stated anyone caught pasting posters would be severely punished. In 1989 before the revolution, the East German government handed down an eighteen-year prison term to an individual who scrawled "Perestroika will yet free us" on a Soviet monument.[27] East German authorities in the first years of the Berlin Wall had guards climb over the wall and paint out any graffiti; later they only erased particularly embarrassing words, while the side of the wall facing East Berlin was kept clean of any street art expression.[28] In pre-perestroika days, the Soviet Union sent to psychiatric wards protesters who publicly displayed placards or banners. In November 1987 in Brashov, Romania, graffiti appeared that expressed the emotions of many Romanians: "It's all the same to us whether we die from hunger and cold or from bullets." The culprits were given long prison terms.[29] On the eve of the Communist party Congress in Bucharest a few months before the revolution, someone wrote the graffito, "Give us our country back" on the statue of Lenin in the main square. Six students were arrested and given prison terms.

In 1988 in Sri Lanka, a society bedeviled by a high level of social and ethnic conflict, a "democratically" elected regime found the president issuing an emergency decree declaring imprisonment or execution of anyone possessing leaflets or posters calling for strikes. This was in response to effective strikes called by opposition extremists. Strikes were commonly announced by posters or leaflets that appeared overnight on buildings and walls.[30] In Chile during the Pinochet dictatorship, distributors of oppositional street art risked their lives. Apprehended individuals were beaten and arrested; some were tortured. Other individuals were fatally shot while hanging posters. One such fatality occurred in July 1988 when a Socialist party militant was shot only one year before the regime's demise.[31] Under Franco, Spain imprisoned activists who distributed illicit propaganda. This offense accounted for the most numerous category of crimes committed under the regime.[32] In November 1989, the Haitian military security killed three opposition partisans who were pasting posters calling for the return to power of former democratically elected president Leslie Manigat.[33] As a result of the FMLN guerrilla offense into the nation's capital of San Salvador in November 1989, the democratically elected government issued a severe new antiterrorist law that mandated four-year imprisonment for anyone imparting subversive propaganda and six years for anyone justifying or publicly defending terrorism.[34] This did not, of course, apply to state terrorism. The Nicaraguan resistance involved in underground street art suffered harsh repercussions. At first, militants faced six months in jail. When the insurrection gained force and became more threatening, the security forces shot those they caught. The government completed the process by painting over the messages.[35]

At a less reactive level in Madrid, the capital of Spain, it was reported in the late 1980s that the governing Socialist party quickly reacted to any anti-Socialist party graffiti that appeared. They instructed cleaning companies, contracted to cleanse the city of graffiti and other propaganda, to give top priority to erasing anti-Socialist signs. In Catalonia, officials concerned about the activities of radical Catalán nationalists who initiated a campaign against King Juan Carlos's official visit in April 1988 had them detained for pasting posters against the visit.[36] Governments respond in a variety of ways to street art.

ADDITIONAL INDICATORS

Other areas of effectiveness can be extrapolated from the preceding chapter. One pertains to impacting the dominant media, either domestically or internationally. Suffice it to state, if street art makes the pages of dailies or weeklies, or is carried on the nightly news, its message has been disseminated effectively. Name recognition is another dimension in assessing effectiveness. Just as in commercial advertising, name recognition is vitally important in politics. In both, one must have a product people want, an attractive program, a colorful personality, charismatic appeal, and something that serves people's needs. Among consumers, recall is highly selective. Similarly, groups, individuals, and parties need name recognition, especially for the political newcomers. One means to achieve this is through a concerted repetitive street art effort. Many regional parties in Spain have established name recognition through extensive graffiti and poster campaigns. Whatever the circumstances, if a society has a spectrum of groups and parties and a tradition of street art, it can provide the interested with information on what is occurring politically. It can enlighten them regarding political campaigns and highlight the deeds and misdeeds of public officials. Like any information, street art offers the citizenry a perspective on what is happening.

Other and sundry factors relate to street art's effectiveness. One such factor is the practice of intimidation street art. It is used as a means to issue warnings to groups or individuals that violence against them may occur because of unacceptable activities or their incorrect ideological proclivities. Basque terrorists in Spain and right-wing death squads in Honduras used graffiti and posters to mark victims and were effective in creating fear. The discussion on the effectiveness of intimidation street art is limited here because of the extensive discussion and examples in the previous chapter. Suffice it to say, individuals and groups have a right to be fearful because death warnings have not been empty threats.

The most egregious example of intimidation street art in the United States is gang graffiti. It arouses a variety of emotions and fears. The graffiti constitute a struggle over territory, serve as a communication network among gangs, evoke intimidation and domination, and destabilize neighborhoods. The appearance of graffiti indicate that residents are losing control of their communities.[37] Since graffiti symbolize gangs and gang violence, a sense of personal danger is engendered; people feel that public space has been commandeered by private groups. For residents in areas where gang graffiti are common or begin to appear, fears arise that the neighborhood is no longer safe, that a violent atmosphere prevails. In a middle-class suburb of San Diego, California, newly scrawled graffiti caused community residents to meet with police to prevent the establishment of gang activity. Police treated the graffiti as the work of visiting gang members.[38] In other instances, graffiti in parks rendered them less attractive and less frequented by the public. Los Angeles International Airport officials, concerned about a marked increase in gang graffiti, feared this indicated gangs were moving in and warned action would be taken to deter the intrusions.[39]

And finally, there are official judgments. In Spain in 1988 a reunion of experts convoked to select the most effective antidrug campaign chose as the winning selection the work of an anonymous graffiti crusader whose message "Do not take drugs, hook yourself on life" was illustrated with a broken syringe.[40]

NOTES

1. See Rita Atwood and Emile G. McAnany, eds. *Communication and Latin American Society: Trends in Critical Research, 1960–1985* (Madison: University of Wisconsin Press, 1986).

2. See Robert Huckfeldt and John Sprague, "Networks in Context: The Social Flow of Political Information," *American Political Science Review* 81:4 (1987).

3. *San Francisco Chronicle,* (Reuters) March 22, 1987.

4. See David William Foster, "Argentine Sociopolitical Commentary, the Malvinas Conflict, and Beyond: Rhetoricizing a National Experience," *Latin American Research Review* 22:1 (1987).

5. *Los Angeles Times,* August 27, 1990.

6. *El País,* October 22, 1989, and *Diario 16,* "Dossier de la Semana," October 22, 1989.

7. *Newsweek,* April 16, 1990.

8. *El País,* August 20, 1987.

9. *Los Angeles Times,* February 21, 1989.

10. For example, news programs on the Intifada were aired on *Spanish TV* during December 1987; see also *Los Angeles Times,* February 21, 1989.

11. *Los Angeles Times,* November 13, 1988, and May 10, 1989.

12. *Los Angeles Times,* March 19, 1989.

13. See *Los Angeles Times,* February–March 1989 and September 4, 1989.

14. *Newsweek,* January 19, 1989.

15. *New York Times,* April 17, 1989.

16. *Los Angeles Times,* June 3, 1989.

17. *Los Angeles Times,* April 27, 1989.

18. *El País,* June 23, 1989.

19. *Los Angeles Times,* February 9, 1990.

20. ABC's "World News Tonight," May 8, 1990.

21. Milos Forman, Opinion Section, *Los Angeles Times,* December 24, 1989.

22. *Los Angeles Times,* December 24, 1989.

23. *CNN coverage,* December 1989.

24. *Los Angeles Times,* December 28, 1989.

25. *Los Angeles Times,* December 27, 1989.

26. See Bill Rolston, "Politics, Painting and Popular Culture: The Political Wall Murals of Northern Ireland," *Media, Culture and Society* 9 (1987), p. 21.

27. *Los Angeles Times,* August 1, 1989.

28. *International Herald Tribune,* November 14, 1987.

29. *El País,* November 24, 1987.

30. *Los Angeles Times,* November 12, 1988.

31. *La Epoca,* July 9, 1989.

32. See Stanley Payne, *The Franco Regime, 1936–1975* (Madison: University of Wisconsin Press, 1987).

33. *Los Angeles Times,* January 25, 1990.

34. *Jornal do Brasil,* November 25, 1989.

35. Omar Cabezas, "The Voice of the People Is the Voice of the 'Pintas,' " in Armand Mattelart, ed. *Communicating in Popular Nicaragua* (New York: International General, 1986), p. 39.

36. *El País,* April 20, 1988.

37. See, for example, *Los Angeles Times,* February 1, 1991.

38. *Rancho Bernardo Journal,* August 24, 1989.

39. *Los Angeles Times,* November 10, 1988.

40. *El País,* January 29, 1989.

Part II

THE IBERIAN PENINSULA

3

Spain: Centralism and Regionalism

Generally, street art in Spain has evolved as a well-worked channel reflecting the varying historical epochs and changing political landscape. Isolated from the European mainstream, Spain nevertheless was affected by the ideological currents of the first half of the twentieth century that traumatized Europe. For example, Spain was besieged by the ideas of the anarchists that found fertile soil among the exploited working class and peasantry in the first decades of the twentieth century. These ideas impacted the labor movement. The anarchists' antisystem, confrontational style contributed to turbulent years of heightened social conflict as sectors and classes struggled over defining the nature of the political system. The dramatic conflict between traditionalism and liberalism, centralism and regionalism, was temporarily repressed by a modern dictatorship in the mid-1920s under General Miguel Primo de Rivera. Unable to withstand the currents and ideas of democracy, the regime surrendered to them. The Republic was born; 1931–1936 was a period of heightened conflict. The attempt to democratize Spain failed, cut short by its Civil War in 1936–1939, a period during which competing ideologies across Europe struggled for continental influence in a prelude to World War II. After experiencing the trauma of the Civil War, Spain settled into an extended period of intolerance under the dictatorship of Franco. Upon Franco's death in 1975 Spain moved quickly to integrate into mainstream European democratic culture. Spain became a member of the European Community (EC) and the North Atlantic Treaty Organization (NATO), establishing itself as a stable democracy.

HISTORICAL SETTING

The Republic, 1931–1936

The checkered political landscape of Spanish history during the twentieth century is recorded in the street art of each era. The anarchists, a powerful influence in the first decades of the twentieth century, were oriented toward confrontational street politics. Their philosophy was to dominate the streets both physically and psychologically. They introduced the political tactic of a general strike and utilized street art to arouse people's emotions. They were prolific producers of street art. Because of the rigid sociopolitical attitudes dominant in Spain and the existing conditions of a feudal system, Spanish workers and peasants became a highly politicized work force. At the beginning of the Republic, half the Spanish population did not know how to read or write. Illustrated posters became an important medium to reach and move them. During earlier turbulent years of bitter social conflict, 1917–1923, Andalusian peasants took the initiative and scribbled on whitewashed walls, "Viva Lenin." [1] The anarchist movement, led by the Confederación Nacional del Trabajo (CNT) and the more moderate socialists, grouped around the Partido Socialista Obrero Español (PSOE) and their workers in the Unión General de Trabajadores (UGT), competed to attract the workers. By the end of World War I, the anarchists numbered 800,000 and the Socialists 200,000. By 1934, there were 1.44 million members in the UGT and 1.58 million members in the CNT, reflecting the growing politicization of the working class. [2] With this large number of organized workers and the fratricidal social conflict, street art became a well-used communication medium that recorded the struggles.

During the brief Republican period, especially the national elections of 1931, 1933, and 1936, street art—posters in particular—became a common medium. Workers wrote graffiti on public transportation to express their sentiments. The Spanish Confederation of the Autonomous Right (CEDA), an alliance of right-wing Catholic parties that won the 1933 elections, utilized street art to popularize their ideas. Some CEDA posters reflected the current fascist thinking in Europe, fashioned toward national issues. These posters implored people to save Spain from the ravages of "Marxists, Masons, Separatists, and Jews." [3] The anti-Marxist and anti-Jewish themes came from Germany. The anti-Mason diatribe was tied to traditional Catholic ideology—Masons were republicans and sought to curb Catholic political power. The antiseparatist, regionalist position reflected the centralist ideas of Spain's traditional right, which viewed regionalism as a threat to Spanish unity and greatness. The question of regional devolution erupted at the beginning of the Republic in 1931 when the left–center won the elections and granted Catalonia home rule. This outraged traditionalists. The conflicts between regionalism versus centralism, church versus state, authority versus freedom, and class versus class were the divisive factors leading to civil war. Each found expression in the street art.

Because of the enormous funds from traditional elites, the right was able to massively produce posters. The right's reliance on posters and graffiti demonstrated their belief in the relevance of street art as a key dimension of psychological warfare, a tactic for stirring emotions. In the emotionally heated general elections of 1936, street art was heavily employed. Headed by the CEDA, the right pasted up large numbers of posters bearing a dictatorial-looking portrait of its would-be governing leader, Gil Robles, with a slogan demanding power.[4] The right's use of street art was paralleled and surpassed by the prolific street art of the left. The left's victory in the 1936 elections sealed the Republic's fate; five months later on July 18, constituted as the Nationalists, the right rebelled, propelling Spain into a devastating civil war.

The Civil War: 1936–1939

During the Civil War, its ferocity, and the death, destruction, and brutality were recorded in dramatic street art. This art was powerful in its messages and aggressive in its orientations. It served as a handmaiden to the emotional forces that took hold throughout the country. The Nationalist movement, the victorious anti-Republican militant force, was a combination of Falangists, Carlists, Monarchists, and conservative Catholics. They were linked through the defense of their heritage, a belief in the old authoritarian Spain.[5] The Nationalists employed street art to inspire and visualize a brighter future, to issue warnings, to educated politically, to castigate, and to take revenge. The latter was accomplished by leaving visual symbols against a marked enemy. For example, one Falangist poster exalting the movement and its future depicted a group of individuals marching, a woman with her arm raised in the fascist salute, and a child held high as the central figure symbolizing the worthiness of fighting for the future. A student, a worker, and a soldier walked in the front rank, all against the background of the Falangist and Spanish flags and the Falange logo—the yoked arrows of the Catholic kings—with white doves in the sky. In Republican areas captured by the Nationalist forces, especially in Andalucía, villages were laid waste under conquering Nationalist troops. Graffiti which read, "Your women will give birth to fascists" was scribbled on walls as symbols of the conquering, revengeful victor.[6] The Falangist motto *Arriba España* (Up with Spain) and *Viva la Muerte* (Long live death) and the Nationalists' *Viva España* (Long live Spain) were slogans liberally scrawled in conquered areas. These epitomized the Nationalist cause, proclaiming that Spain was indivisible and separatism would not be tolerated.

Nationalist groups competed among themselves. They employed street art to advance their cause and increase their influence. Their publicity was harsh and aggressive, their posters prolific and omnipresent. The Carlists, an antiliberal, religiously fervent movement, stood for a powerful king, an indivisible country, and an hierarchical church. They were drawn to the Nationalists by their antiliberal values. Carlist posters proclaimed their message, "If you are a good

Spaniard, love your country and her glorious traditions, enlist with the *Re-quetés* (militia).'' Recruitment themes for the Nationalist forces were ladened with macho cultural overtones: "Young men of Spain—*o castrenses o castra-dos*" (either military or castrated). The Falange's recruitment message was equally threatening: "The Falange calls you—now or never." The ranks of the Falange swelled as the population scrambled to join and escape the slaughter of the conquering forces.[7] The threat was real. One of the first laws promulgated by Franco, the Law on Political Responsibilities, made it an ex post facto crime to belong to leftist political parties, a Masonic lodge, or impede the Nationalist movement. Many citizens were executed for such activities; others received long prison terms.[8]

Nationalists utilized children as subjects in posters to elicit an emotional response toward the "Republican monsters." One poster showed a giant figure of a subhuman worker–soldier with a rifle in his hand standing over the out-stretched, limp body of a young child; the caption read, "Your father was a fascist." Nationalists stressed ties to the Catholic Church, which they con-sidered the heart and soul of Spain. One poster featured a pole-shaped figure with the word *Crusade* crossing to form a cross-like background shadow. It carried the inscription, "Destination."[9] The term *crusade* held a significant connotation because of the close identification between the Church hierarchy and Nationalists. In a collective letter, the Church termed the Nationalist move-ment a crusade, thereby legitimizing the Franco cause.[10]

At the close of the war, the Nationalists used posters to reeducate the citi-zenry. Republican orphans captured by the Nationalists were adopted by the Falange and indoctrinated about the sins of anti-Spanish ideas. Some posters portrayed communists as devils. One showed a huge man with a broom sweep-ing out anti-Nationalist human trash—"the Communists, the Masons, the Sep-aratists." Another showed the giant hands of a hovering communist devil reaching down to rip apart families portrayed by women and their children. They were defended by a Nationalist soldier. A heroic message written across the poster read, "NEVER." A third poster showed a huge Bolshevik with a whip, en-slaving horrified children; and a fourth sketched the progressive metamorphosis of the communist hammer-and-sickle logo, turning it into a skull, the symbolic consequence (death) with a communist system. The poster said, "That's what there is behind communism."[11] When the Nationalists captured Catalonia early in 1939, street art quickly brought the message of Spanification. Posters or-dered everyone to "Speak Castilia—the language of the Empire." The regional language Catalán was forbidden.[12] Under the "New Spain" of Franco the Catholic Church was given an enormous role. One responsibility was keeper of public morals. Posters carried the theme "No immoral dances, no indecent clothes, no bare legs, no heathen beaches."[13] Furthermore, to convey that Spain was now Nationalist territory, Franco's name was painted on the sides of public buildings.[14]

The Republicans also engaged in the widespread use of posters and graffiti.

The anarchists, particularly powerful in Catalonia, made liberal use of street graphics. Trams in Barcelona were repainted with the anarchist colors, black and red. Railroad cars carrying partisan slogans were covered with pro-Republican graffiti. Recruitment posters were popular. One anarchist poster showed three soldiers in battle with the various anarchist organization acronyms imprinted on each soldier's cap—the CNT, the FAI, the FIJI—with the inscription "Each battle an objective—forward—join the forces—a free Spain." [15] Another poster, distributed during the first month of the Civil War, had as the central figure a young woman in workers' clothing with a rifle held high against a background of marching soldiers carrying rifles and the Catalán and anarchist flags. The poster inscription, in Catalán, proclaimed, "The militias need you." [16] The anarchist feminist group Mujeres Libres conducted a morality campaign through posters. In Catalonia's red-light districts, they displayed posters inviting prostitutes to renounce their professions and choose career training courses. Another Mujeres Libres poster was directed at the moral confusion of antifascist militiamen who exploited prostitutes. This poster portrayed an ugly, shadowy militiaman fondling a beautiful prostitute. The implicit message was do not be a hypocrite and exploit people, this is your fight. [17] A dramatic Communist party poster issued in November 1936 showed the giant figure of a man with a flashlight in one hand and a club. He was about to step on and crush a group of citizens illuminated by the light. The poster's message read, "Discover and crush the fifth column without pity." Another Communist poster aimed at agrarian reform portrayed a colossal farmer holding a sickle; another man was plowing. The inscription read, "This land will be yours—we must defeat fascism." [18] The Workers' Party of Marxist Unification (POUM), an independent anti-Stalinist communist party of importance during the Civil War, had a war poster which stated, "POUM—until victory or death." Another POUM poster, aimed at recruiting workers, had the profile of several workers over the backdrop of a sickle. It read, "Workers—POUM waits for you." [19] The Republican Ministry of Propaganda featured a poster of a boat with all the Nationalist bedfellows inside—the Church, the fascist, the military, and the Moor (Arab troops under Franco's command)—crossing the Mediterranean from Morroco to Spain with the inscription, "The Nationalists." An anarchist poster portrayed a giant beast rising: "The beast is nearing—be careful what you say—CNT-FAI." [20]

The Franco Era

The Franco years are difficult to assess because of the closing of political space following the Civil War. Opportunities for resistance were few, and severe punishment awaited those caught engaging in opposition activities. As with most repressive regimes, the type of street art available to the resistance was limited. Graffiti, the most risk free, became a popular tool and opened space for political expression. Walls served to express what was censored by other media. Over time resistance street art became more visual and more widely practiced. The end of World War II enabled resistance groups to organize and carry out activities more freely after France was liberated. After 1945, Basque activists painted walls with revolutionary slogans or planted the Euskadi flag on inaccessible but highly visible locations.[21] Strikes, illegal under Franco, were accompanied by commentary through pamphlets and graffiti. The first sustained antisystem strikes were in 1951. Leaflets and slogans written on walls helped mobilize the people.[22] Working-class neighborhoods where socialists and communists had strength displayed antisystem graffiti, with the communists' hammer-and-sickle appearing on walls. The N-20 (November 20) celebration of Falangist leader José Antonio was met with opposition graffiti, "Do not go—the dudes are full of shit."[23] In 1956, university students opposed to the Falangist-legalized student union, the Sindicato Español Universitario (SEU), wrote "SEU no—free unions" and "Down with SEU."[24] In the 1960s, antisystem graffiti and other opposition activities erupted at the University of Madrid. In 1959 in Barcelona, leaflets were circulated urging people to write the letter *P* for protester on walls; arrests followed the *P* graffiti campaign.[25]

Franco advocates, logically, did not face the same restricted public space. In Andalucía, especially in smaller towns, the continued visual presence of Falangists' and Nationalists' symbols was prevalent. Large graffiti slogans, "Viva Franco," "Viva España," and "Arriba España" were evident and intimidating. Some lasted for years, indicating that no one tampers with prostate graffiti and propaganda.[26] Andalucía, an extremely anti-Franco, antisystem region, was where the Socialists and the anarchists had their power base in pre-Civil War days. Thus, the visual presence of the Falange message symbolized that Andalucía was an ideologically and physically conquered region. Opposition activists who painted street graffiti were severely punished in Franco's Spain. However, written statements, logos, and slogans that supported the dominant ideology were tolerated. For example, young rebels of the Falangist JONS movement rallied around the figure of Manuel Hedilla, conveying their feelings by writing "Hedilla–JONS" slogans on Madrid walls in chalk.[27] The Falangist logo and the face of martyred José Antonio were liberally displayed on walls, and antisystem groups were singled out: "Reds—no," "Carrillo (communist leader)—we will make mincemeat out of you."[28]

The state itself became a sponsor of street graphics. In the immediate post–World War II period when Spain was increasingly isolated and the United Nations was pressuring Franco to step aside, state propaganda machinery in December 1946 printed leaflets and posters announcing Spain would not submit to being a colony.[29] Subsequently, in 1947 Franco proposed a draft law on succession that made Spain a kingdom but gave him rule for life. A referendum held in July 1947 was to demonstrate the popular approval of the regime. The streets were replete with state-sponsored leaflets directing people to vote. Walls were covered with "Yes" posters. Opposition groups such as the anarchists had their own "Vote No" leaflets. Twenty years later another referendum was ordered. The regime decided in a symbolic way that it was time to normalize the succession process through an Organic Law and again prove to the outside world its legitimacy. In the plebiscite people could vote either "Yes" or "No." Giant posters with "FRANCO—Si" accompanied by his profile were printed, along with tens of thousands of Franco photographs and stickers.[30]

POST-FRANCO: THE DEMOCRATIC PERIOD

With the demise of the Iberian authoritarian states, street art experienced a renaissance in Spain and Portugal. New, direct, expressive thought via street art represented a renewal process. What were the social forces at work within Spain and the political claims that exemplified and characterized the street art in this new era? Several factors drove the production of street graphics during the transition: First, a public catharsis engulfed both Spain and Portugal. In the months and years following the democratic openings, street wall expression was prolific. This catharsis against censorship coupled with the emotion of free expression unleashed a torrent of opinions. They offered a spectrum of people's feelings and gave an indication of group forces that might emerge in the new states. For the ordinary citizen in Spain, street art was an easy way to affirm freedom from censorship. It made sacred what the previous regime had forbidden—freedom of expression. Street art symbolized that censorship had gone bankrupt, that free expression and the democratic exchange of ideas had emerged victorious. Groups and individuals that had suppressed their anger and ideas quickly recorded a popular version of their history.

A second factor that drove street art was the string of continuous elections—national, regional, municipal, plebiscites, and constitutional reforms. Street art became an important mechanism for new political posturing and recognition by groups and political parties seeking political space, for injecting ideas into the restructured democratic process, and for establishing political agendas. In essence, the highly politicized street art that emerged served to visualize ideas for debate, convey everyday concerns of groups, and reflect the sociopolitical conflicts and competitiveness of the democratic system.

The restructuring of parties and groups had to adapt to the new composite thinking that emerged in Spain. To become viable, political parties and groups had to reorganize, test public opinion, set priorities, establish identities, and seek support among the citizenry. When parties were legalized in 1977, over three hundred registered. Of the major parties that emerged, only the Socialists (PSOE) were able to claim a semblance of stability and tradition. By 1981, the Partido Comunista de España (PCE), the highly organized, disciplined, and militant communist party, split into three warring factions and parties—the PCE, the Partido Comunista de los Pueblos de España (PCPE), and the Partido de los Trabajadores de España (PTE)—and declined as a viable alternative. Attempting to regain political space, the communists regrouped in 1989 as an alternative leftist movement under the PCE's Izquierda Unida (IU). The Unión de Centro Democrático (UCD), which emerged as the governing party in years immediately following the democratic opening, was unable to establish credibility and splintered into many factions. The Alianza Popular (AP), the major rightist party, was renamed Partido Popular (PP) in 1988. This post-Franco party was founded in 1976 by former members of the Franco regime who pulled together the shattered remnants of the UCD and other old Franco forces. Thus new parties formed, old alliances died, and the right and left tried to establish viable alternatives to the dominating influence of the Socialists, who have governed since 1982.

Regionalism

The third factor that drove the intense use of street art was the emotional question of centralization—the dominance of Castilian culture and politics (Madrid) versus the counteridentities and rights for regional peoples and cultures. Pushed by the phenomenal emergence of regional grass-roots parties, a restructured state moved Spain away from Castilian centralization and toward regional autonomy. Franco had tried desperately to permanently terminate regional identities and culture. He employed mass executions, torture, retribution, and suppression of "non-Spanish" cultures, all in an attempt to cleanse the nation with a surgical cure. The Catalans and the Basques were particularly castigated for their separatist ethnic tendencies. This suppression of regional identities also occurred under King Alfonso XIII in the 1920s. Separatist tendencies were punished by law. Offenses against the unity of Spain included any public manifestation, act, word, written expression, or display of graphic media or flag that was not Spanish.[31]

Franco's triumph of centralization and a single national identity did not survive his death. With the new democratic opening, regionalism, ethnic regional nationalism, and all the long-festering issues pertaining to centralization—past persecutions, policies of Spanification, and national versus regional language and culture—exploded in fury. Centralism had become equated with repression and lack of freedom and, conversely, regionalism with freedom. The regional nationalists, the Catalans and Basques, and to a lesser extent the Galicians, staked out claims by promoting regional power. This evolved into a broad national movement and became the most dynamic and salient phenomenon in Spanish politics.[32] The conflicting claims emerging from this centrifugal pull became one leading theme communicated via street art. Regional nationalists and regionalists used graphics prolifically. They utilized the public space to raise their profiles. The level of consciousness on this political issue evolved to such a point that all the major political parties, in one manner or another, adapted to the political requisites of regionalism to remain viable. Traditional centralists, which include many former Francoists in the PP and Marxist parties, have adapted to this political phenomenon; only the fascists have rejected the trend.

For example, a change in emphasis was most dramatic with the PCE. In the 1980s it placed regional nationalism ahead of class struggle.[33] The Communist party in pre-Franco Spain represented a hard-line leftist position for centralization. Regionalism was viewed as breaking the unity of a strong Spain. To survive and gain political space during the clandestine years, the PCE altered its image by allowing regional communist parties to exist. This policy was designed to benefit from the historical tensions between the periphery and the core. However, Leninist party discipline remained.[34] In the early 1970s, increased opposing tendencies forced the PCE to adapt to the same changing political circumstances confronting political groups trying to establish a national presence. The PCE and other Marxist parties adjusted their political rhetoric and structure to accommodate renewed emphasis on regionalism and regional nationalism. For the 1979 elections, recognizing the multinational, multilingual character of Spain, both the PCE and PSOE supported the concept of decentralization.[35] To reflect stronger regional identity, some national parties emphasized regional organization. For example, the Andalucian branch of the PCE became the Andalucian Communist Party, the PCA. The PCA sponsored street art under this new label and later under its leftist coalition, Izquierda Unida-Convocatoria por Andalucía (IU-CA). The pro-Soviet communist party, the PCPE, became the PCPA, replacing España with Andalucía. Its street art placed the Andalucía flag alongside the hammer-and-sickle. The adjustment by the PCPE to regional interests demonstrated the depth of feeling attracted to regionalism in Andalucía and elsewhere. The more leftist-oriented regional nationalists, including communists, went further. They placed the regional struggle in Third-World terminology: colonies trying to break the hegemonic control of an exploiting center. Various Marxist parties gave greater emphasis to the right of self-determination. It was a common theme often reflected in street art, particularly in the historical regions.

Regional identity is more rooted in Spain because various regional languages serve as an important unifying factor. Marxist parties, and even conservative national parties, adapted to this requisite by addressing the issue in a symbolic substantial manner, giving expressive recognition of various cultures through street art communicated in regional languages, according to regional identities. Despite the adjustment by major parties, regional parties continued to grow. In the general election in October 1989, the regional parties captured 17 percent of the national vote, making them the third major force; only the PSOE and the PP out-distanced them.[36]

In regions with linguistic identities, street art has served to keep regional cultural differences alive. Language is a factor that separates regional nationalism from regionalism. Language is especially significant in the northern historical regions of Galicia, Catalonia, and Euskadi, but it stretches beyond these. Depending upon one's definition, there are five or six linguistic identities: Galician (gallego), Basque, Bable (the old language of Asturias), Aragonese, Catalán, and perhaps Valencian, a language related to Catalán.[37] Catalán is also spoken in the Balearic Islands. Bable and Aragonese are nearly extinct, although small groups are attempting to rekindle an interest as a way to promote a separate identity. Estimates suggest 10 million of Spain's 38 million inhabitants speak a regional language. One way to promote these languages, as practiced in Galicia, Catalonia, and Euskadi, is to increase their visibility and the awareness of them by writing these languages on public walls. Even in Valencia, where the language has deep roots, it was promoted feverishly through street art. Public opinion polls indicate citizens feel more regionalist in Euskadi, Galicia, and Andalucía. The Catalán region is diluted by an influx of Spanish workers into the industrial heartland.[38] Regional identities were strong in the nonlinguistic-based communities of Navarra and the Canary Islands.

Led by the historical regions, the post-Franco constitution allowed regions to establish Autonomous Communities and take responsibility for certain services. This stimulated the evolution of regional groups and political parties of various ideological persuasions. Regional parties became more entrenched and more represented on the regional level than on the national level. In four Autonomous Communities, regional parties have either ruled alone—Catalonia and Euskadi—or in coalition—Navarra and Aragón. In several other regions, regional parties have captured more than 20 percent of the vote.[39] The most significant regional parties included: Partido Andalucista (PA), Partido Aragones Regional (PAR), Unió Valenciana (UV), Unitat del Poble Valencia (UPV), Agrupaciones de Independientes Canarios (AIC), Agrupación Herreña Independiente (AHI), Extremadura Unida (EU), Partido Regionalista del País Leones (PREPAL), Partido Nacionalista de Castilla y Leon (PANCAL), Partido Regionalista Independiente de Madrid (PRIM), Unión del Pueblo Navarro (UPN), Partido Regionalista Cantabria (PRC), Partido Riojano Progresista (PRP), Unión del Pueblo Melillense (UPM), Partido Castellano (PC), and Unión Mallorquina (UM). In addition, there are regional nationalist parties in the three historical regions: in Galicia, the Coalición Galega (CG), Partido Nacionalista Galego (PNG), Bloque Nacionalista Galego (BNG), Partido Socialista Galego (PSG-EG), and Frente Popular Galega (FPG); in Euskadi, Partido Nacionalista Vasco (PNV), Euskadiko Ezkerra (EE), Eusko Alkartasuna (EA), and Herri Batasuna (HB); and in Catalonia, Convergencia i Unió (CiU), Esquerra Republicana de Catalunya (ERC), and the radical Moviment de Defensa de la Terra (MDT). The plethora of multiregional parties was responsible for the proliferation of street art that marked the visual landscape of Spain. Each group used street graphics to advertise its existence, raise the consciousness of the regional citizenship, and pressure major parties and the central government for greater changes and transference of responsibilities.

The quantity of street art produced by these regional parties was abundant. They campaigned nearly year-round, stimulated by the continuous multiple elections. These included the European parliamentary, the Spanish national parliament, the regional parliament, and local elections, each separately convoked. Across the landscape, one could see the acronyms of regional parties everywhere—PREPAL, PANCAL, AIC, PAR. Usually, the stronger the party, the greater the amount of street art. In regions where several regional parties competed, the increased volume of street art was noticeable. Many weaker regional parties were not as visually evident. Such cases would be PRIM, PRP, and PRC. The one region with no regional party presence was Murcia. In the regions of Madrid, Castilla-La Mancha, Cantabria, Asturias, and La Rioja, regional parties had a minimal presence via street art. Party acronyms were painted on highway embankments, bridges, the sides of abandoned buildings, and just about any place that would attract the eye. Regional visibility of street art in one region reinforced it in other regions.

One strategy for gaining political space was through repetitive identification. One would see PREPAL, PREPAL, PREPAL, or EXTREMADURA UNIDA, EXTREMADURA UNIDA, or PANCAL, PANCAL, PANCAL, written everywhere. These parties and others would also launch more elaborate statements and messages such as "Vote PREPAL—it is ours," "Zamora es León—PREPAL," or "León autonomy—PREPAL." The explanation for these latter statements was that PREPAL advocated separating the present León-Castilla region into two Autonomous Communities. Included in León would be the provinces of Zamora, Salamanca, and León. To advance further awareness in these provinces, the Leonist zealots pushed their cause by scrawling out road signs with graffiti that identified the León-Castilla region. They marked out Castilla in the Leon provinces, and León in the Castilla provinces so that they visually become separate entities. PANCAL, on the other hand, favored the continuous union of Castilla and León. This conflict developed with the Autonomous provisions of the 1978 constitution and subsequent Institutional Law for the Harmonization of the Devolution Process in 1981. The latter mandated all provinces be organized within an Autonomous Community, either as a single province or as multiple provinces. Seventeen Autonomous Communities were established. The peripheral regions of central Spain were easy to divide as they had maintained a more historical identity. On the central Meseta, where century-old regional identities had given way to a general feeling of Spanishness, complications arose over the proper divisions. In their street art PANCAL and PRE-CAL reflected messages pertaining to the continuing debate over the division of the Meseta.

THE HISTORICAL COMMUNITIES: REGIONAL NATIONALISM

General Characteristics

Several features distinguished street art in the historical regions of Galicia, Catalonia, and Euskadi from other regions. These included an elevated politicization, a complexity of the issues articulated, and a greater tendency to utilize all four forms of street art. The examples noted here focus mainly on Galicia and Catalonia. The Basque case is given special consideration in the next chapter due to its more complex political-historical circumstances. Themes that dominated in the street art in the historical regions were often strongly anti-system. This tone did not mean that those sentiments represented majority feelings. It simply meant that Marxists, radical leftists, and nationalist groups had a greater tendency to utilize street art as a means for communication on a continuous basis.

As to form, mural expression was more common in the historical regions than other regions. They were illustrative of a new democratic era. In many instances, murals became celebrations of regional nationalism and culture. While politically motivated murals could be found throughout Spain, they did not have the quantity and dominance they had in the historical regions, where linguistic and cultural difference motivated activists. Furthermore, competitiveness exaggerated the production of political murals in the historical regions. Marxists and radical nationalists competed for political space, reinforcing the mural culture. For some, murals became cultural icons that helped fuel the fire of a political-cultural expression demonstrating resistance to the internal hegemony of Spanish culture. What could more visually emphasize cultural differences and identities from Spanish nationalism than linguistic and cultural codes that dramatized the difference between the cultures. The inescapable street art served to demarcate separate sociocultural identity through nationalistic symbols and cultural norms, and to politically educate and induce linguistic literacy. Few could escape the omnipresence of these distinct linguistic symbols.

The acceptance of linguistic separateness was exemplified by the national Spanish parties when they began designing electoral propaganda to meet regional linguistic trends. They captioned street propaganda bilingually or solely in the local vernacular as a means to maintain or gain political space. National parties, the PSOE, the IU, and the PP, each tried to maintain a visual presence and political base in these historical regions by employing linguistic symbols.

In the historical regions, there were differences in intensity, issues articulated, and quantity of street art in each region. In Euskadi, where the struggle was further advanced, the conflict with centralism had broader implications. Nationalistic sentiments were stronger, sectarian divisions more pronounced, and goals redefined more drastically. Euskadi had the most politicized and prolific street art, Galicia the least quantity as it was the region where nationalistic sentiments were weakest. Unlike Catalonia and Euskadi, Galicia is a poor region with little industrial base. Small farms and divided land characterize the region, creating a certain conservatism.

In each of the three regions, nationalistic linguistic roots ran deepest in the small towns and villages. In larger cities, with their cosmopolitan culture, Spanification had its greatest success. This is where identities split and cultures collide. In cities such as Barcelona, San Sebastian, Bilbao, and Santiago de Compostela, the nationalistic feelings were weakest. Those who were educationally ambitious understood that to succeed meant adopting the Spanish language. To increase linguistic consciousness in the urban areas, radical nationalists focused on visual impact with street art, meaning in the cities the politically active groups were especially visual. Activists' posters and murals were written in non-Spanish vernacular or bilingual format. In Galicia, the socialization process of linguistic consciousness in street art occurred primarily in the six urban centers—Santiago, Orense, Lugo, La Coruña, Pontevedra, and Vigo. In Catalonia, street art was displayed more regionwide, although it was heavier in Barcelona and other cities. In Euskadi, street art was everywhere.

Catalonia

Street art in Catalonia was more an alternative channel for nongoverning groups and parties. This was particularly true for the communist parties, radical nationalists, and various marginal groups seeking greater political space. These groups were practitioners of street art on a day-to-day basis. They did not confine their communication to elections or special events as did the major political parties. With the declining influence of Marxist groups late in the 1980s, a corresponding decrease in street art has occurred. The governing nationalist regional coalition, the CiU, a conservative, middle-class nationalism, primarily confined its street graphics to election campaigns as did PSOE, which governs the city of Barcelona.

The presence of nationalist terrorist groups and supporting auxiliaries has been felt in varying degrees. These forces utilized street art as a psychological tactic for conveying their presence, issuing warnings, and making demands. In Catalonia, the nationalist terrorist organization, Terra Lliure (TL), created in 1979, and its principal political auxiliary, Moviment de Defensa de la Terra (MDT), were proindependent advocates. The MDT lacked charismatic leaders and was beset by a schism in 1987 that divided it into the MDT-Independentistes del Paisos Catalans (MDT-IPC) and the MDT-Partit Socialista d'Alliberament Nacional (MDT-PSAN). These radicals did not receive the social support which the Herri Batasuna coalition did in Euskadi. This movement dissolved in 1992 when Terra Lliure gave up the struggle and joined the main stream parties.

The MDT was responsible for the street art surrounding the radical independent movement. In its independence logo, the four vertical strips symbolized each Catalán province; a red star resting above the strips represented the ideological sentiments for a future socialist state. This logo, widely visible on the walls throughout Catalonia, appeared either in a crude monochrome graffiti or placed in MDT wallpaintings and murals executed in polychrome colors featuring the official red and yellow regional colors of Catalonia. The MDT was responsible mainly for the ubiquitous *Visca Catalunya* (Long live Catalonia) and "Independence for Catalonia" slogans that appeared as graffiti or as themes in murals. Murals constituted a subculture movement in itself. The MDT was joined by other leftist parties such as the ERC, various communist parties, and

Latin American solidarity groups in utilizing murals as a channel for expression. These murals did not last as they did in Euskadi; they were more ephemeral. The MDT murals were especially vulnerable to eradication. However, some lasted from weeks to several months. Several Communist party murals in Barcelona painted along highway retaining walls remained for several years. Themes presented in MDT murals and posters often portrayed imprisoned militants, named them patriots and political prisoners, and called for their release. France received vitriolic attacks because Terra Lliure militants taking refuge in France were subject to extradition. When extradition occurred, the MDT and the Committees for Solidarity with Catalán Patriots (CSPC) engaged in campaigns to mobilize opinion against it.

The most celebrated case was Pere Bascompte, assumed leader of TL, who was arrested in southern France in January 1989. Immediately, throughout Catalonia, posters sponsored by the MDT and CSPC were pasted. One poster showed a photo of Pere with various inscriptions: "Catalonia supports its refugees," "No to extradition," "Solidarity with Pere Bascompte," "For the right to political asylum." Another announced a rally to support Pere. On other occasions, the MDT utilized graffiti to celebrate martyrs, "Felix Goñi died for independence," or to romanticize armed conflict, "An armed people—a respected people." Annually, the MDT celebrated the Day of the Catalán Soldier in January. A poster for the 1989 celebration profiled a large hand clutching a rifle and an extended arm stretching out to form an elongated map of greater Catalonia. Linguistic issues were at the core of the MDT's cultural identity. They pushed language vigorously in wallpaintings, "Speak Catalán everywhere." And the MDT, along with other leftist–nationalist groups, used the occasion of the official visit of Spanish King Juan Carlos to Catalonia in April 1988 to stir nationalistic sentiments. Threatening graffiti, "Death to the king— long live the nation," were common. Posters were also created for the occasion. A black and white poster showed a miniature Jordi Pujol, president of the Autonomous Community, who had officially invited the king, sitting on Juan Carlos's lap. The king was portrayed as a giant in comparison to a midget Pujol. The inscription read "Independence."[40] Another black and white poster showed three young warriors masked with the Catalán flag, proclaiming, "The Cataláns do not have a king—Defend the Cataláns—Independence." Other street art announced rallies against the Spanish king. This event proved to be an occasion when nationalists had an opportunity to mobilize public opinion, thus the tremendous utilization of street art.

A common theme elaborated in MDT murals focused on their four-point program, a program akin to the five-point KAS Alternative, which forms the political base for ETA-HB in Euskadi. The MDT program called for "Unification of Catalonia, acceptance of all forms of struggle, defense of the interests of the Catalán working people, an independent nation." The first point needs explanation. Most people see Catalonia as territorially united, but militant nationalists are expansionists. They want unification of all Catalán linguistic provinces. For militants, these encompassed the three provinces of the Autonomous Community of Valencia, or at least the northern two, Valencia and Castellón, the Balearic Islands, and present-day Catalonia. Thus, in MDT street art, particularly in posters and murals, they often designed themes with the elongated map of greater Catalonia. The Pere solidarity posters and the murals spelling out their four-point program contained these elongated maps.

The communist movement has had strong visual presence and support in Catalonia. In the first national elections held in June 1977, they captured 18 percent of the regional vote.[41] Beset by factional infighting, by the depolitization that has occurred throughout Spain following the democratic opening, and by the demise of the Socialist bloc, the communist influence has waned. Until the 1990s their street art continued to be prolific and vibrant, and not confined to elections. They struggled to maintain political space by adapting to the changing sociopolitical and economic realities. During the 1980s, two major communist parties competed for the communist working-class vote, the Partit Socialista Unificat de Catalunya (PSUC); the Catalán branch of the PCE, which had its greatest electoral strength in Catalonia; and the Partit dels Comunistes de Catalunya (PCC), the Catalán branch of the PCPE. The PCC was formed in 1982 in a schism from the PSUC.

Both parties were avid street art communicators and strong competitors. The PCC, the smaller of the two, seemed to be the most visually active practitioner of street art. The party had well-designed posters for the 1986 elections. Each called attention to a particular issue: "Work or subsistence—vote PCC," "For a Leftist Front—vote PCC," "No to NATO—military bases out—vote PCC," "The young will vote PCC," and "Self-determination—vote PCC." This last point reflected the nationalist position. There was a poster with a historical touch, "50 years of Popular Front, 1936–1986—for a United Front," and a more elaborate poster spelling out a four-point program, "For a dignified schooling, For a place to work or subsistence, For self-determination, Bases out—no NATO." The PCC was also responsible for some gigantic murals in the Barcelona area. During the 1989 national elections, the visibility of the PCC as a separate entity continued despite the fusion of the communist parties and the successful electoral alliance of the IU—regionally the Iniciativa per Catalunya (IC), which replaced the PSUC communist label. The visual presence of the IC began in the mid-1980s. Walls came alive with "Iniciativa per Catalunya—IC" as the PSUC tested this name identity and image. For a few years, the IC wallpaintings became the most heavily produced street graphics in the Barcelona area. Its new image won acceptance. Early in 1990, the PSUC disbanded and reconstituted itself as the IC.[42] This constituted its evolution into a mainstream party, seeking to gain political space abandoned by the PSOE on the left.

Traditional May 1 celebrations continued to be an occasion for communist parties to assert their visibility. Murals and posters commemorated the occasion. The theme in 1986 for the PCC and other communist parties was peace because of the NATO controversy. A May 1 PCC poster featured a white dove against a background of workers, along with a list of the PCCs claims, "For a Left-front, For peace, For full employment, The right to self-determination." The smaller Catalán Communist Movement (MCC) stressed not peace in its May 1 poster but workers' rebellion, "100 years of worker rebellion." In 1989 the focus was on Europe and the EC, stimulated by the elections to the European parliament and by Spain assuming the revolving presidency of the Council of Europe. The PCC attacked the EC in its street art by calling for "National sovereignty—renegotiate with the EC." The PCC took a radical position on European integration by not supporting it, like other radical nationalist groups such as the HB.

Linguistic identification was recognized by the communists. Ninety percent of their street art was written in Catalán. Both the PCC and the PSUC featured the Catalán national flag alongside the hammer-and-sickle logo on their posters and wallpaintings. These practices helped demonstrate the depth of regional feeling in Catalonia, and the importance placed on currying favor to regional nationalistic interests, despite the large number of working-class migrants from Spain who flooded into Catalonia seeking employment.

There were many special-interest groups involved in communicating through street art. These included feminist groups, and Latin American Solidarity Committees with El Salvador and Nicaragua, who utilized murals and graffiti. Environmental groups such as the Greens produced mainly posters and occasional green zone murals. Unions announced strikes and demonstrations via graffiti and posters, and anti-NATO, antidraft groups utilized all forms. One anti-NATO mural by the United Committee for Peace profiled hands breaking a rifle into two pieces, the inscription in polychrome read, "For a not so Black Future"; the *not* (no) was arranged in the Catalán language so it read, "No NATO."

A characteristic to note about this street art was the universal use of the Catalán language, more pronounced than in Euskadi where the difficult Basque language was often supplemented by Spanish. Furthermore, the Catalán language is more widely spoken and understood than is Basque in Euskadi. Thus, the practitioners of street art did not need to be concerned about the inability to read the messages as in Euskadi where bilingual presentations were more common.[43] Not everyone was happy with the use of Catalán; often Catalán street art inscriptions were sabotaged by rabid Spanish nationalists who crossed out Catalán words and Spanified the message in graffiti.

Galicia

Galician street art, while the smallest in quantity of the three historical regions, offers an interesting perspective. Galicia attracted various aggressive groups and parties who livened public walls with stinging discourse. There were two general attractions, regional nationalism and the workers. Even though Galicia does not have the industrial development of Catalonia or Euskadi, there was an organized industrial work force built around the important Atlantic sea ports and shipyards. These include the city of Vigo and its port, and the La Coruña-El Ferrol area, the home of the old shipyard industry. This labor force attracted groups seeking to represent the workers' interests—socialists, Marxists, communists, and Trotskyists. Added to this economic characteristic was a regional-cultural identity anchored around the Gallego language. Regional nationalism has roots. Groups and parties emerged to guide, advance, and represent these emotions. At times nationalism and working-class concerns overlapped, forcing Marxists to accommodate to regional nationalist interests.

The intensity of political debate was not as accentuated as in Catalonia or in Euskadi, for regional nationalism had not attracted the depth of support it had in the other two historical regions. Street art reflected this political reality. In Galicia, street art was more limited in the plurality of interests represented and the opportunities presented. The medium was less a day-to-day expression and more oriented around special events and issues, opportunities that facilitated the chance to curry favor and perhaps mobilize public opinion. The event most accelerating street art, beside elections, was the "National Day of Galicia—July 25." It was the day when nationalists and leftist groups mobilized their ranks to compete for visibility and recognition. Four nationalist groups were responsible for the street art: the BNG, the PSG-EG, the FPG and the PNG. The PNG and FPG were products of recent schisms, the PNG from the nationalist conservative party, the CG, and the FPG from the strongest of the left nationalists, the BNG. In addition, marginal communist parties and groups had high visibility via their wall art: the Trotskyist's Liga Comunista Revolucionaria (LCR), the Partido Comunista de Liberación Nacional (PCLN), the Movimento Comunista Galego (MCG), the Partido Comunista del Pueblo Gallego (PCPG), and the Juntas Galegas pola Amnistia (JUGA). For the most part, the nationalist and communist groups developed overlapping interests and demands articulated via street art. The reason for this was that each group had tied itself to an issue of great concern during the 1980s, unemployment and working conditions. The old shipyard industries had become obsolete, resulting in high unemployment. This precarious economic climate and accompanying psychological insecurity were exacerbated by Spain's agreements with the EC.

Murals were a preferred medium for Marxists and regional nationalists. They maintained a semipermanent presence, lasting for months, and were visually dominating. In Spain as a whole, citizens tended to respect murals. They were not seen as scarring the environmental landscape as were posters and graffiti. Leftist groups utilized murals because of their symbolic collective value and because of their visual impact. Mural production was facilitated by the many walls that surround industrial complexes along the waterfronts, and others that form embankments along the highways and streets in the hilly terrain. It was along the seaports and small ocean towns that the greatest quantity of street art was visible. Only the state capital of Santiago could rival the seafront towns and cities in the quantity of street art produced. The main seaport city of Vigo was often inundated with murals during the 1980s; their themes focused on the economy. In Santiago, greater emphasis was placed on the linguistic issue. In both Santiago and seaport towns, these issues were visible mural themes.

The BNG was the most active party in communicating via street art, focusing upon economics, cultural identity, and Spanish repression. The BNG was prolific in its "In Galicia—speak Gallego" theme. This was also pushed by various communist parties such as the PCPG, "Gallego is our language," and the MCG, "In Galicia—only Gallego." The LCR proclaimed, "No repression of independence—national sovereignty," a theme used in many murals by the nationalist and communist parties. Most called either for "Self-determination" or "Independence." As in Catalonia, the various communist parties featured both the red communist flag and hammer-and-sickle logo alongside the regional flag in their street art. Nationalist sentiment was reflected in scrawling out the Spanish inscribed road signs, replacing the words with their Gallego equivalent, or writing "In Gallego" on the sign. Many murals focused on the most urgent issues—industrial dismantling, dislocation, and exploitation. The FPG exemplified these issues in murals with slogans, "Popular struggle against industrial dismantling," the PCE (lm) "We are victims of gigantic corporations," the BNG, "Defend yourself against industrial dismantling," and "For reindustrialization—no layoffs." The fishing industry was also under threat because of the EC agreements. One BNG mural popular in the mid-1980s, profiled four fishermen with their nets and the statement "Defend yourself against the Common Market—the ruin of our fishing industry." Other murals and graffiti supported the Canary Islands fishermen—"Solidarity with the Canary Island fishermen for better wages." These fishermen had protested the government's new fishing treaties with Morocco.

Galicia has had nationalistic independent terrorist groups and auxiliary organizations although their significance was less than in the other two historical regions. When appropriate, they emphasized martyrdom and repression. There were two active terrorist organizations, the Grupos de Resistencia Antifascista Primero de Octubre (GRAPO), a revolutionary Marxist group that had plagued various regions of Spain off and on over the years, and the Exército Guerrilleiro do Pobo Galego Ceibe (EGPGC), a Galicia nationalist group. In 1988, a half-dozen EGPCG members were apprehended after a terrorist attack. The FPG and the amnesty group JUGA quickly took up the issue—posters and murals proclaimed them political prisoners, demanding "Freedom for national patriots." During the National Day celebration in July 1988, this issue was widely profiled by various nationalist and Marxist groups but faded by 1990. Graffiti called for their release. Photos of each individual were pasted on the walls, especially in Santiago, the street art claiming that "Galicia is in chains," shackled by the imprisonment of patriots. "Release the political prisoners" became the theme of FPG and JUGA murals and posters for the July 25 celebrations. Several murals reached back into history and profiled earlier martyrs: "1936—assassinated for struggling for the liberation of the Galician people—

1975.'' Each date had the name and profiled figure of a martyr. Continuing, the FPG had a wallpainting with the inscription "Freedom for Miguel Campuzano." There was also the "Viva the EGPGC" graffito. The BNG, with established political links and solidarity ties to the Herri Batasuna coalition, had wallpaintings stating, "Solidarity with the Basque patriots—no to extradition— vote HB," "No to the extermination of the Basque people—vote HB," and "Galiza (Galicia) and Euskadi in the same struggle—vote HB."

Other groups and themes articulated through street art were anti-Yankee imperialism, a theme found throughout Spain where there were active communist groups; anti-NATO rhetoric, in particular by the propeace group Coordenadora Nacional de Organizacios pola Paz (CNOP) that sloganed "No NATO— bases out"; the Conscientious Objectors, "Military expenditures for social needs—employment, social justice, culture and health"; and the May 1 commemorations by Marxist groups. Others included an organization for the disabled in La Coruña that placed posters in 1988 beseeching people, "Do not isolate us—we like life also" and a local right-wing group Unión Coruñesa (UC) that spent its energies attacking ETA and Marxism, "A dead ETA member—one problem less," and "ETA = bloody Marxism." The MCG raised the Palestine issue during the Intifada with "Viva Palestine," and various feminist organizations attached to nationalist groups celebrated International Women's day by painting murals. There were also right-wing Spanish nationalists who utilized graffiti to deface and counteract street art of regional nationalists. Their murals and wallpaintings were often defaced with "Viva España" or "Traitors."

NONHISTORICAL REGIONS

Andalucía

Themes expressed in street art varied according to regions. They were stimulated by geopolitical considerations and historical memories. Andalucía offers an interesting comparison to the northern historical regions. Andalucía shares with them a fervert regional identity within Spain. While not regional nationalists in the same context as northerners, Andalucía was the first region to suffer a brutal backlash from the Nationalist and Falange forces during the Civil War. The Nationalists aimed to depoliticize and neutralize the leftist-Marxist cancer that had grown there. As a consequence, Andalucía emerged from the long dictatorship more convincingly leftist and socialist in political attitudes than before. They reached a political consensus that the right would play no appreciable role in Andalucía. The region would become solid PSOE terrain with the communists in a secondary role. Thus, in a region heavily dependent upon an agrarian economy, leftist issues were strongly articulated in the street art.

Geopolitical concerns differ from those of the north. The northern regions focus more on France, while in Andalucía, there was more of an emphasis on the historical relationship with northern Africa and the Arab world. These concerns stemmed from traditional links to Arabic culture, the result of seven centuries of Moorish rule; Franco's special emphasis on an opening to the Arab world exemplified by the refusal to recognize Israel; Moroccan workers employed in agriculture; Arab students studying in Andalucía universities; the requirements of oil-poor Spain; and the historical geopolitical interests in Morocco and northern Africa where Spain historically has occupied large tracts of territory and still retains two enclaves, Ceuta and Melilla.[44] Thus, issues on Arab politics and the sensitive question of imperialism were topics strongly reflected in the discourse of the street art.

The issue of colonialism in Andalucía assumed different emphasis than in northern provinces where cultural colonialism was the predominant concern. Andalucía focused on the three colonial enclaves, Spanish Melilla and Ceuta in North Africa, and British Gibraltar. Ceuta and Melilla were the subject of considerable street art commentary. In the mid-1980s, the small Partido Socialista de los Trabajadores (PST) pushed the issue to "Decolonize Ceuta, Melilla, and the Canaries" with more explicit graffiti stating, "Ceuta, Melilla, and Canaries—independent—they are Moroccan." Other anonymous graffiti countered with the claim that "Ceuta and Melilla are Spanish." The issue heated up in 1987 when the PCE began discussing a formal proposal for its Twelfth Congress that advocated Ceuta and Melilla be returned to Morocco.[45] The PCE branches in the two enclaves broke away from their parent organization over the volatility of the issue among Spandiards living in Ceuta and Melilla. They opposed decolonization. The PCE was castigated for its stand via graffiti.

Other Arab issues were articulated. One was the anti-Moroccan monarch commentary directed at King Hassan. Typical "Down with the monarchy" graffiti greeted Hassan when he paid a one-day state visit to Sevilla-in September 1989. This visit generated various graffiti—"Democracy for Morocco" and anti-Hassan posters. One raised the topic of war in the Spanish Sahara where indigenous groups were fighting Moroccans for the right to independence. The poster showed children behind a barbed-wire fence, the inscription, "Hassan—where are the disappeared of the Sahara?—Peace—No military occupation." The small Movimiento Comunista Andalucía (MCA) castigated Felipe González for "Abandoning the Polisario and joining with Hassan the assassin."

The Palestinian question, stimulated by the Intifada, was the subject of commentary. Pro-Palestinian, anti-Jewish and Israeli graffiti were common, such as "Viva Palestine," and "Solidarity with the Palestinians." Anti-Jewish graffiti carried the dollar sign to exaggerate the stereotypical image. The propaganda was evident in other regions as well. Prodemocracy Algerian groups attacked their authoritarian government through graffiti and posters especially after the cancellation of elections in 1992. Libya's Muammar Qaddafi received solidarity support when the United States bombed Libya in 1986. Solidarity concerns extended to Latin America as well. The Central American Solidarity Committee (CSCA) educated the citizenry that "1,500 disappeared in Guatemala in three years—the PSOE government received those responsible for the crimes," and that "January 22 [was] the international day for the Salvadorian people." "Viva free Nicaragua—Yankees out," "Pinochet will fall—Chile will prevail," were common graffiti while murals commemorated the "Tenth Anniversary of the Sandinista Revolution." For the Intifada, the CSCA extended a "Solidarity to the Palestinians" salute. The most recent campaign, begun in 1989, protested celebration of the Discovery of America Quincentennial.

Other and sundry issues articulated in political art called for "Agrarian reform," or "More work for women." Ecological groups were less active in Andalucía than in northern regions. There were graffiti that supported workers' causes—better salaries, strikes, no layoffs, and increased employment. In the port city of Cádiz, sectarian leftist groups were particularly visual in their campaign to educate the workers. No other city in Andalucía had as many murals as Cádiz, many produced by the artistically prolific Trotskyist group, the LCR. Wherever the LCR was active, whether in Euskadi or in the port cities of Galicia and Barcelona, murals were their visual contribution.

Madrid

Madrid, Spain's capital, is the embodiment of Spanish identity and culture, and a magnet for a variety of groups that shower the city with prolific doses of street art. What emerges in other regions, descends upon the capital, making it a repository of demands for old marginal groups attempting to maintain visibility, and nascent groups wishing to assert themselves.

Yesterday's powerful ideological groups of the Republic who are today's marginal groups, Francoists, anarchists, and communists were particularly visible in Madrid through street art. During the privileged years under Franco's dictatorship, the right-wing core embedded itself in Madrid. To them Madrid symbolized the centralist principles of the Nationalist cause. In the post-Franco era, a number of small neo-Falangists, fascists, and Carlists groups emerged, spawned by internal schism and sectarian factionalism.[46] Especially in Madrid they continued to keep their candles flickering through prolific street art. Their posters were plain and uninspiring, with little artistic creativity. These groups did not use murals as a medium. Major themes in their street art were attacking leftists, Marxists, regional nationalists and the democratic system. "Soldier rebel," (advocating a coup) and "GAL kill them—Reds against the wall," were graffiti slogans of these fascist groups.[47]

There was a plethora of radical right-wing groups and hardly a week went by without their visual appearance in Madrid. The Bases Autonomas (BB AA), claimed to be "The third way—neither Marxist or capitalist." They were heavily into graffiti with "BB AA" acronyms liberally sprayed about, especially around the University of Madrid. Other favorite targets were the banks, which they accused of being corrupt institutions. The Nazi cultural organization, Círculo

Español de Amigos de Europa (CEDADE), which was poster-oriented, announced events and offered solutions with such statements as "If you do not believe in parties, do not vote—there is a solution—CEDADE—the national solution." CEDADE also pushed the revisionist theme, claiming gas chambers never existed and that the Jewish genocide was a lie. In February 1989, they lined the walls of Madrid with posters celebrating the centennial of Hitler's birth. The Falange student union organization SEU recruited at various universities using graffiti advertisements, beseeching students to "Join now." They castigated the concept of a united Europe recalling nostalgia for an insular Spain, "Europe = decadence." The Juntas Española, another group, rhetorically asked, "Will our voice be yours?" Traditional Carlists still advocated their ideas of a half-century ago, "Carlism again," "Construct a new society," "Nothing without God," "Faith and Country," "God, Country, Fueros, and King." They also turned to present problems, "A strong hand against drugs," and "A strong hand against ETA."

The Frente Nacional (FN) of Blas Pinar, the main fascist election coalition, advocated "Vote FN," and "Viva España—Vote F/N." The FE de la Jons, whose graffiti could be seen throughout Spain and whose posters appeared regularly in Madrid, massively pasted on the facades of many buildings, especially banks, celebrated a variety of events including, "The Falange National Day— October 29," "Commemoration of November 20—the day of the martyrs" (the deaths of Franco and José António), and election event posters calling upon the people to "Shock the system—vote FE JONS." Fe Jons supported various issues and positions such as castigating regionalism and the breakup of the Spanish state, "León is not Castilla—it is Spain." They advocated the third way, "Neither Marxist nor capitalist," and conducted a constant graffiti-diatribe against ETA, "Now is enough—it is necessary to terminate ETA without negotiations," and "ETA will die." Fascists and ultraright-wing antidemocratic sentiments were summed up in the graffito, "Army to power." Especially prolific was the street art for the Day of the Martyrs, November 20, 1991, in which fascists from around Europe swelled the crowds. Previously, the fascists had a field day with their propaganda when Rudolf Hess died in August 1987. Within hours CEDADE, the Juventud Vikings, and others had posters in Spain's leading cities, with the commentary, "Rudolf Hess—your struggle has not been futile—we will continue it," "Rudolf Hess 1894–1987— he fell for a New Europe—your comrades will not forget you," "Rudolf Hess has died—now he is free," and "Rudolf Hess—he achieved the freedom that democracy denied him."

The anarchists, old antagonists of the Nationalists, were now a small group. However, their followers continued to be militant activists and were highly visible through constant commentaries via street art in Madrid, and in their historical strongholds, Andalucía and Catalonia. They communicated mainly with graffiti. On occasion they produced posters, and at other times murals and elaborate wallpaintings. They advanced many antisystem causes. One traditional issue was nonparticipation in the electoral system. They advocated, "Abstain—do not vote," "Abstain—your vote today—your sorrow tomorrow," and "Abstain—a man is worth more than a vote." One poster sketched a person painting the inscription "Promises by politicians during elections—workers throw them in the . . ." Another poster voiced "Voting—they continue to exploit you." Because of their traditional identification with the working class, anarchists commemorated May 1. They used posters, graffiti, and an occasional mural. These called for and supported "Revolutionary general strike," and announced antisystem demonstrations. Their antipathy toward the military and the state led them into commentary such as, "The military—social parasites," and claims of repression, "Release political prisoners." One elaborate, antidemocratic poster portrayed an obese politician with a cigar named democracy; three puffs of smoke signified the democratic claims of "Fraternity, Liberty, and Equality," but the system was guarded by a line of armed policemen, symbolizing for the anarchists that democracy was repressive. And lastly, the anarchists placed their ubiquitous circled A logo everywhere. The logo was adopted by various rebellious youth as well.

The main body of the communist party made Madrid their center, although their electoral strength was in Andalucía and Catalonia. To change their image remaining from memories of the Civil War, and Franco's persistent negative propaganda, the PCE downplayed its radical past. The traditional color of red and the hammer-and-sickle logo were often absent from their street graphics. The communists were prolific producers of street art, especially using posters and occasional murals. However, murals were not as familiar in Madrid as they were in the northern regions where open landscape was more conducive for painting. For the 1977 elections, the PCE had nearly 30,000 volunteers in Madrid and Barcelona. The UCD center party had but 230.[48] This imbalance facilitated street art placement for the PCE. However, a precipitous decline in membership, volunteers, and electoral strength engulfed the PCE by 1980. In 1981 when the PCE split into three parties, the PCE became the reformist party, the PCPE pro-Soviet, and PTE the personalistic party of former communist leader Santiago Carrillo. This split led to tremendous competition reflected in the quantity of street art. During the 1986 elections, various communist parties, especially the PCPE and the PCE, were the heaviest producers of posters in Madrid. Many posters were placed side by side in billboard style. This propaganda competition financially bankrupted the parties.[49] This led to a substantial decrease in the volume of communist street art which was evident up to 1992. In Barcelona, where the main communist parties still had electoral strength, their youth wings engaged in painting murals and wallpaintings. Several gigantic murals graced the highway embankment walls.

Fusion among most communists prior to the 1989 general elections helped end the costly competitiveness. A new focus in street art reflected an image aimed at recapturing the lost electorate. It was a formidable task. The working-class movement was in general much weaker. Old industrial factories had closed, the workplace had changed, the standard of living had improved. Consequently, the old language of class conflict had lost its evocative power to postmodern values. In adapting to these changes, class struggle was replaced by the evocative power of regional identity, social issues, relationships with the European Community, and by a new emphasis on the authentic leftist alternative to PSOE. During the 1989 national elections, the PCE was obsessed by the idea that all reference to communism should be dropped by the IU. The hammer-and-sickle did not appear in its street propaganda. Its theme was "A leftist alternative." [50] The PCE proclaimed its new ideological Program Manifesto in August 1988. This replaced the 1975 document. The new manifesto gave recognition to changed political circumstances fourteen years after Franco. In it, the PCE reasserted its definition of Spain as a plural nation-state composed of different regions and nationalities. They defended the right of self-determination and the free union of all peoples within a federal state. [51]

Other groups also made their presence known in Madrid via street art. The antidrug movement, headed by the mothers, marched each week in the Plaza del Sol. Supported by grass-roots neighborhood associations, they took their antidrug campaign to the public via wall graffiti. Some were elaborate commentaries on the danger of drugs; others simple slogans, "Drugs kill." Other graffiti messages demanded government action, "We do not want heroin— without protection—do not pay your taxes." Founded around 1986 in Madrid, the Okupación movement consisting of the Asamblea de Okupas was composed of alienated youth. They occupied abandoned buildings, turning them into homes. Graffiti advertised their movement and communicated their concerns. Their logo was splashed liberally. The Okupas represented an alienated, jobless generation, with strong antibourgeois, antisystem rhetoric and action, concerns expressed in the graffiti "If they won't give you a future—fuck the present," or "Bourgeoisie swing, your time is short before dying."

Other issues were debated on public walls: "Abortion—legal and free," or "No to abortion." Animal rights groups attacked animal abuse research at the universities. They attacked the sacred culture symbol, the bullfight, communicating through graffiti that "It is not art, but cruelty." Sundry environmental groups left their messages on walls. Human rights abuses surfaced periodically. An investigation into the disappearance of a young man (Nani) while in police custody, turned into a media focus. It resulted in the graffiti, "Barrionuevo, (Minister of Interior) where is Nani?"

NATIONAL CAMPAIGNS AND ISSUES

War and Peace Issues

Concerns around war and peace caused a national discourse that resulted in prolific quantities of street art during the 1980s. These concerns were provoked by President Ronald Reagan's bellicose policies. As a consequence of World

War II, the Spanish had deeper anti-American feelings than most European countries. Many in Spain did not view the United States as liberators of fascism as many Europeans did. On the contrary, they believed United States military and economic agreements with Franco in the early 1950s propped up a dying regime, ended its isolation, and extended its life. With the democratic opening, the issue of Spain's membership in NATO surfaced and Spain joined in 1982. This issue, which decisively divided Spain, was exacerbated by Reagan's aggressiveness in Latin America and Libya, and his cold war confrontation with the Soviets. Spain was divided. Many did not want to be brought into an East-West clash. In 1986 when the NATO referendum occurred, the "Sí" versus "No" option was energetically debated on public walls throughout Spain. This campaign is discussed more fully in the next chapter on the Basques. Suffice it to state that NATO membership was approved by a bare majority of the electorate. However, the street art outpouring resumed in earnest in 1987–1988 when the lease on American military bases in Spain came up for renegotiation. Many demanded that the bases be dismantled. Graffiti, posters, and murals screeched out, "Bases out," "Europe without missiles—Spain without bases—PCPE," "Not one base, not one foreign soldier, neither Russian nor Yanki—UCE," and "Neither NATO, nor the Warsaw Pact—CNT." These messages reflected deep sentiments, substantiated by polling data that showed the majority of people wanted a reduced American military presence.[52]

President Reagan caused great contention within Spain. He was portrayed as unstable, warlike, and dangerous. During his 1985 visit, he was greeted with the standard "Reagan go home" graffiti. Thousands marched in anti-American demonstrations and walls resonated with anti-Reagan, anti-American slogans. When Reagan ordered the bombing of Libya, it resulted in another wave of anti-Reagan rage, "Reagan = fascism," "Death to Reagan." The anti-Reagan, anti-American sentiment was manifest with Latin American solidarity groups as well. These groups sprung up to protest United States intervention in Central America and the Caribbean, and human right abuses. Graffiti and posters announced demonstrations and special events for solidarity groups. In Euskadi and Catalonia, murals ensured the visibility of this issue and kept it before the public. Nicaragua received the greatest support. In the late 1980s many murals commemorated the "Tenth Anniversary of the Sandinista Revolution." Graffiti stating, "Yankis, leave Nicaragua in peace" were common. Latin American solidarity groups focused not only on Central America and United States intervention but also on military regimes, especially on Chile. Due to the youth sectors of the communist parties, Chile was the subject of much street art. They kept up a steady street art campaign focused on Chile. "Chile will prevail," "Pinochet get out," and "Pinochet assassin" were typical slogans. Some murals were stylized in mural art characteristic of the Chilean left. Cuba was also an elevated focus by the 1990s. Pro- and anti-Castro groups squared off in street art propaganda battles when the Cuban leader made an official visit to Spain in July 1992.

War and peace had its domestic side in the national debate. The draft and mandatory service were issues that engulfed the entire country. They touched a broad segment of the population—students and their families—and raised emotions and a corresponding commentary via street art, acts to influence public opinion. A variety of grass-roots organizations sprung up to push this issue. Among the groups were the Mili KK, who favored the antimilitary graffiti, "The Mili kills—Mili KK," "Do not go to the mili—object," "Do not let them cut your life," "The mili—no thanks," "Less mili—more work"; the Movimiento de Objetores de Conciencia (MOC) carried these messages in their murals and slogans, "Neither Mili nor missiles—social services," and "The women do not want to go to the barracks"; the Asociacion de Insumisos, "Disobey the draft laws"; the Assembei Antimilitarist (Valencia), "Neither military nor substitute service"; and the Anti-NATO Commissions with their well-placed murals. These single-issue groups were joined by leftist student groups associated with the communist and socialist parties and by the CNT. Each contributed to the profuse street art, keeping antidraft sentiments visually present into the early 1990s. The successful campaign resulted in an abrupt decline in support of obligatory military service; only 12 percent supported it in 1989, compared to 50 percent in 1975 and 74 percent in 1960.[53] The issue reached such awareness that in the 1989 national election, the major parties issued policy statements on draft reform and alternative service.

The PSOE

Another national issue that initiated a great deal of street art messages was the anti-PSOE campaign. In 1982 for the first time, PSOE, the former leftist party, won the national elections. This left a broken, fragmented political right and communist left. The party won again in 1986 and 1989, becoming the dominant party. The right was handicapped by its antidemocratic past and collaboration with the Franco regime. The communists, decimated by internal struggles and splits, by their nondemocratic past, and by the breakup of the Socialist bloc, offered no threat to PSOE hegemony. In the mid-1980s, discontent with the PSOE arose over many issues: Europe's highest unemployment rate, Spain's poor infrastructure, social problems with drugs and crime, a retreat from the left, increasing dispute with its labor sector, the UGT, the high living standards of certain cabinet members, corruption, and just the general discontentment that accompanies ten years in office.

The result found a visual reflection in street art. An ad hoc anti-PSOE campaign came from various sectors to become national in scope, strenuously pushed by the IU. This campaign had various manifestations. Radical regional nationalists, especially in Euskadi, held PSOE, the governing party, responsible for not meeting their demands. Therefore, Euskadi had particularly heavy anti-PSOE street art, often equating PSOE with fascism, and other human rights abuses and repression, "PSOE = GAL."[54] Parallel slogans and sentiments were expressed by radical groups in Catalonia. Other radical groups joined the campaign. The fascist groups produced a stream of anti-PSOE propaganda. The anarchist CNT entered the campaign with the slogan "PSOE = fascism"; others wrote "PSSOE" to symbolize the Nazi SS, or "PSOE = 3 Reich." In 1988–1989 as national elections loomed, and as corruption charges surfaced, graffiti linking PSOE to corruption appeared in the form of "CORRUP$OE P$OEZ." This campaign continued into the 1990s. In the winter of 1988, when PSOE began its party congress in Madrid, a graffiti campaign erupted with "CorruP$OE in Miami—olé," taking after the popular TV series "Miami Vice" which was translated in Spain as "Corruption in Miami." The IU made government corruption one of its campaign issues. One week prior to the general elections in 1989, the anti-PSOE corruption lobby enhanced its propaganda in Madrid with two posters. One poster message read, "PSOE corrupt," and a second more elaborate statement read, "PSOE too corrupt—throw them out." The increasing split between PSOE and the labor movement resulted in an abundance of street art against PSOE, "PSOE—traitor to the workers" or "PSOE—Selling out labor." The most prolific national outpouring of anti-PSOE street art occurred in late 1988 when organized labor called a general strike on December 14 to protest against government policies. Street art everywhere announced the "14-D" strike, an event that successfully paralyzed Spain.[55] This process was repeated during the general strikes of spring 1992.

The Marginalized

Several other issues and activist groups acquired national reach through their street art. Various feminist organizations, headed by the national Asamblea de Mujeres, carried out campaigns on public walls. Several of their regional organizations painted murals to give a more direct personal and emotional touch. Euskadi was the region with the most feminist street art. The provinces of Murcia and Albacete were also rich in feminist street art employing mural and graffiti commentary pertinent to women. The wide-ranging messages included: pro-choice, "The right to legal and free abortions"; suggestions that women "Report assaults, rapes, and any physical abuse," or retaliate against physical acts, "No aggression without an answer"; naming men responsible for specific acts, "Sergio Pino is an aggressor"; advocating "Women organize," "Castrate rapists," "Struggle against macho repression," "Emancipate women"; celebrating "International Women's Day"; and urging support, "Women vote No" (NATO referendum), "Women with the strike" (December 14 general strike). Lesbian groups were active as well. Posters addressing this issue were prolific in Madrid in 1992. Women's role in the formal political process became a recognized issue. This was exemplified in the 1989 general elections. All parties featured women candidates. The "PSOE strategy" of reaching out to women was exemplified by President González's wife Carmen who successfully ran for a seat from Cádiz.[56] Other parties followed suit. The HB coalition profiled a revolutionary women as one of its principal poster images. Other major parties emphasized women candidates.

The environment, drugs, and crime on the street were issues that drew national commentary. Crime had become a concern in the 1989 general elections and all major parties made policy statements on it. Drugs and crime received the most prominent street art commentary in Madrid and Euskadi. The environmental issue was explosive and engulfed Spain. It had different manifestations in different regions, but was most pronounced through street art in the northern regions. Illustrative of this issue was an event in the mid-1980s that produced prolific graffiti and some posters on a national scale, the Riaño project. Riaño, a pristine valley, was destroyed by a dam construction project. Environmentalists saw this as wanton destruction of an important habitat. "Riaño lives" graffiti were prolific on public walls during 1987–1988. Other dam projects, such as Omana in León, were the subject of environmental demands articulated through graffiti.[57] Even with increased environmental consciousness, the Green movement remained politically weak. They did not win a seat nationally or in any Autonomous Community. However, their occasional street art did call attention to environment issues. The controversial nuclear issue received a lot of attention. Nuclear-free zones, designated by politicized towns and cities, called attention to the danger with official signs or graffiti stating, "This area is nuclear free." Nuclear power plants have been the subject of several campaigns. In the Burgos area antinuclear murals and graffiti demanded closure of the Garoña nuclear power plant. In Euskadi, as is discussed in the next chapter, the controversy over the Lemóiz nuclear plant led to emotional confrontations, the closure of the plant, and abundant street art commentary.

And lastly, there were what can be called the 1992 issues. Each of these was subject to street art commentary. The year 1992 was significant in Spain from four perspectives: the economic integration of the EC; the Olympics; the World's Fair; and the Quincentennial of the European Discovery of the New World. The economic integration of Spain into the EC was not a divisive issue. However, as 1992 approached and with the signing of the Maastricht Treaty in 1992, apprehension arose. Economic integration received attention during the 1989 European parliamentary elections. The PSOE campaigned vigorously through posters, to identify itself with the concept of Europeanism. They campaigned with the twelve gold stars against the blue background logo, the symbol of a united Europe. Other major parties followed suit. However, in the historical regions of Catalonia, Galicia, and Euskadi, strong anti-EC campaigning took place via street art. Radical regional nationalists opposed integration as did marginal communist parties. The HB coalition campaigned against the EC, while the PNV campaigned for it. This contrast generated many posters and murals by the HB. In Catalonia, the PCC campaigned for a renegotiated treaty, believing the EC meant a loss of national sovereignty. This position was adopted by other marginal, radical groups. Fascists saw it as "No 92—Hispanic genocide," and the anarchists, "92 = dirty business," "Sabotage 92."

The anti-Olympic movement did not generate a great deal of street art commentary, except in Catalonia. The Catalonia radical nationalist groups attacked the Olympics, calling them the "Spanish Olympics." The anarchists also entered the "No Olympics" campaign. However, the Quincentennial generated a variety of commentary. The Commissions Against the V Centennial Celebration organized to oppose the term *discovery* of the New World. They sought to counteract this celebration, pointing out the tragic consequences of European conquest. Graffiti and murals proclaimed, "Do not celebrate the V Centennial," "Be against imperialism—no to the V Centennial," "500 years after— the genocide continues—religion, crown, and money," and "No to the V Centennial—accomplices to assassinations—do you want to celebrate a genocide?" Adding their voices to this campaign were various youth wings of the communist parties. The anarchists stated a negative position on three 1992 events, the EC, the Olympics, and the Quincentennial.

NOTES

1. Stanley Payne, *Falange: A History of Spanish Fascism* (Stanford, CA: Stanford University Press, 1961), p. 5.

2. Antony Beevor, *The Spanish Civil War* (New York: Peter Bedrick Books, 1982), pp. 20–21.

3. Ibid., p. 33.

4. Ibid., p. 39.

5. A clarification of the use of the term *nationalist* in this study must be made. The term *Nationalist* began with the Civil War and refers to the pro-Franco forces. In the post-Franco era, the nationalists are the regional nationalists or micro-nationalists who have defined varying degrees of separatist positions in the historical regions of Catalonia, Galicia, and Euskadi.

6. Beevor, *The Spanish Civil War,* p. 76.

7. Ibid., pp. 81–82.

8. Robert Clark, *The Basques: The Franco Years and Beyond* (Reno: University of Nevada Press, 1979), p. 82.

9. José Luis Vila-San-Juan, *Asi Fue? Enigmas de la Guerra Civil Española* (Barcelona: Ediciones Nauta, 1971), p. 248.

10. See Juan Linz, "Opposition to and Under an Authoritarian Regime: The Case of Spain," in *Regimes and Oppositions,* 2nd ed., Robert Dahl, ed. (New Haven, CT: Yale Press, 1973).

11. See Beevor, *The Spanish Civil War.*

12. Ibid., p. 249; and Ronald Frazer, *Blood of Spain: An Oral History of the Spanish Civil War* (New York: Pantheon Books, 1979), p. 485.

13. Beevor, *The Spanish Civil War,* p. 262.

14. Payne, *Falange,* p. 234.

15. See Juan Antonio Perez Mateos, *Entre el Azar y la Muerte: Testimonios de la Guerra Civil* (Barcelona: Editorial Planeta, 1975).

16. See Vila-San-Juan, *Asi Fue?*

17. Beevor, *The Spanish Civil War,* p. 89; and see Martha Ackelsberg, *Free Women*

of Spain: Anarchism and the Struggle for the Emancipation of Women (Bloomington: Indiana University Press, 1991).

18. See Perez Mateos, *Entre el Azar.*

19. See Vila-San-Juan, *Asi Fue?*

20. Ibid.

21. Clark, *The Basques,* p. 103.

22. Max Gallo, *Spain under Franco* (New York: E. P. Dutton, 1974), p. 211.

23. *Boogie,* no. 5, December 15, 1988.

24. Gallo, *Spain under Franco,* p. 234.

25. Ibid., p. 254.

26. The data on the early 1960s came from personal observation during a year's residence in Spain, 1960–1961.

27. See Payne, *Falange.*

28. *Boogie,* no. 5, December 15, 1988. Santiago Carrillo was the head of the Spanish Communist party.

29. Gallo, *Spain under Franco,* p. 174.

30. Ibid., pp. 334–40.

31. Pedro Pascual, *Partidos Políticos y Constituciones en España* (Madrid: Fragua, 1986), pp. 60–61.

32. See Richard Gunther, Giacomo Sani, and Goldie Shabad, *Spain after Franco: The Making of a Competitive Party System* (Berkeley: University of California Press, 1988).

33. *El País,* May 16, 1988. This was dramatically formalized at the PCE XII Party Congress in February 1988 when the IU was accepted as the electoral vehicle for the PCE.

34. Eusebio Mujal-León, *Communism and Political Change in Spain* (Bloomington: Indiana University Press, 1983), pp. 91–92.

35. Gunther, et al., *Spain after Franco,* p. 253.

36. *El País,* October 31, 1989.

37. The Valencian language is closely related to Catalán but some Valencian nationalists define it as a separate language and, therefore, the basis for a separate cultural identity from Catalonia.

38. See *Tiempo,* February 22, 1988.

39. *ABC,* January 29, 1989.

40. *El País,* April 14, 1988.

41. Mujal-León, *Communism,* p. 157.

42. See *El País,* April 1–7, 1990.

43. *Los Angeles Times,* January 1, 1991. Stanley Meisler, a correspondent in Spain, reports that 90 percent of the 6 million Catalans understand the language and 64 percent speak it.

44. Payne, *The Franco Regime,* pp. 426–27.

45. *El País,* October 12, 1987.

46. See Payne, *The Franco Regime.*

47. A discussion on GAL, a right-wing terrorist group, follows in the Basque chapter.

48. Gunther, et al., *Spain after Franco,* p. 66.

49. *El País,* December 27, 1987.

50. See *El País,* October 21, 1989; and *Diario 16,* October 22, 1989.

51. See *El País,* August 2, 1988.

52. *Tiempo,* February 22, 1988.

53. An *El País* poll, October 9, 1989.

54. The discussion on the Basque's anti-PSOE campaign is taken up more substantially in the following chapter.

55. See *El País,* December 16 and 22, 1988.

56. See *El País,* September 24, 1989; and *Cambio 16,* October 23, 1989.

57. *El País,* March 4, 1989.

4

Basque Nationalism:
Center–Periphery Conflict

Basque nationalism is a movement opposed to the hegemony of a dominant Spanish culture. It is an attempt to shape and strengthen the feelings of loyalty of a subculture with its own historical memory and culture, and to transform it into a self-contained national force. Street art has played a role in this process. What best characterized Basque street art was its expression as the collective consciousness of the people. Basque nationalists—the first generation represented by the PNV, the second by the ETA-HB movement—have used street art as one means to increase linguistic visibility, to oppose the Spanish state, to carry out psychological and cultural warfare, to establish a collective memory, and to build a nationalist movement. For radical Basques, linguistic nationalism, the belief that a common tongue creates community, has been an important stimulus for utilizing street art to raise linguistic consciousness and literacy.

The value of street art is exemplified in the amount of effort spent in its production. It was placed in highly visible areas along the major highway embankments, within large cities and rural towns, and extended into Navarra province where Basque nationalists have a special interest. Street art was not just an urban phenomenon. The ETA-HB movement had deep roots in rural small town life where traditional Basque culture and nationalism were the strongest. Those who eradicated radical Basque street art faced physical retaliation. Street art was a contest for symbolic authority, a way to strip away the symbols and myths of the dominant Spanish culture and loyalty, and to establish Basque symbols and norms. Murals were common and had a greater permanency than in any other case in this study due to their iconic value to the political imagery of Basque nationalism, especially for radical Basques.[1] Murals reached a saturation point by 1989. Having accumulated over the years, they formed an inescapable aspect of the Basque landscape. However with radical nationalists' predominance increasingly weakened, there was a dramatic drop in street art production from 1989 to 1992. Few new murals were evident and many older ones were worn away by the environment.

THE BASQUE HOMELAND: EUSKADI

The Basque region is located in northern Spain and southern France where Euskera, the Basque language, is a strong foundation for ethnic nationalism.[2] But what should constitute Euskadi is controversial. Basques live in seven provinces, three in France, four in Spain. Three historical provinces presently compose the Spanish Basque Autonomous Community (CAV). They are Vizcaya, Guipúzcoa, and Alava. A controversy smolders over whether the province of Navarra, now a separate Autonomous Community, should be included as part of the greater Basque community—a principal goal advocated by radical Basque nationalists. Basque nationalists' interest in Navarra stems from the historical relationship between Navarra and the other Basque provinces. The ancient kingdom of Navarra included the greater part of the Basque region. This gave unity political coherence and created a historical memory nationalists hope to replicate.[3] Thus, Basque nationalists place a historical and symbolic value on Navarra; Navarra to them is the cradle for Basque unity and identity. The northern towns of Navarra have retained their Basque character. It is this historical vision of joining Basques together in a separate state that drives the most radical nationalists. Navarra, however, rejected this concept, chosing to form its own separate Autonomous Community in 1982.[4]

Political profiles of the Spanish Basque provinces vary. The coastal provinces of Vizcaya and Guipúzcoa are more politically liberal and nationalistic. Alava and Navarra expressed weaker commitments to nationalism.[5] These differences were exemplified by the split positions of the four provinces during the Civil War—Vizcaya and Guipúzcoa militantly resisted the Franco Nationalists,[6] Alava and Navarra immediately joined the Nationalists—and by the voting trends in the post-Franco era.[7] These ideological divisions were reflected in the street art as well. The industrial metropolitan area of Bilbao and the small towns of Vizcaya and Guipúzcoa were inundated with street art. Alava, representing the conservative side of Basque nationalism experienced much less. The Navarra case was more complex. The province was more politicized than Alava because militant Basque nationalists, as well as Spanish liberals and conservatives, struggled for its political and cultural soul. For the Spanish right, Navarra is inseparable from Spain, its symbolism rests as the cradle of traditional patriotic values. Radical Basques and Spanish traditionalists, which both extract historical symbolism from Navarra, inudated Navarra and the capital of Pamplona with street art. Both sides sought to define issues and attract support.

The last parts of the equation are the French provinces of Soule, Basse Navarre, and Labourd. They are primarily rural with a combined population of

200,000. Unlike the Spanish Basques, the French experienced a nonrepressive democratic tradition. Consequently, the French Basque outlook was not nationalistic like their Spanish relatives. However, militant nationalists on both sides of the border interpret Euskadi as consisting of all seven provinces. Radicals want this dream fulfilled; they are separatists.

Nationalism is not a recent goal nor the exclusive feeling of a small minority. It stems from centuries of trying to maintain an identity in the wake of conquests and repression.[8] Under the 1979 Autonomous Statute, the three Spanish provinces formed a Community with a parliament in Vitoria. The radical Basques, feeling the statute did not achieve self-determination, campaigned against it. This attitude was reflected in their street art that advocated "Full autonomous government," and "Vote against limited autonomy." Despite different goals and tactics, Basque nationalism has popular support. This has been reflected in the various elections over the past fifteen years. Basque parties have overwhelmed Spanish parties. Only the PSOE survived politically. Since the November 1986 elections for the autonomous parliament, the nationalist parties won 70 percent of the regional vote.

HISTORICAL SETTING

Early Nationalism

The modern version of Basque nationalism finds its origins in the nineteenth century when in 1895 Sabino Arana, the father of modern Basque nationalism, formulated a nationalistic platform and founded the PNV. Nationalists trace their roots to Arana. He saw the Basque nation composed of peoples from the seven provinces, with Euskera the official language. Arana evolved the first slogan of the new nationalism, *Jaungoikua eta lagi-zarra* (God and the Old Laws).[9]

Art and politics are a cultural tradition among Basques. During times of repression, Basques turned to music and art for community expression.[10] In the 1920s political art was an important manifestation of identity. During the 1930s— a decade of grave turbulence—street art activism accelerated. The PNV became the main standard-bearer for the Basque nationalist cause, and an avid producer of street art. The years of the Republic were a period of rapid expansion for the party. It had been primarily a party of Vizcaya, but in the 1930s it mobilized a significant following in Guipúzcoa. Auxiliary groups became active. The Women's Patriotic Association (EAB) expanded membership and related activities.[11] The PNV became the premier party in Euskadi. It won 45 percent of the regional vote in 1933 and 35 percent in 1936.[12] PNV ideas rested on a conservative, middle-class religious ideology that limited its ability to represent all classes and groups. Nonetheless, the PNV grew because it functioned like a resistance movement that opposed the dominant Spanish culture. Thus, the PNV represented the nationalist interests in this era; Basque nationalism was not fractured along class lines as it was in Catalonia.[13] The PNV movement involved itself in all aspects of social life through a variety of activities, such as the *batzoki,* or PNV community hall, which combined political with cultural and culinary activities.[14]

The PNV built an extensive propaganda fund and carried out widespread publicity.[15] In May 1931, a General Statute of the Basque State proposed an autonomous regional status. The PNV launched the most intensive campaign in Euskadi history to garner support for the proposal. The PNV and its proponents produced five thousand large mural announcements, distributed more than four million posters, and dispersed several million leaflets.[16] Although rejected by Navarra, the statute was implemented in the other three provinces following the general elections in 1936 and approved by the Spanish national parliament, the Cortes.

In general, the era of the Republic was a time of much street graphics. *Gora Euskadi* (Long live Euskadi), one of the most common slogans found in the lexicon of Basque nationalists today, often written in graffiti, was a PNV motto developed during the Republic. For the 1936 elections, the PNV's slogan was "For Christian civilization, for Basque liberty, for social justice."[17] One poster, artistically designed, carried the artist's signature, Uralde '36. It had the Basque flag diagonally dissecting the poster with a young man carrying the flag, his body hidden by it, only his face showing. He was shouting the PNV slogan which was written across the top of the poster, the script in Spanish, not Euskera. At the bottom of the poster was the PNVs standard slogan, *Gora Euzkadi,* written in Basque.[18] Each clause of the slogan differentiated the PNV from other ideological struggles and defined their position: "Christian civilization" differentiated the PNV from the anticlerical ideology of leftist Popular Front, "social justice" distinguished it from the right, and "Basque liberty" asserted its goal of regional autonomy.[19]

The Franco Period

Basque nationalism received tremendous impetus from the Spanish Civil War. Pro-Republican Basques of Vizcaya and Guipúzcoa bore the brunt of the fascist onslaught. The most heinous event was Guernica. On the afternoon of April 26, 1937, German war planes bombed the town as people went to weekly market. This tragedy, forever recorded in Picasso's masterpiece, *Guernica,* is an eternal flame for nationalists. Its message is recorded in the region's graffiti and murals, a reminder of past injustices and a warning against future repression from Spanish nationalists.

Basque nationalism became radicalized as a result of Franco's policies. Autonomy granted in 1936 was rescinded when Franco militarily subdued the region. In the name of Spanish civilization, Franco's government initiated a policy of crushing Basque nationalism. Public meetings were banned and the use of the Basque language prohibited. These policies tried to induce a culture of silence upon the Basques. The result was the evolution of a new generation of militant nationalists, spearheaded by the ETA movement. This served to break the culture of silence imposed by the dominant Spanish system, and project the vision conceived by Arana. Franco's intolerance created a reaction among Basque youth and stimulated renewed nationalistic sentiments. Thus on July 31, 1959, ETA emerged. For these new nationalists, the PNV seemed passive and tolerant toward Franco's policies and cultural repression, and too conservative in its nationalistic vision. ETA began a process of defining its ideology and declaring its intention to create a separate identity and collective memory by making all Basques ethnically conscious. Through this process, the fatherland would be preserved, and an independent Basque state would result.[20]

Some of ETA's first activities consisted of study groups, circulating propaganda, and writing graffiti.[21] For example, shortly after its formation, the ETA acronym began to appear on walls in the larger cities.[22] Graffiti writing, as well as defacing monuments to Franco, were early forms of ETA underground resistance, before it became hardened to the armed struggle.[23] These graffiti were often noted in the underground publication *Zutik,* giving them broader dissemination.[24]

ETA activists were responsible for reintroducing street art as a popular tool of political education and a means for intensifying psychological tension.[25] These nationalists established a tradition that became a trademark of the propaganda activities by radical nationalists in the post-Franco era. It was a popular tool subsequently adopted by other groups who did not want to lose the psychological battle for the streets to ETA-HB. Street art became one symbol of a re-awakened nationalism. In the first graffiti, ETA acronyms and catchy slogans were the order. The symbolic mathematical formula, "$4 + 3 = 7 = 1$" for the unity of all seven provinces, became commonplace.[26] A variation of the theme in Basque, *Zazpiak Bat* (out of seven, one) was also used. The symbolic emblem of ETA, an axe entwined by a snake, the axe symbolizing the armed struggle, was a common graffito. Often the logo was designed in black and red colors, with the ETA acronym written underneath.[27] The Basque word *EZ* (no) was one that loomed large in the graffiti of the final years of underground activism against Franco. *EZ* has a broader connotation than just no, it represented a complete rejection, and a readiness to fight against Spain, its political system, and dominant culture. *EZ* connoted the radical's rejection of all post-Franco political reform; *EZ Konstituzioa,* (No to the Spanish Constitution) was a graffito profusely displayed during the early years of the post-Franco period.[28] The reverse side of the EZ campaign was the common slogan, "Fatherland and Liberty."

In December 1970, a Spanish military court tried sixteen ETA militants. This political event was known as the Burgos show trial. It catapulted ETA into the consciousness of the nation, raised international attention, and dealt the Franco regime a severe propaganda blow. A mass-mobilization was organized, demonstrations, general strikes, rallies, occupation of churches, manifestations by the Basque clergy and prolific propaganda, all designed to repudiate Franco's regime. Opposition to the trials spread outside Euskadi. For example, authorities closed the University of Madrid to thwart planned solidarity rallies. Street art accompanied this illegal mobilization process. Heroes and martyrs were created. ETA became a political fact, obtaining national recognition and a following among reawakened Basque nationalists.[29] Right-wing supporters of Franco responded with their own counterattack. They utilized graffiti to castigate ETA and liberals. Basque church officials were targeted for particularly harsh attacks: "Red Bishops to Moscow" and similar themes were typical of their graffiti rhetoric.[30]

ETA had its setbacks. Weakened by mishaps of its initial attempt at armed struggle, and the imprisonment of leaders following the trials, ETA moved to strengthen nationalism by pushing for a Basque National Front (FNV). This was to be a multiclass front composed of all Basque nationalists, the core composed of PNV nationalists.[31] The slogan for the front was *BAI,* a word with a double meaning. *BAI* means "yes," while the acronym stood for *batasuna* (unity), *askatasuna* (liberty), and *indarra* (strength). It emerged as an important graffiti theme. With Franco's death and the transition to democracy, extensive wallpaintings, murals, and posters became new forms for commentary.

During the Franco era, it seems, ETA and supporting groups had several objectives: to rally the Basque people in opposition to Franco and the Spanish state; to advertise to the Franco government the presence of an active nationalist movement that sought to demoralize and destabilize the regime; to intensify the level of tension through rhetorical discourse; and to clarify to the Basque masses the distinction between the new nationalistic feeling of ETA and the traditional nationalism of the PNV.[32] As a complement to ETA strategy, a campaign of counterviolence was launched at the Franco regime. Thus ETA gave violent expression to Basque nationalism. An often evoked ETA motto, "With the warriors of yesterday and today," expressed one generational sentiment, while the PNV motto, "Euskadi free and in peace," illustrated the other. Through protests and demonstrations, selective violence and street art, traditional media use, education, and social activities, a rebirth of spirit took root and a deep bond of ethnic identity grew even though the various nationalists came to differ in their approaches, goals, and tactics. Whatever relationship can be inferred between cause and effect, one ETA objective was clearly accomplished, Basques became fervent nationalists.

COMPETING VIEWS

Basque Nationalism: Ideological Alternatives

Beginning in the 1960s, the PNV was challenged by the new Basque nationalist left, ETA, and the *abertzale* movement. The ETA-HB movement, anti-system advocates, rejected both the Spanish state and the reformed autonomous

system. Radical nationalists, or *abertzales* (patriots), who postulated independence, articulated a position which PNV rejected. The PNV pushed for modi-
fications in the system. The abertzales were unwilling to accept the constitu-
tionally sanctioned division of regional autonomy. As a rejectionist movement,
ETA differed from the PNV by renouncing parliamentary tactics. They favored
revolutionary violence and a commitment to some form of socialism. The PNV
was middle-class, reformist, and capitalist.[33] The PNV, which had dominated
nationalistic sentiments since it was founded in 1895, was thus confronted with
an alternative view. A more radicalized, class-conscious vision made a direct
appeal to workers. In 1968, ETA acknowledged the working class by creating
a Workers Front to complement its Political, Economic, Military, and Cultural
Fronts.[34] For May Day 1970, ETA introduced the slogan, "Worker Unity."
Thus began a campaign to unite workers with the nationalist struggle.[35] Posters
and murals by abertzale groups carried this theme.

In the early 1970s ETA split over tactical differences, resulting in ETAm
and ETApm. The ETAm believed in armed struggle with no accompanying
mass movement, ETApm espoused a combination of political and military
struggle. Several years later ETAm altered its position due to political circumstances. "Freedom or death" and "Revolution or death" became the slogans
that distinguished ETApm from ETAm.[36]

A scrambling for political space occurred in the period immediately after
Franco. Political groups and their ideologies competed to measure the political
sentiments. On the left, radical socialists found a number of groups, parties,
and unions. Some floundered for lack of support, others found fertile soil. In
an attempt to coordinate support among various Basque socialists, the Koordi-
nadora Abertzale Sozialista (KAS) was formed in 1975.[37] It was composed of
two Basque labor unions, Langile Abertzale Batzordea (LAB) and Langile
Abertzale Komiteak (LAK), three small socialist parties, and ETApm. The
composition of KAS changed over time. ETApm withdrew and created its own
political party, the Euskal Iraultzale Alderdia (EIA), and an election coalition,
the EE. ETApm dissolved itself in 1982 and turned exclusively to democratic
participation through the EE, leaving the armed struggle to ETAm. The EE
contested the 1977 elections, winning 5 percent of the regional vote. Other
abertzale socialist parties' victories added to the total, giving the radical left 11
percent. By 1979, the range of abertzales contesting the elections expanded.
The HB coalition, formed to challenge the 1979 elections, won 13 percent. All
abertzale parties won 21 percent.[38]

The ETAm was the inspiration for the founding of HB. It was formed to
give radical nationalism a new mass-political base to complement ETA's armed
struggle and compete with the PNV, the PSOE, and the EE in the electoral
arena. The HB carried into the political arena ETA's no compromise with Madrid.[39] When ETApm withdrew from KAS, KAS became dominated by ETAm.
By 1989, KAS included the Gestoras Pro-Amnistía (amnesty sector), Jarrai
(youth sector), Egizan (feminist sector), LAB (labor sector), ASK (popular

sector), and Eguski (ecology sector).[40] The organizational structure of the ETA-HB-KAS movement had evolved. Street art, especially murals, became a significant component of the political activism of KAS. Some murals and posters carried the KAS collective sponsorship, such as a freshly painted mural done in the town of Bermeo in 1989. Its aesthetic design consumed the broad sweep of a long wall. It featured the KAS logo, a raised fist, and carried the words *HERRI BATASUNA* across its length. Spaced across the bottom was the identification of each KAS sector (with the exception of ETAm), with each group's logo placed above the group's name. Other KAS street art displayed a collective-group sponsorship—*Jarrai* (KAS) for example—while others had individual sector sponsorship on issues pertinent to that sector. Each sector supported the electoral ambitions of the HB and the issues it articulated through its street graphics. The core of the radical left nationalist position was thus in place by the late 1970s. It consisted of ETA, the HB, and KAS and their auxiliaries. The organizations were mutually supportive and linked.[41]

An established PNV alternative now existed, constituting a formidable challenge to the symbols of ethnic Basque nationalism and to the field of electoral participation. The ETA-HB-KAS movement succeeded in redefining the political discourse, shaping the terms of the national debate, and replacing the PNV as the sole motivating force of Basque nationalism.[42] This condition persisted until the early 1990s when ETA-HB became increasing isolated. In redefining the political discourse, ETA sought to impose a war environment on Basque society and the Spanish in general. Violent acts, more pronounced since the democratic opening than during the Franco years, conveyed a total rejection of the existing system. The *ala* (either-or) and the prominent *EZ* (no) terms, often expressed in street art themes, communicated this message.[43] This war mentality also found expression in messages of intimidation graffiti. *Chivatos* (informers) were publicly identified in graffiti. Some were marked for execution for treasonable activities. Joseba Zulaika, in his book *Basque Violence* relates one such story which occurred around 1972. Carlos, the bus driver in the village of Itziar, was labeled a *chivato*. One morning the town awoke to find ''Death to Carlos'' graffiti. One day while making his bus run he was murdered. The graffiti remained on the town walls for three years, a chilling reminder to others who might stray.[44]

ETA and supporting groups redefined their ideology and interests over the years. ETA declared itself a socialist revolutionary Basque movement, while others advocated a Third World anticolonialist strategy.[45] The debate within and without the organization broadened by introducing differing policy dimensions. National liberation and self-determination became goals. ETA shifted from opposing the Franco state and raising the nationalistic consciousness of the Basques, to a goal of independence. Class struggle became a dimension of this redefined ideology. Elimination of the capitalist system became a requisite for resolving national rights for it was seen as the principal enemy of the national rights of the people. ETA believed repression occurred as a result of consolidation of the capitalist system. Therefore, one must destroy the bourgeois system, eliminate private property, and the salaried worker.[46] Those positions coupled with the practice of violence became an albatross for the movement by 1990.

ETA-HB utilized street art to help build a mass movement and raise consciousness by converting every Basque into a patriot. This call did not go unanswered by opposition groups who were swept into the media fray of street art communication where positions and counterpositions were defined and redefined. Graffiti, wallpaintings, and murals became an accepted fact of political communication. Groups and parties that did not participate lost opportunities to educate and attract support. ETA and its partisans set the tone for the street debate. Their initiative and aggressiveness in projecting ideas was a fact of the political landscape. The ideology of ETA-HB-KAS was depicted in graffiti such as, "There is no independence without socialism," "Expropriate the banks and the large landowners," "Class struggle," and the esoteric, "If the rich also cry, help them." Capitalism, the banks, and the military were particular points of reference for antisystem ideology.[47]

These ideological maxims were attractive in Euskadi, one of the most highly industrialized areas of Spain where class politics were an issue. Industry had lured Spanish workers to Euskadi. This clientele attracted the PSOE, the communist parties, and various sectarian groups of the left. All competed for the loyalty of the workers. This competition enriched street art, drawing numerous Spanish national parties into this visual process. The radical Basques adjusted their strategy to this reality. Spanish workers were not castigated as unwelcomed foreign guests, which would have made them scapegoats for Basque nationalism, but accepted in the name of repressed peoples of the world, a strategy based on class origin and solidarity. This strategy served the long-range goals of radical Basques to undermine the capitalist system and link workers to the radical cause.[48] Spanish workers were seen as possible allies in a world-wide solidarity effort. In this case, Basque nationalism was de-emphasized and socialism emphasized. Spanish workers were seen as possible converts to Basque acculturation.

One recurring debate among Basques was whether to define Basque nationalism along class or ethnic lines. In the 1980s two active producers of street art in Euskadi were Marxist parties which were schisms from ETA, the Movimiento Comunista de España (MCE-EMK), a Maoist party expelled in 1966 as ETA-Berri, and Liga Comunista Revolucionaria-Langileria Komunista Iraultza-ilea (LCR-LKI), a Trotskyist party expelled in the early 1970s as ETA VI. These expulsions were the result of emphasizing Marxism and class struggle at the expense of Basque nationalism, and a willingness to make alliances with Spanish groups and parties in the name of solidarity; a concept rejectionist Basques abhorred. Socialism over nationalism was abhorrent to the abertzale nationalists. The term *Spaniards* became a disparaging label. Radical nationalists used it for those who sold out; that is, for those who were willing to make cause with Spanish groups. For example, during the 1970s the MCE slogan was, "Spanish independence confronting Yankee imperialism." Both LCR and MCE came full circle, becoming more accepting of Basque nationalism, electorally supporting the Herri Batasuna coalition, and understanding the value of self-determination in its confrontation with Spanish imperialism. The street art of these two groups by the 1980s was heavily oriented toward reinforcing the ETA-HB movement.[49]

Sectors of the ETA-HB maintained a Third World identity. This ideological definition views Euskadi as a colony struggling for liberation against a dominant capitalist system that exploits the colony and suppresses nationalistic interests.[50] This view persisted despite the fact that Basque provinces were the wealthiest in Spain. According to some Basque scholars, ETA studied the liberation struggles of Third World countries.[51] National liberation was thus symbolically tied to the image of a colonial people struggling to overcome external domination. The quest for national liberation was carried forward rhetorically with the themes, "Self-determination," "Sovereignty," and "Liberation," which were frequent slogans of ETA-HB-KAS street art. Self-determination was a non-negotiable demand of ETA's "KAS Alternative," whose terrorist campaign was justified on the basis that the struggle was a nationalist liberation war and, therefore, violent means were justifiable. These were interwoven into what became known as the five-point KAS Alternative, which was liberally painted on the walls throughout the Basque region. HB was often the sponsor of this KAS Alternative graphic commentary that would be written out point by point to visibly engage the citizenry. HB partisans often made reference that self-determination was a basic right of the United Nations Charter.

Voting played a role in the self-determination campaign, and the slogan, "Do not give them a truce—vote HB" was one of many graffiti messages of radical Basques. It was the theme of a 1986 Jarrai election poster which showed youth fighting security forces in the streets. In the early post-Franco period, ETA did not accept the concept of electoral participation within the Spanish system, rejecting an approach embraced by the PNV. The founding of HB represented a change in strategy, voting was now a rejectionist tactic. HB elected officials refused to participate in the national Cortes or in the Autonomous parliament. They formally took their seats only at the grass-roots local level.

To stress the concept of repressed people, the radical Basque nationalists emphasized solidarity issues in their street graphics. The preferred forms were murals, wallpaintings, and graffiti. Murals have an imposing visual impact and symbolic value for radical nationalists for street art carries a Third World, socialist aura. HB partisans, along with the MCE-EMK and the LCR-LKI, systematically advanced solidarity themes in their street art through the end of the 1980s, giving importance to global issues. Pro-Qaddafi and anti-Reagan graffiti appeared after Reagan bombed Libya in 1986, "Death to Reagan," "Reagan's an assassin" were typical. Graffiti supporting the M–19 guerrilla rebels in Colombia who seized the Supreme Court building in Bogotá in 1985 and died in a bloody shoot-out ordered by President Bétancur read, "Bétancur assassin—EPL Colombia will be victorious." Some of these graffiti were signed. These graffiti slogans were endemic in Euskadi as well as other major cities in Spain. The majority of HB and affiliated-group-sponsored solidarity murals and wall-paintings related to the conflict in Central America. They expressed anti-American intervention feelings along with ardent pro-Sandinista sentiments. The strong Nicaraguan ties stemmed from the HB-linked Solidarity with Nicaragua Committee. In addition, the HB maintained a representative in Nicaragua. In the late 1980s the delegate was Izaskun Larreategui, wife of an important HB leader.[52] This push for solidarity came from ETAs strategy for the HB to establish concrete solidarity agreements of mutual assistance in Latin America.[53] As the global picture radically altered, Latin American solidarity themes, so prominent in the murals of the early 1980s, began to disappear. The last burst solidarity motifs were murals to commemorate the tenth anniversary of the Sandinista revolution in 1989.

The HB-KAS-ETA View

The HB-KAS dominated the expression of street art, making its message visible throughout Euskadi. They sponsored elaborate, artistic productions, utilizing various themes, styles, and colors. HB's street art activity was facilitated by ETA liberated militants who worked full time to coordinate propaganda. The HB-KAS-ETA street art often had multiple sponsorship. Auxiliary supporting groups maintained separate identities, as did the HB, KAS, and ETA. For the HB-KAS-ETA street art, there were several categories of expression: a collective tone, a coalition tone, as well as a mixture of the two. The collective expression was found in posters, wallpaintings, murals, and graffiti that showed HB designation with no other sponsorship. An excellent example could be seen from 1986–1992 in the fishing village of Bermeo. The concrete sea wall protecting the harbor was painted in multicolored horizontal strips of blues, grays, and greens with "Herri Batasuna" written in bold letters. Many other murals carried just the HB sponsorship. Especially prominent were solidarity themes, others propagandized against NATO, or advertised HB electoral support. Most posters that supported the HB were HB sponsored as were graffiti. Typical of the graffiti were "Vote HB—make them afraid," "Hit them hard—vote HB," "Herri Batasuna—your alternative for a free Euskadi," "Defend your people—Vote HB," and "KAS Alternative—HB." Wallpaintings were also common. A popular one was the KAS Alternative, a fully formed five-point program that carried HB sponsorship. In addition, KAS-sponsored graffiti were collective in identity. The KAS acronym was the most common and could be seen throughout Euskadi. There were more elaborate KAS signed graffiti, such as, "More car bombs—hit them in the guts until they negotiate or they leave—KAS."

The coalition expression of HB and KAS was manifested through individual group sponsorship by HB-KAS auxiliary groups, and through supporting radical parties that were not formal members of the coalitions. These groups and parties produced murals, wallpaintings, posters, and graffiti that identified their group, or raised an issue, with or without mentioning the HB. If they mentioned HB, it was for advocating voting for the HB coalition. The LAB, the KAS-HB labor sector, was one such example. It mainly contributed murals. The KAS ecology group Eguski had a number murals that focused only on ecological questions. The KAS feminist organization Egizan manifested a marginal visual presence. However, the Jarrai youth sector of HB-KAS was an active group, especially in painting the ETA logo, "ETA—Jarrai," advertising itself, "Jarrai," and producing simple murals and posters that appealed to the youth, "Youth—break your marginalization—vote HB." Jarrai backed the KAS-HB policy of "Boycotting French products," focused on education and language "For Basque public education," campaigned for "The Spanish army out," and was an active participant in the anti-NATO crusade. The LCR-LKI and MCE-EMK, electoral supporters of HB, produced enormous quantities of murals, posters, and wallpaintings, more than any Basque nationalist party except for HB. Some of their street art was for HB electoral support, many others were articulating their particular concerns. The visual array from groups backing the HB gave it the image of having widespread grass-roots support. It was an image with merit. This abundant output of street art illustrated that the HB was not a marginal force. By the mid-1980s, the HB was the largest Basque leftist political party, and the third largest political force behind PSOE and the PNV. The HB has elected a significant number of mayors, councilmen, and regional and national parliamentarians.

ETA-designated street art was more limited than the HB. Because ETA was an outlawed organization, it was illegal to produce complimentary public graphics. The risks were greater in putting up pro-ETA propaganda. Most ETA public art was graffiti, consisting of simple spray-painted slogans and statements. The ETA logo formed part of the message occasionally. At times, pro-ETA slogans were signed HB, KAS, ETA, and especially Jarrai. However, mostly there was no signed sponsorship. The most common ETA slogans spoke to state terrorism, repression, and amnesty issues; for example, "You are the fascists, you are the terrorists," "Total amnesty," "The police assassins," "The car bomb is the solution against more repression," and "More car bombs and shootings until they negotiate or they go." A focus in the late 1980s was the campaign to protest accelerated arrests and expulsions of ETA exiles living in France. A series of raids in October 1987 and spring 1992 had resulted in the roundup of numerous ETA operatives. Graffiti and other public art called for a halt to this "State repression." The most common graffiti written under various group sponsorships, were "No to the extraditions of Basques refugees." These graffiti could be seen systematically throughout Euskadi in the major Basque cities and in the numerous small towns. However, the most common ETA graffito remained the slogan, *Gora ETA* (long live ETA), seen not only in Euskadi but also throughout Spain.

The PNV, Non-Abertzale View

As the oldest established nationalist party, the PNV had its own tradition of using street art. PNV again turned to its use in the post-Franco era, relying on posters and wallpaintings. During the immediate transition period, PNV street art focused on issues. Themes dealt with autonomy and restoration of the region's traditional economic rights and *fueros*. In 1978, the PNV mounted a campaign involving demonstrations and rallies with accompanying street art to advance these issues. Posters proclaimed, "Madrid—the millions come from here," a statement highlighting the importance of the Basque economy and how it subsidized the rest of Spain.[54] In 1979 for the Basque Autonomous Statute referendum, the PNV mounted a street art campaign resonant with slogans. The central slogan was "BAI (yes) for the Statute." The "BAI" was attached to a series of slogans produced on posters making claims of what passage of the statute would mean for Euskadi: "I will lift up Euskadi with BAI," "I will resolve a problem of centuries with BAI," "I will bring peace to Euskadi with BAI," "I am going to recuperate my culture with BAI," and "I am going to give life to Euskera with BAI." The PNV postulated that without the statute military intervention might occur. They saw the statute as a first step to independence.[55]

Following approval of the statute and the elections for the Autonomous parliament, the PNV became the governing party. Its street art became subdued, supporting the PNV's electoral efforts through bland posters and unimaginative wallpaintings with little focus on substantial issues. During the 1986 national elections, most PNV street art advertised itself and its governing role. Well executed wallpaintings with the PNV logo on a white background ordered, "Vote for PNV-EAJ."

One factor that affected the PNV use of street art was the loss of important sectors of its youth movement. They grew impatient with the party's traditionalism and left for alternative nationalist groups. Many joined HB-KAS. Youth were important in placing street art. The PNV had to rebuild its youth sector, the Euzko Gastedi del Interior (EGI). By the mid-1980s, it was the second most active youth sector behind Jarrai for producing street art.

After 1986, the PNV came under increasing competition and pressure from HB electoral gains. In addition, they suffered a severe blow in 1986, when ex-president of the Autonomous Community, Carlos Garaikoetxea, bolted the party and created the fourth nationalist party, the Eusko Alkartasuna (EA). This schism galvanized the PNV into greater street art efforts. Based upon my observation, there was an increase in murals and wallpaintings by the PNV and the EGI during the period 1987–1990. This output was stimulated by European and national elections of 1989, and the autonomous parliamentary elections in 1990. The PNV became more aggressive, creative, and issue-oriented in its street art. Murals and wallpaintings were common. They utilized more creative colors than the standard red, green, and white, following the aesthetic trend set by HB-KAS street art. For example, a basic mural for identification had the simple PNV-EAJ acronym painted against a background of abstract blocks in pastel colors. This gave PNV a creative, modern image.

In their election propaganda for the European elections, the PNV and HB differed fundamentally. The PNV supported the EC, utilizing its golden twelve star symbol, the HB rejected the concept. For the annual celebration of the PNV, "Alderdi Aguna—88," murals advertised party support for European integration. A painted Basque flag served as background. Superimposed on the center third of the flag was the blue and gold star flag of the EC, and inside that flag was the PNV logo, symbolizing Euskadi's future was linked to a united Europe. Wallpaintings with "Euskadi—PNV—Europe" emphasized the point. To meet the competitive challenge of the abertzales, the PNV, led by the EGI stressed independence as a reason to vote for them. The new propaganda stated, "Vote PNV = independence," or "PNV—Independence— $4 = 3 = 1$," with other variations. This PNV focus reflected its concern over HB's political development. Other PNV election murals and wallpaintings read, "Vote PNV—vote peace," and "It is the moment of the youth—vote PNV." Keeping on the youth theme, the EGI joined the chorus of antimilitary, anti-draft advocates, painting murals showing a soldier profiled as a pig, tapping his foot in boredom, with the inscription, "Neither military nor soldiers." The EGI's antidraft campaign begun in 1987 with, "Do your thing—object."[56] The PNV's feminine sector, the EAB, occasionally produced murals pertinent to topics of interest. Abortion was a frequent theme.

While PNV made modest use of street graphics, HB, EE, and EA reinforced their identities through street art activism. While elections provided an event to educate the citizenry, HB, EA, PNV, and EE did not confine their street graphics to elections. Nonelection issues and events were articulated as well. Thus, a continual flow of street art expounded issues, events, and party agendas. EE street art mostly consisted of wallpaintings and some murals. During elections it was supplemented by posters. For the Autonomous Statute campaign of 1979, the EE supported the statute. They had their own slogans which were dispersed through street art. The posters stated, "With the statute the political prisoners will come home," "With the statute, Navarra will become part of Euskadi," and "With the statute, the security forces (Spanish) will leave."[57] During the 1980s, the EE concentrated its street art on elections. For the 1986 general elections, the EE slogan was, "The force for reason." The party's specific issues, most visible in murals, included an array of anti-NATO, antimilitary, proecology, and economic themes. Their murals called for, "Divide the work—stop unemployment" and "A 30-hour work week," proposals designed to alleviate the high unemployment besieging Spain and Euskadi. Other murals proclaimed, "Military—No," or spoke to the issue of intolerance, to the creation of national parks, or to an end to pollution problems. The EE suffered a dramatic decline in the 1990 autonomous elections. They schismed into two factions, one was absorbed by the EA and one by PSOE. EE disappeared as a separate electoral entity.[58]

The EA, the newest nationalist party, followed the requisites of political expression in Euskadi by establishing a presence through street graphics. It emerged as a strong electoral competitor to HB and PNV in Guipúzcoa. It achieved electoral presence in Navarra in 1984 when the regional PNVists were expelled by the PNV national executive committee. They subsequently joined the EA. This eliminated PNV electoral existence in Navarra during the 1989 national elections. During the first several years of existence, EA street art mainly consisted of placing its acronym throughout Euskadi as widely as possible. The acronym in red, green, and white—the national colors of Euskadi—was designed within the party's logo. EA also produced wallpaintings on a green and red background with the party name, "Eusko Alkartasuna," emblazoned across them. During the 1989 elections, EA's Vitoria partisans painted a series of creative semiabstract murals throughout the city. These called attention to EA's electoral efforts with slogans such as, "Euskadi—strength." Other 1989 electoral murals featured a simple, arcing rainbow with the message, "Vote Carlos Garaikoetxea—EA." Other murals showed an abstract triangle drawn onto the image of the Euskadi flag, with the words, "Euskadi—strength."

The Spanish View

In addition to Basque nationalists, visual commentary came from the Spanish parties active in the larger cities. The PSOE, the IU-PCE, the AP-CP-PP and the CDS (UCD), all tried to maintain a visual presence and a political base. PSOE, the only viable Spanish party in the region, did not relinquish the visibility and communication it achieved via street art. Its propaganda mainly dealt with elections. As a consequence of volatile ethnic and class struggles, the IU-PCE, recognized there was a political opportunity. They tried to maintain a street presence, but lacked an appreciable base and visibility in Euskadi because their Basque branch, the MCE-EMK bolted over the question of regional nationalism. This left the IU-PCE with no political structure in Euskadi.[59] Only during national elections did one encounter IU posters. The AP-CP-PP, and CDS, were considered pro-Franco Spanish nationalists and consequently did not have much political space in Euskadi, their past haunted them. They were ideologically opposed to what Basque nationalists represented and they garnered no appreciable long-term support. The PP made modest gains, winning one national parliamentary seat each in Alava and Vizcaya in the 1989 elections.

PLACEMENT: PRO- AND ANTI-BASQUE PUBLIC ART

The political emotions surrounding the question of Basque separatism could best be captured and put into perspective by taking visual note of the street art in provinces adjacent to Euskadi and in major Basque cities. To the west of Vizcaya is the province of Cantabria with its popular coastal resort city, Santander. Cantabria's street art paled in quantity when compared to that in Euskadi. The graffiti, however, were some of the most emotional found anywhere in Spain. It typified the strong, anti-Basque nationalist sentiments found in and outside Euskadi. These strong anti-Basque feelings stemmed from the support the AP-CP-PP enjoyed in Cantabria and Santander and from the activity of neofascist groups. In the national elections of June 1986, PSOE won the province. However, the CP received more than a third of the votes. In the 1989 general elections, the two parties split the vote almost equally. Right-wing support provided the context for anti-Basque propaganda. In Santander, no pro-Basque posters or graffiti were evident during the 1986 or 1989 elections, although pro-Basque and ETA graffiti did extend into the industrial city of Torrelavega. It was also common in Barcelona, Madrid, and in Andalucía, Galicia, and Valencia. Basque street art, thus, was not confined just to Euskadi. For example, for local elections in June 1987, the HB garnered more than 30,000 votes in Catalonia, and street art was used to lobby the citizenry.[60] Outside Euskadi, the HB forged election alliances with small, radical parties and presented itself as an antisystem rebellious party. Its street art and slogans read, "Rebel—vote HB," "Be against repression—vote HB," "Against the state—vote HB," and "Vote HB and make them afraid."

The most virulent graffiti in Santander were directed toward the Basque nationalists, including the Basque Catholic Church. Many right-wing Spanish nationalists had deep enmity toward Basque Catholic priests. In Santander, the anti-Basque graffiti accused Basque priests of being, "Red priests—priests of HB." This sentiment reflected the long-standing animosity between pro-Franco followers and the Basque Catholic Church. Many Basque priests supported and thus lent legitimacy to the actions of militant nationalists during the Franco era.[61] In 1960, 339 Basque priests met and sent a letter to their bishops denouncing the atrocities committed by Franco's police.[62] Subsequently, some priests joined ETA and actively resisted the regime. ETA was tagged as communist influenced. When ETA officially proclaimed itself socialist, pro-Franco nationalists proclaimed the virtue of their cause. To them Basque priests were communists aiding ETA-HB subversives. In the 1970s, billboards and campaign posters in Navarra stated that bishops recommended voting for parties of the left.[63] Thus, emotional feelings found an expressive outlet in graffiti. Anti-ETA graffiti proclaimed, "Death to ETA," "GAL will kill ETA," and "No negotiations with ETA—to the firing squad." In 1988, when the wealthy industrialist Emiliano Revilla was kidnaped by ETA as a means of replenishing its coffers, Santander and the surrounding highways were resonant with graffiti attacking Revilla for paying the ransom and aiding ETA. Insults were the order, "Revilla—traitor" and "Revilla—homosexual."

The old northern highway that connected Santander to the French border passed through Euskadi as it weaved and climbed its way to the French border. The Santander to Bilbao section of the highway was two lanes and heavily traveled. Because the highway was a crucial artery and provided a captive audience, propaganda-producers flocked to paint their messages. During the 1980s, this highway offered the greatest variety of the most emotional and heaviest concentration of street art in Euskadi. Only the cities of Bilbao and Pamplona, and the San Sebastian-Tolosa highway could rival this street art. The propaganda contained both pro and anti-Basque, anti-ETA statements, as well as a full enunciation of the social and political issues the various groups espoused. However, for the most part, the pro-Basque nationalists controlled the commentary. Some pro-Spanish groups had penetrated portions of the highway, however, in small Basque towns anti-Basque propaganda was non-existent.

For Spanish nationalists a favorite tactic was painting the Spanish flag, a symbolic message this was Spanish territory, not a Basque homeland. Instead of painting over the Spanish flags, Basque nationalists simply turned the table on the territorial issue by writing *Abajo* (down with) across the flag. Other anti-ETA graffiti stated, "Enough deaths—peace now." Peace was an important theme. Public opinion polls in Euskadi showed people rejected ETA violence which has claimed more than 600 lives since 1968. The more strident, anti-ETA graffiti called for "Judge the guilty—no more traitors," and "No amnesty for terrorists."

Putting up murals in Euskadi became frenzied. Murals became so important to the HB-KAS-ETA movement that they moved into the realm of mass production. They precut stencil forms which the cadre used to draw their design. Although the design was often the same, color combinations and size varied. Murals were most numerous along highways where space was available along the numerous embankment retaining walls. By 1989, the San Sebastian-Tolosa highway had more than 100 murals, the Amorebieto-Guernica-Bermeo road more than 75, the highway from San Sebastian to the French border more than 50, the city of Irun more than 25, Pamplona more than 30, Lezo about 30, Amorebieto around 20, the Bilbao area more than 100, and the Bilbao to San Sebastian road too numerous to count. There were in 1989 more than 1,500 murals. Since then, few new murals have been painted and many old ones have worn away.

SELECTED ISSUES: MID-1980s

War and Peace

Anti-American, anti-Reagan themes were particularly prevalent and constituted a whole subcategory of street art. *El País* reported that of all NATO members, the Spanish had the least sympathetic feelings toward the United States.[64] Reagan inflamed the anti-American emotions when he ordered the bombing of Libya. Both the left and the right attacked him. In graffiti and wallpaintings he was vilified with such accusations as *Reagan Hiltzaile* (Death to Reagan), "Reagan an assassin," "Reagan a terrorist—Libya will be victorious," and "Guernica and Libya." "Guernica and Libya" graffiti were most prominent along the Bilbao-Amorebieta-Guernica-Bermeo corridor. Anti-Americanism was expressed even before the Libyan incident. This street art castigated "Yankee oppressors," and advocated "Yankees out of Central America."

The NATO referendum added to anti-Yankee sentiments. Groups led by the Anti-NATO Commissions, the HB, and the EE, headed up the no position. NATO won a slim majority with a 52 percent yes vote. In Euskadi, the no vote received 62 percent, the highest percentage in Spain.[65] Only two other regions voted against NATO. Graffiti were an important medium for airing one's opinion on NATO. There were many simple statements, "Yes NATO" or "No NATO," or "Vote for NATO." There were pro-NATO graffiti, "No neutrality—NATO." However, much of the Basque regional graffiti proclaimed, "Get out Reagan—NATO no," "Do not sell out to the Yankees," "If you want peace—vote no," "NATO is organized terrorism of the North Atlantic," "Yankees out of Spanish territory," and "Vote for peace—NATO no." Anti-NATO murals depicted exploding bombs and missiles raining on Spain. Messages on several Bilbao murals, sponsored by the Ecology Collectives summed up the situation with humor, "What do you do in case of a nuclear war—kiss your children good-bye." Even in Vitoria, the most politically conservative of the three Basque provincial capitals, numerous anti-NATO murals adorned city walls. Few towns were without at least one anti-NATO mural or wallpainting. Even in hamlets such as Itziar, population less than one thousand, anti-NATO murals were apparent.[66]

Basque feelings on NATO reflected the general antisuperpower, antiwar attitude. Thus, anti-Gorbachev graffiti also appeared, simply, "No Gorbachev," and/or referred to the Chernobyl meltdown. Some Basques focused on the nuclear issue, both its peaceful use and military application. A cleverly designed poster read, "Nuclear no thanks, nuclear energy neither civil nor military, neither in Chernobyl nor here." The poster was embellished with antinuclear logos, the smiling face of the sun, and the logo of the Basque ecologist group, Sol. Each logo was bordered with "No to nuclear" written in three languages—Spanish, Basque, and French. Large murals by the MCE-EMK pinpointed the danger, "Yesterday Harrisbourg [sic], today Chernobyl, tomorrow Lemóiz?" The depth of the antinuclear feelings was expressed with "Nuclear-Free Zone" signs and graffiti in Basque towns.

The antinuclear issue has deep emotional roots. Since the mid-1970s, Basques fought the construction of nuclear plants. They regarded them as dangerous capitalist adventures. The nuclear plant at Lemóiz became a rallying point. It was judged by many to pose the greatest environmental threat in the region. Its construction was a hotly contested issue during 1978–1982. ETA played a leading role in the debate, sabotaging the plant, and killing two of the plant's chief engineers. In March 1978, two hundred thousand joined in a protest demonstration. This issue was well reflected in street art. During this period, slogans carried a rejectionist reference, "Lemóiz EZ" and "Either Euskadi or Lemóiz." Other graffiti called for "Lemóiz—demolition." The Lemóiz-nuclear issue raised ecological awareness in Euskadi.[67] This issue allowed the ETA-HB movement to assert itself for several years into one of the most volatile popular mobilizations. ETA made headlines through its spectacular and controversial actions. In addition, the issue was kept visually present through occasional murals painted to commemorate Gladys, a woman killed in one of the anti-Lemóiz demonstrations. In the town of Ondarroa, a huge mural for the 1989 elections carried the antinuclear theme, "No nuclear—vote HB—working community—we will defend you." Adding to the antiwar sentiments was the 50th anniversary of Guernica in 1987. Commemorative murals were painted in numerous towns and cities, many featured the white dove and motto, "Freedom and Peace." Antimilitary feelings, prevalent throughout Spain, had an ironic twist in Euskadi. Jarrai's street art stressed chauvinistic nationalism, calling for "A Basque army." Jarrai was not opposed to the concept of a military, only a Spanish army. On the other hand, the EE opposed the military per se, "The mili does not jib, neither Basque nor Spanish."

The Environment

In few countries were environmental issues as vividly expressed in the street art as in Euskadi. They were strong environmental advocates, both from the radical HB and conservatives. It was an issue no one could escape. For the HB, the environment was a fundamental issue since the group's formation. Environmental groups such as Sol, Ametz, and Eguzki actively advanced the ecological issue through murals. The Sol (sun) logo appeared on many ecological murals. A somewhat typical mural, sponsored by the HB in the town of Amorebieta, had a rainbow arch and the Euskadi flag painted multicolored providing a background for the message, "Green zone—parking for everyone." A huge mural near the town of Markina, bearing the Sol logo showed the evolution of humanity disappearing into a vapor. In Mondragón, Eguzki's murals called attention to the river pollution. To emphasize the environment and a nonbellicose image, the HB utilized the symbolic rainbow in some of its murals and posters. The rainbow was either drawn in an arc, or rainbow colors were painted straight across the mural to fill the background. This nonbellicose symbolism was related to HB's campaign for peace. It argued that peace would come when Madrid would negotiate and allow self-determination. In 1988, when HB began an intense "Negotiate Now" campaign and ETA agreed to a temporary truce, hundreds of murals with rainbows were produced to support the campaign. These rainbow-peace images sharply contrasted with other HB graphics that were militant in image and message.

Concern over pollution was also tied to questions of industrialization. Bilbao epitomized the problem of exploitation of the natural environment. Its air is heavily polluted with industrial waste; the Nervión river, which bisects the city, is fouled with industrial effluents. Basque environmentalists seized on this exploitation to shape their street art. It particularly served the propaganda interests of the HB whose partisans depicted the capitalist system as ravenous, irresponsible, and covetous of excessive profits. Murals depicted people choking on air pollution. Death and financial exploitation were common themes. The popularity of environmental issues embraced additional concerns: saving the coast from wanton development; preserving the marshes and estuaries—"Save Oyambo"; developing and maintaining green belts, city parks, and plazas; and cleaning up polluted rivers and the air. All this was summed up unequivocally in the graffito, "Contaminated industries must be controlled."

Referendums and Elections

As a part of the transition process, referendums were an important indicator in defining citizen attitudes; deep feelings of Basque nationalism were in evidence. For example, only the Basques rejected the 1978 national referendum ratifying a new national Constitution. In three referendums—the constitutional, the autonomous statute, and NATO—graffiti were a common medium for expressing opinions. For these referendums, the choice was simple, "Yes or No for the Constitution," "No or Yes for regional autonomy," or "Yes or No for NATO." There were elaborate companion messages to why a particular position should be selected. Partisans for both sides often crossed out the others' "Yes" or "No" and put in the opposite word. This occurred frequently for the 1986 NATO referendum. While the Basque provinces voted against the Constitution and against NATO, they did approve the 1979 statute creating an autonomous region. This satisfied moderate nationalists. The national government made major concessions by granting Euskadi power to levy taxes, run schools, teach Euskera, manage television and radio media, and to set up its own regional police force.

In Euskadi, the 1989 general elections inspired an outpouring of street art. In quantity, artistic sophistication, and the spectrum of issues articulated, it surpassed the electioneering of 1986. Several factors contributed to this increase. During the 1989 elections, of the several political symbols at stake, one belonged to the HB. Since 1979, the HB had demonstrated steady electoral strength, a symbol of the increasing radicalization of the Basque electorate and the success of its political discourse. There were indications though that perhaps HB had peaked. The government purported that public opinion polls indicated HB would lose support. The changing international scene and the breakup of the Socialist bloc added to the government's optimism and to the anxieties of the HB-ETA movement. Radical socialism was being discredited, a divided Europe united, and the issue of NATO became less significant. Another factor was the increasing readiness by Basques to support protests against ETA violence.

The first test for HB's staying power were the European parliament elections in June 1989. The HB vigorously campaigned on the exclusive issue of opposition to European integration, in particular to the EC. Confirming PSOE's prediction, the HB suffered an electoral setback. According to a critical internal HB document, this caused consternation. Taking advantage of its success in the European elections, PSOE advanced national elections to October 1989. The HB, believing it had stressed an anti-European emphasis too strongly, readied for the national elections. Mural production was prodigious. HB militants worked feverishly, hoping to stem the recent decline. The party produced a series of six posters that were posted throughout cities and towns. The artistic creativity and use of colors in these street graphics were the most sophisticated of the decade. LAB and Gestoras Pro-Amnistía, and especially Jarrai, were particularly active in producing murals and wallpaintings. This production was complemented by other electoral supporters, the MCE-EMK and the LCR-LKI. For the 1989 elections, Jarrai's street art consisted of numerous murals and wallpaintings with the slogan, "We are a nation." The motto was taken from the earlier ETA-HB expression "Out of Seven—One," a goal to make the Basque nation coterminous with Basque culture. Despite this abundance of street propaganda, HB suffered a reverse, and a symbol was pierced. The second political symbol at stake was the emergence of the EA. This was its first opportunity to win national representation and establish an image that it offered a viable option. As the new entry, it needed to be competitive and establish a visual presence. EA surpassed the visible presence of both PNV and EE in street art for the 1989 elections. The EA was successful, winning two seats to the national Cortes, half the number of HB and equal to that of EE.

Abertzale Issues

Nonelection campaigns and sundry issues articulated by abertzale groups added to the proliferation of street art. In 1988, the HB began one of its concerted campaigns to lobby the Spanish government to begin official talks with ETA. Murals and wallpaintings erupted with "Negotiate—Yes," in bright colors and often with a rainbow. Other murals pushed additional negotiation demands, "Self-determination," while 75,000 posters spelled out the five-point KAS Alternative. In March 1989, when talks broke off and ETA resumed its violence, HB plastered Euskadi with posters which read, "The governing PSOE has not kept its word—IT DOES NOT WANT PEACE—without negotiation there is no solution." These posters were featured on the front page of *El País*.[68]

The second issue that generated a barrage of street art was the government policy of dispersing concentrations of ETA prisoners to prisons throughout the country. HB-KAS viewed this as an attempt to break prisoners' spirits and morale and their continued commitment to ETA. Gestoras Pro-Amnistía led the antidispersal campaign. Posters were pasted informing people about the government program. One 1989 poster portrayed a map of Spain indicating the name and location of each penitentiary and the number of ETA prisoners in each. Similar posters continued to 1992. In towns where the HB had greatest influence, prisoner dispersal posters became part of the 1989 election propaganda. In Hernani, posters were hung on the City Hall. Each poster contained a photo, the prisoner's name, and the prison where he or she was detained. In Tolosa, posters were strung like a banner across the main street bearing the prisoners' names and prison locations. In Bermeo and Ondarroa, similar posters were strung across the town plaza. These prison dispersal posters were prevalent in Leso, Lekeito, and Pamplona as well. The posters were locally produced and varied from town to town. In Ondarroa, an especially emotional mural featured the fingers of a hand, painted red, clutching onto prison bars. The issue was related to a previous campaign to oppose French extradition of Basque militants. Murals, graffiti, and posters pressured to stop these extraditions. Particularly popular in the towns near the French border from San Sebastian to Irun was a retaliatory campaign to boycott French products.

In many respects, through its street art, the HB-KAS movement articulated the broadest spectrum of issues of any political entity in Spain. These included anti-NATO, anti-EC, antinuclear, antipollution, antitorture, antiextradition, anti-PSOE, anti-Spain, antiprisoner dispersal, as well as the boycott of French products, socialism, self-determination, green belts, and amnesty. There were also various concerns over economic issues. Additionally in 1989, there was opposition to construction of a highway to link Navarra to Guipúzcoa. The HB based its opposition on environmental concerns and possible use of the highway by NATO forces. Graffiti warnings marked the area under dispute.

History taught citizens to regard physical threats voiced via graffiti seriously. For instance, in 1980, through threats—some via graffiti—ETA took steps to eradicate cinemas showing sex films. Many threatened changed their programming.[69] One of the most persistent concerns of HB-KAS-ETA during the 1980s was drugs. They led an antidrugs, antitrafficking campaign. Murals, graffiti, and posters focused on this issue viewed as a conspiracy to subvert Basque youth. The ETA enforced its campaign by intimidation—death threats, bombings, and other physical means.[70] Suspected drug traffickers were singled out, death threats conveyed via graffiti, and at times carried out. The campaign began in earnest in 1980. Fashionable bars suspected of drug trafficking were warned to cease their activities. In some cases where the ETA was not satisfied, facilities were attacked and those responsible eliminated.[71] The campaign continued throughout the 1980s. Rumors that two Vizcayan industrialists were accused by ETA as drug traffickers were confirmed in graffiti. They were executed in 1988 by ETA.[72] In the town of Lezo, the names of alleged drug traffickers were marked on the public walls, other graffiti called for their executions. In several cases, neighbors organized to expel the drug traffickers from their homes, which they marked with the graffito, "Here lived a trafficker."[73] In addition to death threats to *chivatos* and drug traffickers, threats occurred over street art eradication. These were sort of sacred icons to the ETA movement and one did not remove its political signs. In 1982, for example, the mayor of Itziar had the word *Independentzia,* an ETA sacred sign, erased from the walls. This elicited a leaflet in response, accusing him of being a *chivato,* a warning that could carry the death sentence.[74]

In other cases, local political disputes with the HB have led to physical threats. In the town of Huarte (Navarra), the nonaffiliated mayor fled after receiving threats in graffiti expressed on town walls. The mayor accused Jarrai of the graffiti, stating that the HB affirmed that the street was theirs.[75] Furthermore, Jarrai utilized posters in San Sebastian to threaten three newspaper reporters for writing injurious articles against ETA. Posters called them "Dogs of the pen."[76] Another group targeted for threats were ex-ETA combatants who had left the struggle to reinsert themselves in society. Conversion from participant to observer was tantamount to treason for the ETA. Various ex-ETA members who abandoned the armed struggle received death threats; some were executed.[77] The most celebrated case was the assassination of ex-ETA militant Yoyes in 1986 as she strolled in her hometown. "Yoyes chivata" and "Yoyes traitor" graffiti had marked her destiny.

CITIES: PROTRACTED CONFLICT

Three cities are worthy of special attention when analyzing Basque street art and nationalism: Guernica, because of the emotional and symbolic feelings attached to it; Pamplona, because of its complex political dynamics; and Bilbao, because it symbolized capitalist and colonial exploitation for radical Basques. In each of these cities, antiestablishment commentary was particularly virulent, directed against the security forces, the capitalist system, and the national governing party, the PSOE and its leader, Felipe González. The police and Guardia Civil were subjects of a particularly vitriolic treatment and a concerted campaign to drive them out was being waged by radical Basque nationalists.

Guernica

Murals were popular in the Guernica area, especially along the Amorebieta-Guernica-Bermeo highway. In 1989 more than 75 murals were in place with environmental, antinuclear, anti-NATO, peace, electioneering, and pro-HB themes. The PNV, not particularly active in producing murals, had several, as did the EE and the EA. Groups belonging to KAS such as Jarrai were active, as were the small sectarian Marxist parties, the MCE-EMK and LCR-LKI. In the late 1980s, Jarrai was particularly active, endorsing the HB, supporting the ETA-HB antidrug campaign, "Drugs No—Jarrai (KAS)," and graffiting the ETA logo, "ETA—Jarrai"; they were probably responsible for the many "KAS" graffiti or "KAS = Peace" slogans. Several feminist-sponsored murals were also present. There were no murals by major Spanish parties, the PSOE or the PP. This seemed to be the case throughout Euskadi. In Guernica itself, an anti-NATO mural, particularly apt for Guernica, portrayed an attacking dive bomber, a clever reminder of the ravages of the Civil War on the 50th anniversary of the Guernica carnage. Other murals throughout Euskadi commemorated this event.

Anti-PSOE street art had its own emotional themes in Euskadi and Guernica. The Socialists were singled out as a target of the radical's rage for two reasons: First, radicals generally ignored other parties in their street art, but not the PSOE. As the only Spanish party able to maintain a strong level of support in Euskadi, mainly among Spanish workers who radical nationalists wanted to win over and acculturate, the PSOE constituted a threat. Second, when the PSOE became the national governing party in 1982, all animosities felt toward the Madrid government were directed toward them. According to the radical view, the PSOE was nothing more than a continuation of its fascist predecessors. They were seen as new fascists repressing Euskadi, refusing self-determination, responsible for the violence afflicting Euskadi, and trying to win public allegiance through deceptive reforms. When the PSOE forged a joint agreement in the late 1980s condemning ETA terrorism, it was signed by the major Spanish and the Basque parties except the HB, thus isolating the HB; radical antipathy increased toward PSOE. The anti-PSOE messages were engraved on walls in the SS form, "PSSOE," for the Nazi SS.

In Guernica these anti-PSOE sentiments were expressed in posters with photos of police repressing demonstrators. Such brutality was attributed to the Socialists. A poster depicting police repression, sponsored by the Gestoras Pro-Amnistía, chose a title with a cynical twist, "This is the 'Good Way' of PSOE." Other posters showed the profile of Joseba a young ETA militant, who allegedly was martyred while in police custody in 1981. The poster placed responsibility for the murder on the PSOE government. Other posters and graffiti carried similar messages, "Here they torture—war," and "Death to the police." The issue of police intimidation was at the heart of the radicals' campaign. The national police were an occupying Spanish force, repressing popular sentiments. "Repressive security forces—to the firing squad" was expressed often in graffiti. This repressive police theme further appeared in pro-ETA graffiti. Especially common was an acronym designed message which read, "GAL = PSOE." GAL was a paramilitary organization active from 1983 to 1986 and alleged to comprise security personnel responsible for murdering ETA militants living in safe exile in France. The poignant message was state terrorism—that without PSOE approval GAL could not have operated. The hostility was manifested further in graffiti that called for "Death to PSOE" and accused the PSOE of being "Equal to terrorists," "They torture," and "They assassinate." The HB election posters had PSOE the villain, "Give PSOE the coup d'etat—vote HB." For the radicals, the PSOE was the essence of the Spanish state.

Pamplona

Navarra's political complexity is interesting because of the city's symbolic value both to ardent Basque nationalists and right-wing Spanish Nationalists. Pamplona is the capital of Navarra. There, the HB was an ardent campaigner, pasting posters, painting murals and wallpaintings, and writing graffiti, its presence as visible as in any other Basque city. Other parties vigorously campaigned as well. The quantity of street art probably surpassed that of other cities. Murals were not as numerous as in Euskadi, but in 1989 there were a minimum of 40–50 murals in Pamplona. The HB saw Pamplona as key to Navarra's incorporation into Euskadi. The Autonomous Statute allowed absorption of various communities at any point. This occurred through a formal process requiring local legislative and plebiscite approval. Thus unification was a political process achieved by manipulating public opinion. HB activities were counteracted by the strong presence of PSOE and the UPN, a conservative Navarran party that proposed Navarran nationalism and opposed Basque nationalism. The UPN, in an election alliance with the PP, won a plurality in the 1987 Navarra autonomous elections and again in the 1989 national elections. The PSOE had strong roots among the industrial workers.[78] Thus, in Pamplona the emotional clash between Spanish history and current political conflict over nationalism came together as in no other city. In this city, opposing parties on the Basque question meet on neutral ground, and Navarran, Basque, and Spanish parties divided the electorate. Animosity from the Franco era with its Basque-fascist antagonism was emotionally displayed here, and the radical Basque-PSOE conflict raged. Political divisions were reflected in distribution of Navarra's five parliament seats. In the general elections of 1986, PSOE and CP each won two seats, and the HB captured one.[79] In the 1989 general elections, HB lost its only seat, the PP-UPN coalition gained one, and PSOE maintained its two seats. The HB, the only Basque nationalist party with significant support, won 11 percent of the vote.[80]

The emotional charges and countercharges ignited via street art in Pamplona paralleled those of Guernica. The most prolific graffiti were the "PSOE = GAL" statements, elaborated to include "González = Mitterand = GAL," and "The government is guilty of assassinating ETA." French President François Mitterand was accused of turning a blind eye to GAL's activities in France and castigated for his extraditions. These statements reflected ETA's deep concerns as it adjusted to counterterrorism. The graffiti sought to build support to pressure against GAL's activities. ETA's own terrorism was immortalized in a barrage of anti-ETA graffiti, "ETA assassins," commentary not often seen in Euskadi. There were graffiti that equated the CP-PP to fascism, "CP = fascists," while the fascist Fe Jons were active with such slogans as, "Do not negotiate—ETA to the firing squad."

Radical partisans covered a range of issues. Some graffiti called for amnesty. The most common was, "Amnesty" or *Amnesty Osoa* (complete amnesty). In 1988–1989, the city was replete with street art protesting the prisoner dispersal policy. The "KAS" acronym was often written as was the five-point "KAS Alternative." The alternative has varied over the years; as articulated in Navarra, it called for total amnesty, self-determination, incorporation of Navarra, withdrawal of the national police force, and full democratic rights.[81] In 1988–1989, just as in Euskadi, the HB partisans carried out a street graphics blitz to lobby Spain to negotiate with ETA. Posters were an important medium for HB propaganda in Pamplona. HB posters outnumbered the opposition's. Prominent were posters portraying the martyred Joseba. One Joseba poster featured only his photo and name; another a short synopsis of his militancy, arrest, and death; and a third profiled him behind prison bars. Other HB graphics carried anti-NATO, antinuclear, and environmental themes.

In 1988, King Carlos's first formal visit to Navarra stimulated emotional anti-Juan Carlos graffiti and posters by radical Basques, just as his visit had done in Catalonia among radical Cataláns. Thousands of HB posters showed Juan Carlos and Franco standing side by side waving, with the message, "OUT" in large letters.[82] Social issues were also depicted. A unique mural pertained to women. It was painted in the old section of the city in 1986 by Aizan, the feminist organization linked to HB-KAS. The message said, "It is clear that if you do not change the women, the mentalities, the structures, the laws . . . we will continue being . . . ." (puppets). The idea of puppets was made explicit by showing two women being manipulated by strings. "Vote HB" was written in two corners of the mural. The issue of women's rights was prominently displayed in Euskadi, more so than in other regions of Spain. The street art on the feminist issue was more a big-city phenomenon, although in Mondragón the Egisan-KAS group was especially active. The women's issues most articulated in Euskadi were the right to abortion, denouncement of male aggression, and in San Sebastian murals celebrating lesbianism.

Many Spanish groups actively articulating issues through street art in Spain were also active in Pamplona. For example, there were "anti-mili," antidraft, antiapartheid, anti-Lemóiz, anti-dam construction, antidrug themes. In addition, solidarity with Nicaragua murals was sponsored by ASKEPENA. Posters by the Basque nationalist neighborhood organization, Comites Abertzales Socialistas (ASK), urging people to study Euskera were also in constant evidence.

Bilbao

In street art, Bilbao was the most heavily politicized of the three Basque provincial capitals. Of the two other capitals, San Sebastian had only moderate displays of street art—some murals and fairly heavy pro-ETA-HB graffiti and posters in the old historical core, the one section of San Sebastian with heavy street art. The visible space was dominated by the territorial demarcation of ETA-HB-KAS. Vitoria, a quiet orderly city, had little graffiti and many clean walls, a phenomenon not found in many other Basque towns and cities. Political posters were common at election times, placed on approved designated spaces, and a number of murals painted by the EA for the 1989 elections were visible. Ecology was the most salient street art issue, but there were anti-NATO, antimilitary draft murals, various feminist murals, as well as murals by the anarchist labor organization the CNT. The CNT was mostly active in Vitoria and Bilbao, utilizing murals in 1986 with the messages, "Your vote legitimizes a military and nuclear society," and "Do not vote—give them what they deserve." Regarding political parties, the PNV and the EA rather than the HB dominated the street art; Jarrai which was so visible in Vizcaya and Guipúzcoa during 1988–1989, had little presence in Alava and Vitoria. The HB had some visible presence. For the 1986 elections, it emphasized that the HB was the channel for the protest vote; one mural appealed, "With your secret vote, you can change many things," another took a different tact, "Many have given their lives for the liberation of Euskadi, you can give your vote—vote HB." The HB did not win a parliamentary seat in Alava.

Bilbao carried some of the same contrasting political emotions seen in Pamplona. The variety of groups and parties involved covered the Spanish and Basque spectrum. This was due mainly to the fact that Bilbao is an industrial city with Spanish workers and a broad mix of class and ethnicity. Street art visibility was facilitated by numerous constructed walls throughout the city. For example, the polluted Nervión river that dissects the city center is channeled by concrete walls highly visible from the roads running along both sides. Likewise, the highways leading in and out of Bilbao are lined with concrete embankments. Every available space seemed covered with political slogans, statements, murals, and wallpaintings. Being an industrial city, it attracted the plethora of sectarian leftist parties as well as the major Spanish and Basque nationalist parties.

The intense competition spread everywhere in Bilbao. No structure was sacred, not even the city's monuments and cathedrals. These were badly defaced with graffiti and posters. An interesting perspective on street art communication pertained to the activities of the CP. Under Franco, pro-Franco advocates were adamant that defacing public buildings and monuments not occur. However, under the democratic system, the CP and neofascist groups were guiltiest of this in Bilbao. They placed posters and scrawled graffiti on monuments and on the cathedral. The cathedral in the city's historical center became an arena for contrasting political positions and their accompanying graffiti battles. The most virulent anticlerical graffito read, "Priests to the gas chamber." Most street art emanated from leftist groups. They contained class conflict themes, extensive environmental messages, and radical Basque issues. A rare mural with ETA sponsorship was evident in the old city as were many ETA logos signed by Jarrai or Jarrai-KAS. They also sponsored anti-PSOE graffiti and wallpaintings. Similar to the historical central core of San Sebastian, in Bilboa the visual space along the narrow pedestrian streets of the city's core were predominantly controlled by HB-KAS partisans and sectarian Marxist parties. These liberated zones were predominantly marked off in the Basque language.

For the most part, the Spanish communist parties had a low profile in Bilboa despite the class presence of a Spanish proletariat. They were not able to compete with PSOE and the Basque left for the political allegiance of the workers. The MCE-EMK and the LCR-LKI, on the other hand, were very active, painting murals on several themes: anti-NATO, antinuclear, antidrugs, and electoral support of the HB. In the late 1980s, large murals by the MCE-EMK castigated capitalism, "Be against capitalists' terrorism." They also castigated PSOE. A mural portrayed a man, identified as PSOE, laying off workers. This reflected Spain's high unemployment rate, the highest in Europe. The Socialist party and the CP-PP had a presence. Spanish workers supported the PSOE, giving the party a base. However, the CP-PP was rather weak, gaining only 10 percent of the provincial vote in both 1986 and 1989 elections.[83] The CP-PP utilized posters and billboards but at times some of their most prominent billboards were defaced with graffiti, "Terrorists." This referred to state terrorism during the Franco regime. The PNV had its strongest roots and electoral strength in Vizcaya and this was reflected in the street art where there were many PNV-EAJ wallpaintings. In essence, Bilbao and its environs conveyed, through street art, the depth of emotion for Basque nationalism, as well as a spectrum of Spanish sentiments. This spectrum was reflected in the electoral statistics in Vizcaya in the 1989 general elections; the PNV had 28 percent, the PSOE 21 percent, the HB 15 percent, the PP 10 percent, and the EE 8 percent; the EA and the IU trailed.[84]

NOTES

1. See Joseph Zulaika, *Basque Violence: Metaphor and Sacrament* (Reno: University of Nevada Press, 1988).

2. Ibid., p. 16.

3. Ibid., p. 17.

4. Robert P. Clark, *Negotiating with ETA: Obstacles to Peace in the Basque Country, 1975–1988* (Reno: University of Nevada Press, 1990), p. 23.

5. See Robert P. Clark, *The Basque Insurgents: ETA, 1952–1980* (Madison: University of Wisconsin Press, 1984); and Zulaika, *Basque Violence*.

6. See Stanley Payne, *Basque Nationalism* (Reno: University of Nevada Press, 1975).

7. Ibid., p. 164.

8. Ibid.

9. Payne, *Basque Nationalism,* p. 74.

10. See Robert P. Clark, *The Basques: The Franco Years and Beyond* (Reno: University of Nevada Press, 1979).

11. Payne, *Basque Nationalism,* p. 109.

12. Ibid., p. 148.

13. Ronald Frazer, *Blood of Spain: An Oral History of the Spanish Civil War* (New York: Pantheon Books, 1979), p. 379.

14. Zulaika, *Basque Violence,* p. 18.

15. Payne, *Basque Nationalism,* p. 120.

16. Ibid., p. 120.

17. Frazer, *Blood of Spain,* p. 540.

18. Rafael Borrás Betriu, *Los que No Hicimos La Guerra* (Barcelona: Ediciones Nauta, 1971), p. 250.

19. Payne, *Basque Nationalism,* p. 146.

20. See Gurutz Jáuregui Bereciartu, *Ideología y Estrategia Política de ETA: Análisis de su Evolucíon Entre 1959–1968* (Madrid: Siglo Veintiuno, 1985).

21. Clark, *The Basque Insurgents,* pp. 35–37.

22. Ibid., p. 27.

23. John Sullivan, *El Nacionalismo Vasco Radical, 1959–1986* (Madrid: Alianza Editorial, 1986), p. 65.

24. Ibid., p. 76.

25. Sullivan, *El Nacionalismo,* p. 85.

26. See P. Janke, "Spanish Separatism: ETA's Threat to Basque Democracy," in *Contemporary Terrorism,* W. Gutteridge, ed. (New York: Facts on File Publications, 1986), pp. 135–66.

27. Zulaika, *Basque Violence,* p. 328.

28. Ibid., pp. 303–4.

29. See Sullivan, *El Nacionalismo,* ch. 4.

30. Ibid., p. 129.

31. Ibid., pp. 91–92.

32. Ibid., p. 85.

33. Payne, *Basque Nationalism,* p. 242.

34. Zulaika, *Basque Violence,* p. 324.

35. Clark, *The Basque Insurgents,* p. 46.

36. Sullivan, *El Nacionalismo,* p. 96.

37. Ibid.

38. Clark, *The Basque Insurgents,* pp. 111–12.

39. Zulaika, *Basque Violence,* p. 323.

40. *El País,* April 30, 1989.

41. See recent published documents, *El País,* December 27, 1987.

42. Robert P. Clark, "Euzkadi: Basque Nationalism in Spain since the Civil War," in *Nations without a State: Ethnic Minorities in Western Europe,* Charles R. Foster, ed. (New York: Praeger, 1980), pp. 88–94.

43. Zulaika, *Basque Violence,* pp. 169, 184.

44. Ibid., pp. 83–85.

45. Jáuregui, *Ideología y Estrategia,* pp. 142–44, 162.

46. Clark, *The Basque Insurgents*, ch. 2.

47. *El País*, June 21, 1987.

48. Jáuregui, *Ideología y Estrategia*, pp. 168–72.

49. See Sullivan, *El Nacionalismo*.

50. Jáuregui, *Ideología y Estrategia*, pp. 196–200.

51. See Clark, *The Basque Insurgents;* and Sullivan, *El Nacionalismo*.

52. *El País*, December 23, 1987.

53. *El País*, January 3, 1988.

54. Sullivan, *El Nacionalismo*, p. 255.

55. Justo de la Cueva, *La Escision del PNV* (Bilbao: Txalaparta Argitaldaria, 1988), pp. 114–15.

56. *El País*, November 15, 1987.

57. Justo de la Cueva, *La Escision del PNV*, p. 114.

58. *El País*, July 7, 1992.

59. *El País*, March 14, 1988.

60. *El País*, June 16, 1987.

61. See Mujal-Leon, E. "The Left and the Catholic Question in Spain," *West European Politics* 5:2 (1982), pp. 32–54.

62. Jáuregui, *Ideología y Estrategia*, pp. 130–31.

63. Richard Gunther, et al., *Spain after Franco: The Making of a Competitive Party System* (Berkeley: University of California Press, 1988), p. 229.

64. *El País*, March 6, 1986.

65. *El País*, March 13, 1986.

66. See Zulaika, *Basque Violence*.

67. Ibid., pp. 364–65, note 1.

68. *El País*, April 2, 1989.

69. Janke, "Spanish Separatism," p. 161.

70. See for example, Zulaika, *Basque Violence*, pp. 343–47.

71. Janke, "Spanish Separatism," p. 161.

72. *ABC*, December 29, 1988.

73. *El País*, June 23, 1988, and July 9, 1988.

74. Zulaika, *Basque Violence*, p. 315.

75. *Cambio 16*, October 23, 1989.

76. *El País*, January 4, 1988.

77. Zulaika, *Basque Violence*, p. 327.

78. *El País*, June 12, 1987.

79. *El País*, June 24, 1986.

80. *El País*, October 31, 1989.

81. Clark, *The Basque Insurgents*, pp. 86, 97.

82. *El País*, February 6, 1988.

83. *El País*, June 24, 1986; and *El País*, October 31, 1989.

84. *El País*, October 31, 1989.

"Eternal Loyalty!" Peronist poster produced by the Metalworkers' Union for Loyalty Day, with bust profiles of Juan, Evita, and Isabel Perón. (Buenos Aires, 1975)

Poster announcing November 1 march against U.S. military bases in Spain. (Madrid, 1987)

"There are 11,000 girls from age 11–17 in prostitution, just in Recife." Graffiti written by the Street Children Movement, informing about the problems facing street children in their daily struggle to survive. (Recife, Brazil, 1989)

A cacophony of wall painting placed on a harbor wall includes the announcement of the National Patriotic Day of Galicia on July 25, and a popular demonstration against the dismantling of industry. (Vigo, Galicia, 1988)

"Respect for young women, better education, better salaries for youth." A mural produced by the Organization of Youth for Liberty. (Rio de Janeiro, 1989)

Silhouetted poster profiles of the "disappeared," produced by las Madres de Plaza de Mayo. (Buenos Aires, December 1983)

"Patriots, we will win." Herri Batasuna election mural. (Basque Country, 1989)

Mural promoting an "Antiimperialist popular front of the left." (Buenos Aires, 1986)

"Would you celebrate a genocide? No to the V Centennial." Mural protesting the fifth centennial celebration of the discovery of America. (Pamplona, Spain, 1989)

"No aggression without an answer." A Mara-Mara feminist organization wall painting. (Amorebieta, Basque Country, 1989)

"The people's habitat will not be destroyed." LKI communist mural. Pamplona, Spain, 1988)

"Do not go—Object." An antidraft mural. (Pamplona, 1988)

Part III

SOUTH AMERICA: THE SOUTHERN CONE

5

Argentina: Hyperarticulation and Competition

Probably in no Latin America country have graffiti, posters, and wallpaintings constituted such a popular expression as in Argentina. Its pervasiveness made it seem that every wall, street corner, public transportation station, church and cathedral, and building facade had been taken over by street art commentators. The producers cut across the political spectrum from left to right, encompassing conservative, moderate, liberal, and radical points of view, and class and ethnic interests. It was dominated by Peronism, a multiclass, multi-ideological movement anchored in the labor movement, the premier political force over the last half-century. In this highly organized and articulated society, groups raised questions about the system, challenged dominant values, suggested alternative policies and modes of action, defined social reality, provided social commentary, rallied the people, and created their own psychological and political environment. Participation was constant, regardless of whether the political system was authoritarian or democratic. The prevalence of street art was stimulated by the hyperpoliticized and polarized conflict among the social forces—military rule, social tensions, and a powerful populist movement—and by the unstable political system characterized by cyclical swings between authoritarian and democratic regimes.

The evolution of street art is tied to the development of Argentina as a nation. Modern Argentine history can be divided into two eras, 1870–1930, and 1930 to the present. The first epoch saw Argentina transformed from an insignificant underdeveloped nation to a prosperous and culturally acclaimed one.[1] By the 1920s, Argentina was the world's eighth wealthiest state, surpassing Spain, Switzerland, and Sweden.[2] The educational system expanded and a high level of literacy evolved. A cultural development made Buenos Aires one of the cultural centers of the world.[3] It was a leader in Latin America in introducing representative democracy: the epoch was one of the increasing democratization when many European nations were struggling with the concept. However, it was also a time of increasing class conflict and working-class articulation.[4]

The second era was characterized by instability, military domination, authoritarianism, decline of democracy, evolution of the Peronists, development of a powerful labor movement, increasing polarization, and economic retrogression. By the 1980s, Argentina was saddled with one of the world's largest international debts, ranked 78th among the world's wealthiest countries, was characterized by hyperinflation, had a deteriorating educational system, and its international image as the most civilized Latin American country had been besmirched by the dirty war.[5] It arrived at this retrogression through a tortuous path. The 1930s, the Infamous Decade, were characterized by authoritarian rule, political repression, economic reform, and industrialization.[6] The 1940s began with a reimposed military intervention, a regime within which Juan Perón garnered increasing influence. From there, Argentina witnessed the rise of the Peronist movement, led by the charismatic duad of Juan and Evita Perón. Their support was generated from the working class. Beginning in 1946 they ruled in tandem over an authoritarian system until Evita's untimely death in 1952. Juan Perón was overthrown in 1955 by a military coup that led to a partial democratic opening after twenty-five years of various authoritarian governments. The Peronists, the largest single political bloc, however, were proscribed from 1955–1972, and their leader Perón forced to live in exile in Spain. The military became the power broker and governed during 1955–1958, 1966–1973, and 1976–1983, interspersed with democratic openings. The sequence was the legalization of Peronists in 1972; the return of Peronists to a governing role, 1973–1976; a coup and subsequent dirty war; the Falkland/Malvinas War of 1982 with Great Britain; and finally the 1983 democratic opening. President Raul Alfonsín, elected in 1983, was the first civilian head since 1928 to transfer the presidency to another elected civilian, Carlos Menem in 1989.

HISTORICAL SETTING

The Early Decades

Street art has been closely linked to the popular discourse that evolved out of Argentine political and social protests. At the turn of the century, the Socialist party was the first party to bring posters into electoral campaigning.[7] The Socialists recognized the value of combining art and politics to bring immediacy to communication. In 1896 the Socialist party began running candidates for national Congress in an electoral system riddled with fraud. With the reforms in 1912, the electoral system opened, and the Socialists and Radicals (UCR) emerged as competitors for political control in Buenos Aires. During the pre–1930 era, posters and handbills were employed by various parties to inform and elicit support. The Socialist party had a well-defined program—

universal and unrestricted suffrage, honest elections, women's rights, minimum wage, an eight-hour working day, and restrictions on child and female labor. In the first election of 1896, they published 20,000 copies of their programs and pasted up 8,000 posters on the walls, fences, and buildings in Buenos Aires, trying to inform the working class. Lectures, pamphlets, and posters became standard campaign tactics. A tradition was born.[8] Socialists took to plastering posters in billboard style. Pictorial and nonpictorial posters were utilized. The pictorial posters were aesthetically pleasing; they would carry a slogan and the wording "Vote for the Socialist Party."[9] The party did not have a monopoly on posters. As the electoral process became more open and competition among parties more intense, street art activism increased. By the 1920 elections, Radicals, Socialists, and the Democratic Progressives were plastering the city walls with colorful posters.[10] In 1919, when Radical leader Hipólito Yrigoyen—elected president of Argentina in 1916 and again in 1928—realized the value of this mass media, he had his portrait plastered throughout the country.[11] By 1928, Radical election posters had become quite sophisticated. Some announced events and rallies, others carried candidates' names. For example, a sophisticated poster showed a giant UCR locomotive roaring down the tracks with the slogan, "Nothing will stop its advance."[12]

Two ideological political foes utilized street art to battle for their causes. The Liga Patriótica Argentina was a conservative nationalist association, founded in 1919. Made up of young aristocrats it was concerned with combating Marxism and anarchism and placed an emphasis on Argentinism and Social Catholicism. The Liga became one of the most powerful political groups during the early 1920s. They were evangelicals who learned the value of street politics and publicity. They delivered speeches on street corners, passed out pamphlets, pasted posters, produced banners, and held rallies and demonstrations. The Liga spread their ideas with poster-posting brigades. In one campaign in January 1920, the brigades posted an estimated 50,000 posters entitled, "Defense of the Fruits of Labor." These were posted throughout towns and rural areas proclaiming the constitutional "right to self-defense" against attacks on property and life. This was in response to a widely disseminated anarchist poster. The Liga posters caused controversy. Some feared citizens would take the law into their own hands. In 1929, the Liga caused further controversy when Liga president Manuel Carlés began a campaign to oust president Yrigoyen. Posters went up proclaiming the "Hour of Vengeance" had arrived and Argentines had to choose between the fatherland and a government that disregarded the law. Police tore down the posters and arrested some Ligists. Another right-wing nationalist group that opposed the Yrigoyan administration, the Republican League, contributed to the campaign by disseminating antiadministration posters.[13]

The Liga's primary nemesis, the anarchists, were also practitioners of street art. The movement was especially influential up to World War I. Its politics were the streets. Slogans and street propaganda accompanied their actions. For instance, a banner with black lettering against a white background at a demonstration for unemployed laborers in 1910 carried a common anarchist message, "We demand the distribution of the surplus."[14] This anarchist slogan, which found its way into their street art, was an inflammatory message that stimulated the Liga poster response. Posters to neutralize opponents' posters.

Following the 1930s that began with a military coup, the resulting chain of events brought a populist military colonel to prominence, Perón, and changed dramatically the political landscape. The change carried with it a popular culture of extensive street art communication. Peronism rested upon a popular base of working-class adherence. Graffiti became one of its political expressions. Essentially, political graffiti in Argentina had its origins in class politics and was directly linked to the political evolution of the workers and the dynamics of their popular culture during the transition to Peronism. Graffiti were symbolic of class politics, an expression of political will evolving out of the opposition and protests of the working class against the dominant political elite and their culture. The utilization of graffiti was helped in a significant way by the massive demonstrations initiated by the unions and workers in October 1945; these forced the military to reinstate Perón. This gave power to the charismatic colonel who had cultivated workers' favor since being named minister of labor in 1943. The workers' identity had been previously silenced by the oppressiveness of a dominant class elite; theirs had been a culture of silence. When the demonstrations erupted over the forced resignation and imprisonment of Perón by the army—he held at the time the simultaneous positions of minister of labor, minister of war, and vice-president of the country—the workers asserted their own symbolic power through massive street demonstrations of a magnitude not often seen.[15] The workers' movement made visible that which had been invisible. Massive graffiti writing by the workers was one form of their "disrespectful" action. Newspapers reported—all anti-Perón except *La Epoca*—ghastly stories of blasphemy committed by the workers as they marched through the streets in the days leading up to the grand October 17, 1945, demonstration.[16] Workers wrote pro-Perón slogans in chalk on building facades, walls, and most outrageously for the dominant class, on national monuments. A new popular behavior was in the process of being legitimized. Their graffiti, a testament to protest, announced that an oppressed subculture of the workers had surfaced. Their public graphics were established as a permanent fixture of the sociopolitical environment over the next decade under the tutelage of the Perón regime.[17] And it penetrated the totality of society. Middle-class parties such as the Radicals and others absorbed this communication into their repertory.

The Peronist Era

Perón immediately became a candidate for the February 1946 elections when the military stepped aside and allowed open presidential elections, the first since 1928. The United States considered him profascist. Argentina was one of the few Latin American countries to remain neutral during World War II; it was seen as harboring pro-Axis sentiments. Consequently, the United States opposed Perón's election. The United States ambassador, Spruille Braden, took a proconsular attitude. This made him an issue in the campaign. Handbills, no doubt orchestrated by Perón, flooded Buenos Aires, ridiculing him as the "Al Capone of Buenos Aires," or "Cowboy Braden." [18] Braden left the ambassadorship to assume the Latin American policy-making desk at the State Department. Two weeks before the elections, the State Department issued the infamous *Blue Book,* detailing the nation's military collaboration with the Axis powers, and accusing Perón in particular of involvement. [19] The American attempt to help the opposition Democratic Union (UD) misfired; Perón used nationalism to invigorate his campaign. The UD had employed electoral posters with the slogan "For liberty against Nazism." The *Blue Book* was explosive. Walls everywhere erupted with the Peronist's new shibboleth, "Braden or Perón." [20] Furthermore, the opposition produced a poster of Perón holding up a worker's sweaty white shirt as a flag, the inscription proclaimed, "The Sweaty One—the new fatherland colors." This insult against the workers was turned into a popular symbol. The followers of Perón were baptized the *descamisados,* the shirtless ones. This emblem of pride is still carried by working-class supporters of the Peronist movement. [21] Perón was elected with 54 percent of the vote.

Under Perón street art and public events were elevated to a high symbolic level to demonstrate grass-roots appeal. October 17 developed into Loyalty Day. It was a time of rallies, popular culture, and face-to-face communication between the Perons and masses in the Plaza de Mayo. Posters advertised and commemorated the event. The government became a key producer of posters. A 1950 poster, artistically stylized in the European design of the times and signed by the artist, profiled a strong striding figure of a worker against a sky background. [22] The unions, removed of their independent leadership by Perón, were semistate appendages. Thus, union posters were in fact government sponsored. Slogans and posters identified the spirit of the movement, "Perón keeps his word, Evita dignifies it," and "The lady of hope." More elaborate clichés included, "The land belongs to those who work it," and "Argentina should be neither exclusively rich nor excessively poor." [23]

With Evita's prodding, women became more politicized. The Peronists pushed a women's national suffrage bill and Evita became the symbol for women's political action. Posters declared, "Women can and should vote—Evita Duarte Perón," or the same message with, "Viva Evita." [24] Nationalism was also an issue. When Perón nationalized the British railroads, the event was celebrated with street graphics. Gigantic posters rang out, "Now they are ours." [25] New presidential elections were held in November 1951. A repertoire of slogans and street graphics guided the process. Several Peronist sectors, the unions and the women's sector, attempted to offer the vice-presidential nomination to Evita. It was stridently resisted by conservative and military forces. The campaign began during a *cabildo abierto* (open meeting) with slogans, posters, and banners proclaiming, "Perón-Eva Perón," "The ticket for the Fatherland," and "Perón keeps his word—Evita dignifies it." Wallpaintings summed it up, "Perón-Perón, 1952–1958."[26] It was a short campaign, Evita declined the nomination and sick with cancer, died July 26, 1952.

Although the 1946 elections were open and democratic, Perón quickly moved to inaugurate an authoritarian regime. To debilitate the opposition, he denied them traditional mass communication. The airwaves were Peronist controlled, the print media was taken over or intimidated into silence, public meetings were restricted, underground newspapers and pamphlets sought out by the police, and the placement of posters by the opposition repressed.[27] After Perón's 1951 reelection and the death of Evita, Perón ran into increasing difficulties. His most serious miscue was the confrontation with the Church in 1954. Slogans quickly found their way into the communication rhetoric. Church supporters coined, "Christ or Perón," and the Peronists, "Perón yes—priests no," "Divorce," and "Neither clerics nor communists." Denied access to the established media, the Church took to the underground with pamphlets and leaflets. Leaflets made easy handbills that could be fastened on walls. For Corpus Christi day, June 1955, the Church produced half a million leaflets announcing the event. Despite government prohibition, the walls rang out with Christ the King. In September, Perón was ousted by a military coup.[28]

POST-PERÓN ERA

Following Perón's overthrow, the era was dominated by the military through either direct or indirect rule. Street art grew in importance partly as a medium against the military's attempt to purge the Peronist movement. The movement was proscribed. Peronist unions were intervened, their leadership purged. Unable to engage in electoral political activity, the workers returned to the streets to assert their symbolic power and challenge the right and legitimacy of the military to proscribe them.[29] Strikes and general strikes, demonstrations and violence marked the era. Graffiti announced the events and commemorated victims of repression. To challenge the military's hegemony over the traditional media, the Peronists increasingly turned to street art as an underground medium. Other collectives joined the process as the military proscribed all opposition activity during times of direct rule. Even during periods of democracy, street art became an accepted dimension of popular expression, even used by the establishment groups despite the availability of electronic media.

The political swings in the post-1955 era caused definite cycles in the utilization of graffiti, wallpaintings, and posters. They were related to the cyclical swings between authoritarian and democratic regimes. The military had a pathological fear of popular forces and sought to cleanse the country of disruptive street graphics, among other things. The Peronists represented the one organized challenge to the military's dominant power. They reverted to popular forms of expression which rattled the nerves of the armed forces. As an underground medium, street graphics advertised to the public and the military that an active opposition existed. When the democratic cycle returned, graffiti were supplemented, and in instances dwarfed, by the larger, more sophisticated wallpaintings and posters. Wallpaintings particularly dominated because they had a more professional quality, stood out because of their large size, creative application, refinement, and visual appeal. Posters were more ephemeral, often pasted over by commercial ones or worn away by the climatic elements.

The Resistance

The Peronists were antisystem during 1955–1972 because the military had irrevocably stated Peronism was proscribed.[30] The Peronist unions formed a movement called The Resistance, the core composed of a bloc of Peronist unions, the "62 Organizations."[31] They used demonstrations, protests, and general strikes; street graphics were also a popular tool for informing about their issues and events. Several events in 1964 stimulated a massive production of street art. Throughout the 1960s it was common to see large painted "Perón lives" graffiti. In 1964 this was replaced by "Perón returns." Perón hinted he would return from exile in 1964 during a nonmilitary regime period. The walls resonated with a *Perón vuelve* campaign. The military had its way, Perón was prohibited from entering Argentina.[32] The second event was the unions' "Battle Plan." Launched in 1963, and more vigorously in 1964, it attempted to pressure the government to adopt economic policies more favorable to the workers, and to remove all restrictions on Peronist political activities. The unions carried out work stoppages, seized factories, and scrawled graffiti on them symbolically as liberated zones.

The full fervor of discontent toward the system, the military, and the restrictions on Peronists erupted in the late 1960s. It resulted in a groundswell of grass-roots support that had the effect of expanding the ideological base of the movement by adding a leftist sector. A military coup in 1966 inaugurated another era of direct military rule under the tutelage of Juan Carlos Onganía, an admirer of Franco. He declared his intent to remain in power indefinitely. He banned all sociopolitical activity. He intervened in the national universities using strong armed police tactics to expel students and professors suspected of "communist" sympathies, and he crushed the general strike called by the CGT. Students and intellectuals had been sectors alienated from the Peronist movement. Perón had during his first administration cleansed the universities also, expelling thousands of professors and students. Consequently, students and intellectuals became hostile and anti-Peronist. This changed with the Onganía regime. The Peronists began to attract support from sectors which had formally inclined toward small leftist parties. Perón encouraged the development. The movement slowly absorbed a significant left-wing sector, a core of youth and university students who saw in Evita a true revolutionary figure. They reassessed the Peronist movement, resulting in a revitalized youth sector for the Peronists.[33]

Antisystem street art dogged Onganía from the start. Walls came alive with symbols of opposition. When a student was killed in Córdoba in September 1966 during demonstrations, antiregime students produced posters and plastered them on the main city artery, renaming it Avenue Pampillón after the martyred student.[34] In 1967, university walls in particular, and some street walls in general, spouted with procommunist revolutionary symbols to honor Che Guevara who was killed in Bolivia. "Che lives," "Che the revolutionary," "Long live the memory and exemplary life of Che," were typical graffiti slogans. The commemorations to Che violated the political landscape in a country governed by a fervent anticommunist regime. The government was unable to repress these violations of public space.[35] The Cordobazo in 1969 relegated Che to a secondary role; more pressing was the groundswell that eroded the regime's legitimacy.

The Cordobazo, May–June 1969 in Cordoba, was one of the great popular eruptions of the century. It unleashed a cycle of violence that traumatized Argentina for the next decade.[36] There emerged from this confrontation a reinvigorated Peronist movement, a new left, and a guerrilla underground that raised the emotional level of politics, the process of which culminated with the dirty war. The elevated level of violence and the increasing politicization had its parallel growth in street art. The country became awash with street art, a temporary abatement occurring only during the first several years of the next military era, 1976–1983. The Cordobazo initiated the process. Street barricades went up and liberated zones, heavily demarcated with graffiti, were held for hours and several days. The chaotic, war-zone environment gave protesters the ability to carry out a visual graffiti assault throughout the city in a "war of the walls." Graffiti slogans declared, "The barricades close the streets but open the way," "Obedience begins with consciousness: consciousness with disobedience," "Violence is the patrimony of everyone, liberty is for those who fight for it," "Burn me an American," "Onganía, who USA'd you?" and at the School of Architecture, "Do we want to plan misery?[37] Similar but less serious outbursts occurred in other cities, with street art serving as signs of protest and as short-lived political catharses. Antigovernment propaganda, "Onganía—dictatorship," and "Selling the country out" were part of the deluge.[38] The visit of Nelson Rockefeller on a fact-finding mission added fuel to the fire. Street art recorded the hostility with the typical anti-American graffiti. Most significantly, the Cordobazo and subsequent events spawned four guerrilla groups that engaged the military in a violent war of attrition.

The two most important guerrilla organizations that emerged were the Montoneros and the Ejército Revolucionario del Pueblo (ERP). The Montoneros, along with two other groups, Fuerzas Armadas Peronistas (FAP) and Fuerzas Armadas Revolucionarias (FAR) were Peronist groups. They saw in Perón the possibility of a popular revolution. Disgruntled with the old traditional left and establishment-oriented unions, these youth, primarily in their early twenties from middle-class backgrounds, adopted Evita as their revolutionary symbol.[39] Montonero posters declared, "If Evita were alive she would be a Montonero."[40] These groups worked to bring the military to its knees and allow Perón's return. ERP on the other hand, was a non-Peronist, Trotskyist-Guevarist group that saw Peronism as a false bourgeois liberating movement. They emphasized continental solidarity and liberation and took Che as their symbol. ERP opposed Perón. Each group became prolific producers of graffiti. When the system opened again in 1972, wallpaintings and posters complemented the graffiti. At first, much of the street art was simple identification graffiti, "Montoneros," "FAR," and "ERP," or graffiti that identified the groups with their symbolic icons, Evita or Che, like ERP graffiti commemorating Che's death, "October 8—Day of the Heroic Guerrilla." Slogans were added, "Perón or death" and "Socialist Fatherland." Issues began to be articulated, especially dealing with human rights and repression. Moreover, the Montoneros and ERP began to accumulate vast sums of money by kidnapping industrialists for ransom. This gave them the resources to print an underground medium and utilize sophisticated posters.

An event that focused attention on the new left and added to the rising level of violence and retribution was the Trelew massacre. This episode quickly became the motif for street graphics commentary and the symbol of martyrdom. Guerrilla groups utilized this cold-blooded massacre by the military as an effective antisystem tool. It brought scorn on the military and sympathy for the guerrillas; it was the culminating incident in a chain of events that forced the military from its governing role. The guerrillas had their martyrs and it was a boon for the leftist cause. The martyrdom occurred at the Trelew naval base in August 1972. Scores of guerrillas from the four groups were being held at several military bases. In a daring breakout, some escaped, including important leaders, but others were recaptured and taken to Trelew where sixteen were executed in their cells. The military justified their action by asserting they were attempting to escape again. However, four survivors gave witness to the military's false claim. Four victims were women, raising the level of emotion attached to the event.[41]

Radical leftists seized upon this event to enhance their position. Clandestine posters with the photo of each victim, along with the name and organization, were placed on public walls. At the top of each poster in bold lettering was, "Gloria to the heroes of Trelew." There were many graffiti that focused on the same theme as well as posters that celebrated them after the 1973 democratic opening. The artistic quality of the posters was poor, but the message was clear-cut, universal, and devastating. This martyrdom caused a tremendous psychological impact. The posters personalized the victims and confronted the citizenry visually with a moral dilemma. Victims were no longer faceless individuals. Massive graffiti complemented the visual socialization process. "Remember Trelew" kept the citizenry's conscience riveted to military brutality.

The event was commemorated annually in street art over the next few years. It was occasionally recalled in graffiti in the 1980s during the first years of the democratic opening when human rights abuse became an even bigger issue.

Both ERP and Montoneros continued to attack the military during the interlude between military regimes, 1973–1976. ERP mounted a spectacular attack on the Monte Chingolo military base outside Buenos Aires in December 1975. The Montoneros carried out a similar raid in the northern city of Formosa. Both the ERP and Montoneros commemorated their fallen comrades, "Formosa—12 Montoneros fell for liberation," and "Glory to the heroes of Monte Chingolo—ERP." When the Montoneros were proscribed in 1975, their graffiti declared, "With proscription there is no pacification—J. Perón—Montoneros."

A far greater tragic martyrdom followed the failure of the Peronist restoration, 1973–1976. During this restoration state terrorism continued to unfold. When Perón died in 1974, nine months after assuming the presidency again, the mantle of government passed to his vice-president, his third wife, Isabel. She was a weak leader who fell under the dominating influence of Minister of Social Welfare José López-Rega, an ultraright protofascist type.[42] A diabolical figure and an ideological rightist, he instituted the precursor to the military's dirty war. He formed the Argentine Anti-Communist Alliance which began a clandestine campaign to eliminate leftists and opponents. Consequently, López-Rega became the focus of antiregime graffiti. Some illustrated him as a pig. In general, street art commentary of this brief period reflected negatively on the Peronist regime. Isabel was the target of vicious commentary. However, the right-wing countered with their own activist campaign placing pro-Isabel slogans, "Isabel or death—long live the Fatherland," "Isabel—leader or colony," "Nothing without Isabel," and even the women's branch of the Peronist party contributed occasional posters, "President by will of the people." As it became increasingly clear a coup was imminent, anticoup graffiti commentary began to appear on walls. Some read, "Another 55 will not occur," recalling the 1955 coup that removed Perón.

The return of the military in 1976 intensified the all-out attack on the left. The military sought to exterminate Marxist and leftist influence. It instigated a brutally repressive strategy leading to the death and disappearance of more than 10,000 individuals in a campaign termed the *dirty war*. A human rights movement headed by las Madres de Plaza de Mayo emerged to challenge the military morally, demanding an accounting of the disappeared. Las Madres started when a group of mothers and grandmothers of the disappeared began a weekly vigil in 1977 in the Plaza de Mayo. Hand posters personalized the experience. Each woman held a photo affixed to paper or cardboard with the name and date of her disappeared. To heighten the visual impact, women wore white kerchiefs tied over their heads; embroidered in colored thread on the kerchief was the name and date of the disappeared kin. The white kerchiefs became the group's most significant symbol. The military felt compelled to make its message public on metropolitan walls. When the Inter-American Human Rights Commis-

sion came on a fact-finding mission to hear testimony on human rights violations, the military, unable to prevent the visit, wrote its official account and
plastered Buenos Aires walls with a state-sponsored poster, "We are right and
human."[43]

During this period, street art went underground. From the first six months to
a year after the coup, there was a vigorous outpouring of antimilitary resistance
graffiti.[44] However, it receded as repression became overbearing and the opposition neutralized. Graffiti such as, "The moral and order of the military is
hunger and repression of the people," was typical. Graffiti began to reappear
more prolifically in the early 1980s as discontent built and spilled over into the
streets with demonstrations. The walls also came alive in 1982 with state encouraged street art to support the Falkland/Malvinas War. The mobilizing slogan, "the Malvinas are Argentina," was painted over a blue and white (national colors) map of the islands. Prime Minister Margaret Thatcher, the British,
and Secretary of State Alexander Haig were points of attack in posters. Haig
was portrayed as selling-out Argentina. A poster by the "2nd of April Reserv-
ist" group made the United States the point of scorn while also recruiting
volunteers for the war.[45] When casualties began to mount, street art commemorated them; right-wing nationalists made the dead their martyrs to nationalism.
When the war proved a disaster, the military regime collapsed. The walls castigated them in a stream of anti-armed forces sentiments that did not cease
during the succeeding Alfonsín era.

Martyrdom and Human Rights

Martyrdom, part of the political folklore is symptomatic of the divisions that
have traumatized society. In 1983 when the military was forced to step aside,
a catharsis of posters, graffiti, and wallpaintings demanded accountability for
human rights violations. The human rights movement rallying cry, *que apar-
ezca* (reappearance), was proclaimed continually in the street art. Las Madres
and other human rights groups used martyrdom in their street art to pressure
the government for a full investigation. To keep the issue visible, las Madres
continued their weekly marches with their hand-held posters of the disappeared.
Throughout Buenos Aires posters and graffiti kept the issue in the forefront
with a *Nunca Mas* (never again) slogan. An astute and psychologically powerful visual presentation occurred in December 1983 during the first day of the
restoration. Overnight thousands of human-size posters with the silhouetted figures of the disappeared outlined in black on white paper appeared, posters
produced by las Madres. The silhouetted figures indicated the range of human
forms of the disappeared—children, teenagers, women and men, pregnant women,
and couples. Within the appropriate figure corresponding to the physical characteristics of each beloved one, a family member came and wrote the name
and date of the disappeared. This tremendously personalized the national tragedy to all citizens. It created intense interest. People stood by the thousands

looking at the figures, reading the names on this ephemeral victim's memorial. It was the beginning of the process of educating the nation to face the terrible drama that had fallen upon the most civilized South American country. Nobody could escape its consequences. Grief and guilt were embedded in the collective historical memory. The major media fixed on these silhouetted posters; extensive commentary, photos, and television images carried the message to the four corners of the nation.

The emotional level was heightened by victimization of children. Children disappeared when security forces seized young couples or pregnant women. A high percentage of victims were women.[46] The children of parents who disappeared were put up for clandestine adoption. Relatives of missing children began a campaign to locate them. Posters immediately appeared to bring an awareness of this tragedy. On December 10, 1983, in celebration of International Human Rights Day, a poster depicted a lost child in a pensive mood standing on the sidewalk deep in thought, "My grandmother is searching for me—help her find me—the Grandmothers de Plaza de Mayo." An August 5th poster for Children's Day showed a pensive child sitting on the curb with the silhouetted figures of a young couple walking along the sidewalk. The pensive thought, "I am sad and I wait—and I am going to keep looking for you mommy and daddy, and for all the disappeared parents . . . I will promise you papa, there will be justice."

Human rights had not abated by 1990. Las Madres continued their quest for accountability and retribution. Annually, las Madres celebrated a twenty-four hour Resistance March. In December 1989, downtown Buenos Aires was plastered with its large-size las Madres posters, aesthetically pleasing, with the year's theme, "We will not forget—we will not forgive." Posters, as well as wallpaintings, announced the event and invited participation in the Resistance March. One poster was more rhetorical, "Do you know where they are now, those that tortured and assassinated your children? Do you know what position they have or their activities? Where they live?"

Unions had their martyrs, as did political parties, leftist and rights groups, and the military. The turmoil of the late 1960s and early 1970s resulted in the assassination of three secretary-generals of the CGT, Augusto Vandor, José Alonso, and José Rucci, all Peronists. Each it seemed was a victim of leftists Peronists. Commemorative posters acknowledged them from time to time. One for Rucci in 1975 had his photo and the statement, "Argentine and Peronist." Heads of individual labor unions also were martyred. When Saul Ubaldini, current CGT secretary-general narrowly escape an assassination attempt shortly after the inauguration of Menem, the neighborhood around the CGT filled with pro-Ubaldini wallpaintings painted in national colors with the commentaries, "Ubaldini is CGT," "Ubaldini the loved one—the people are with you," and "Ubaldini patriot—loyal to the Argentine people." Evita herself was considered the first Peronist martyr, a victim of cancer and of the political struggle. When she died her embalmed body laid in rest in the headquarters of the CGT.

When the military coup of 1955 occurred, her body was confiscated and hid by the army in a cemetery in Milan, Italy. The mystery of Evita's body and its return was a salient issue until 1972 when it was finally delivered to Perón in Spain. Each year on the anniversary of her death, posters are pasted to commemorate her.

The Peronists

One outpouring of Peronist street art came with the catharsis of the democratic opening in 1973. Full Peronist participation was permitted for the first time since 1955. By 1973 the movement encompassed a broad ideological spectrum from the fascist right to the Marxist left, various leadership combinations were emphasized in the street graphics to project a particular ideological preference, to individualize and personalize a Peronist image, or to push a coined phrase and message. Each Peronist union, faction, or group sought to individualize its ideological position by emphasizing differently the importance of the three Peróns in the hierarchical triumvirate. Leftists and Marxist Peronist factions and unions highlighted the symbolic figure of Evita, totally ignoring Isabel and often Perón, although not at first when he supported the leftist sector. For instance, a 1973 Montonero poster for Loyalty Day singled out Perón, "President Perón—the loyalty and the struggle of the people will make it possible," Evita though, was the darling of the Peronist left. She was the heroine-villain of class and ideological politics, and she divided Argentine sentiments more than any other figure. She symbolized class differences.

Numerous unions used her symbolic figure in their propaganda. In some posters, Evita was depicted as a solo figure with the emphasis on her as a revolutionary symbol. This role had its origins in her tirades against the oligarchy and her "Death or Perón" slogan. Her revolutionary image was sealed forever during her famous speech in Plaza de Mayo just before her death as she stood stricken with cancer. With her dazzling movie star image behind her, and her hair pulled back in a more subdued revolutionary style, her remarks left a legacy, "Peronism will be revolutionary or it will be nothing." Other statements added to her image, "The era of privileges, of select minorities, has ended, because the consciousness of the people has awakened."

In the decade of the 1970s, these slogans were seized upon by radical leftists to make the claim that this tradition was the real ideological root for Peronism. Peronism to them should be revolutionary socialist. For the 1973 elections, the Peronist Youth sector pushed its revolutionary cause through "Evita—Cámpora—Montoneros will bring back true Peronism."[47] One union poster symbolized, "Evita—the eternal flame of social justice," another portrayed Perón and Evita as "Symbols of national unity," while a Peronist Youth poster which silhouetted the profile of Evita called her the "Symbol of youth." Convoking Evita's name was thus a call to action. She symbolized an ideology, a class, and political action. Conversely, Evita was villain-enemy to the conservative upper class, much of the bourgeois, right-wing Peronists; she elicited especially strong emotional reactions among the military. Evita was a popular cult figure who symbolized different things to different people.

Peronists of conservative, right-wing, and fascist bent ignored the figure of Evita. Instead, they choose Perón's third wife, Isabel, who was inclined toward the conservatives. She was given prominence alongside Perón who was often portrayed in his military uniform. This emphasized the hierarchy of leadership authority, "verticalism." To try and hold its position, the right-wing, after Perón's death and Isabel's ascension to the presidency in 1974, stressed traditional hierarchical authority, the unquestioning loyalty to the supreme figure, in this case, Isabel. Posters produced by the Orthodox faction highlighted Isabel as the principal figure. However, leftists answered with "Isabel—traitor" graffiti. In essence, the two wives of Juan Perón represented the right and left ideological positions within the movement. Other Peronist factions and unions individualized their posters by stressing the unity factor, the triumvirate of all three figures. Some unity proponents visually emphasized Evita over Isabel or vice versa, but still the theme was unity. This was evident in some 1973 election posters when strong psychological symbols were employed visualizing Evita in a celestial setting symbolically giving her blessing and loyalty to the movement through the living figures of Juan and Isabel. When Perón died in 1974 the same ethereal setting was reemphasized for commemorative events such as Loyalty Day, placing Perón and Evita in the heavens extending their support and loyalty to Isabel. Other posters portrayed just the solo figure of Perón, or Isabel, or Evita. Graffiti and wallpaintings mirrored the emphasis placed upon each Perón figure. Whatever the combination, this symbolic manipulation was oriented toward giving cognitive recognition to the symbol of Peronism, the ties between masses and leaders. Certainly up until the mid-1980s, the various sectors glorified one of the three Perón figures: Evita was symbol of the underclass, Juan the composite nation, and Isabel the right.

The 1983 presidential elections were the first in the movement's history when none of the triumvirate was a candidate. The leftist faction was a spent force and thus the figure of Evita did not appear often although her spirit was still invoked by many unions. Other factions and unions had ambivalent feelings about emphasizing Isabel for although she was titular head of the movement, she was not popular with the masses, was not a candidate, had remained in exile in Spain, and took no active part in the elections. She retired from politics shortly thereafter. Her figure faded although some Isabel loyalists utilized her figure. It was the grand safe figure of Perón himself that dominated the street art.

The Peronists lost the presidential election. With no Perón figure to guide the movement and offer a focus, the movement fell into an internal leadership struggle. For Peronists, the struggle for the internal soul of the party among various factions resulted in a profuse flourishing of street art. In the mid-1980s various factions and leaders prepared for internal elections and leadership recognition. The intraparty strife erupted between the Orthodox and the Renewals. Each faction used graphics to advance its cause. In 1985, the first internal elections were held in the Federal Capital district. An outpouring of posters and wallpaintings made a colorful street art exhibit of Peronist propaganda. The Renewals won these elections. Next, the energy shifted to Buenos Aires province where the campaign was particularly intense.

The province was considered key in the struggle for internal party control. Postponed several times, the province's internals were held in November 1986. An incredible outpouring of street graphics occurred. Every bridge embankment, over- and underpasses, wall, and interurban rail station, was flooded with propaganda as the factions tried to attract loyal Peronists. Added to this outpouring was the weak reemergence of the Peronist left that tried to demonstrate it was a viable sector. It began an intensive graffiti and wallpainting campaign to advertise its existence. The Orthodox represented the right-wing and tied its symbolic historical claim to the Perón-Isabel roots, "Yes to Isabel Perón—86" spouted on the walls. The Renewals represented the progressive center and emphasized the Perón-Evita historical roots. The left focused on the patron figure, Evita. The Revolutionary Peronist Youth took up the leftist cause, resulting in a massive reappearance of Evita's figure in street graphics of 1986. Her name, slogans, face, and figure adorned many posters. In July 1986, during the celebration of the anniversary of her death, at least sixteen different profile posters were pasted throughout Buenos Aires by labor unions and leftist groups. Massive graffiti accompanied the posters and "Evita lives" or "Evita lives—Montoneros," "Evita *vuelve* (returns)" were common.

The internal struggle was only one category of street art, albeit in 1986, the most important according to the quantity of production. The party and its various internal factions also tried to maintain a collective image. They commented on national issues and thereby established credibility that the Peronists were a serious governing political alternative. The credibility gap was difficult to overcome because of the reorganizational chaos within the party over leadership. To try to rebuild credibility, the party produced a series of collective issue posters with statements, "You do not combat the problem of drugs with repression, it is prevented through social justice." They wrote graffiti and produced posters that declared, "Yes, Peronism does have alternatives," a response to the Radical charge that it did not. These latter posters and graffiti advertised popular assemblies, announced speakers who would expound to interested citizenry on party ideas. Even if the popular assemblies were not well attended, the posters announcing them created the image that the party was alive intellectually and engaged in finding answers to society's problems. This intellectual imagery campaign was summarized with the maxim, "Peronism is on the move," a headline that appeared in street graphics throughout Buenos Aires.

THE DEMOCRATIC RESTORATION

Trends

With the 1983 restoration, street art social commentary shifted to include broad areas of concern. The walls became a historical repository of the issues with which the democratic system had to grapple. These included economic, political, and moral matters. The principal moral issue revolved around the human rights atrocities. Another moral issue was divorce. Economic issues were hyperinflation, economic redistribution, and debate on the huge international debt left over from military rule. Political issues entailed national and regional elections, elections for union officials, internal elections within the various political parties, and democracy itself. An unsponsored poster on inauguration day summed it up, "Democracy—now you have it—guard it." Each of the debated issues and elections found a visual outlet through street graphics where the battles raged continually.

Several trends were apparent in street art during the 1983–1990 period. One was the continual expansion in the number of groups communicating their views via street art. Each year during this period, the propaganda wars on the city streets escalated until reaching a crescendo in 1989. Those groups which were badly repressed or weakened, or had their organizational structures devastated, recovered slowly, some faster than others. As greater numbers of groups, parties, and factions engaged in this activism, they elevated the quantity and intensity of street graphics. Further augmenting the process was that in a politicized society like Argentina, new groups, new alliances, and splinters from old collectives form, break apart, and reform, in a continual struggle for survival, recognition, and greater leverage. Each group used street art to advertise its metamorphosis, its identity, and its realignment.

A second trend was the shift in emphasis in 1986–1987 in the visual placement of street art from the Federal Capital to the surrounding province of Buenos Aires. In December 1983, immediately following the inauguration of Alfonsín, the intensity of political pressure was directed toward the Federal District where groups lobbied the national government for immediate action. As the initial period and its issues faded, the shift occurred in visual placement. The political power of Buenos Aires province is awesome and dwarfs the combined influence of the rest of Argentina. The political importance of this province has meant that over the years a prolific amount of graffiti, posters, and wallpaintings have accumulated as groups have sought to influence the citizenry. The quantity of street art in the province increased in 1986 by a quantum leap for two main reasons: the gubernatorial elections in October 1987 and the internal elections and factional strife within parties, each vital for the political fortunes of the participants.

Chronicled Themes and Issues

The first issue was the November 1983 elections fought between the two dominant parties, the Radicals and Peronists. Street art served the partisan electoral cause by supporting candidates, sloganeering, and pushing specific issues germane to their parties. The Peronists emphasized nationalism. Posters proclaimed Alfonsín the Coca-Cola candidate. They showed him holding a Coca-Cola bottle with the statement, "Alfonsín—President, together the Yankis will win—Coca-Cola—Juventud Peronista." The UCR countered with popular images of Alfonsín. Posters depicted him talking to the multitudes, or stressing leadership, "Alfonsín now—the man we need."

After Afonsín's inauguration, the street art refocused on the second issue, the burning question of human rights, a demand for a full inquest into human rights violations. In response, and to the military's incredulity, Alfonsín set up a commission to investigate the dirty war. Some twelve hundred military and security personnel who had participated in human rights abuses were identified in the commission's final report, *Nunca Mas*. Trials for the nine ruling junta members who governed during this era began April 1985. The trial elicited much street graphics commentary and debate—statements demanding trials for all those tinted with crimes uncovered by the commission; declarations of "No amnesty—neither partial nor otherwise," "Judge the guilty"; inflammatory slogans, "Death to the fascists," "Death to the assassins," "Death to the military"; and just a steady stream of antimilitary commentary. There was the summarizing slogan, *Nunca Mas* (Never Again). The antimilitary campaign sought to arouse public consciousness, destroy the military's credibility, and settle old scores by seeking political retribution, an attitude that emerged from fifty years of direct and indirect military rule. One of the most astute displays of graffiti was carried by the major media the next day; it occurred the night before the trials on April 22. An unidentified group painstakingly wrote on the famous obelisk in downtown Buenos Aires the names of each of the twelve hundred individuals named in the commission report. Included were the infamous nine ex-junta officers, the controversial ex-chief of police Ramón Camps, and Captain Alfredo Astiz, who was identified in a celebrated case as responsible for the death of a Swedish teenager. A graffito message accompanied the names; "all should be tried and none granted amnesty."[48]

On the other side, promilitary and ultranationalists issued threats and death threats via street art against Alfonsín, the commission members, particularly commission President Ernesto Sábato, and human rights groups. All were tagged "Bolsheviks," "Sábato Bolshevik," or more intimidating statements "Death to las Madres." The facade of the offices of las Madres de Plaza was the target of intimidating graffiti; one graffito stated, "Camps will return."[49] Camps was former chief of police responsible for much state violence. Camps' supporters in the ultraright-wing nationalist sector declared, "Camps a patriot—there were no excesses—only justice—the nationalists." This graffito was accompanied by the cross logo of the fascists. After conviction of ex-junta members, the Alfonsín government hinted about placing a cutoff date to terminate the indictments and trials of the lower-level personnel "who were only carrying out orders." This became known as the *punto final* (final point). Spearheaded by las Madres and leftist groups—the Partido Intransigente especially active in producing prohuman rights street art—the walls in 1986 were covered with posters, wallpaintings, and graffiti lobbyed for "No to the punto final." Graffito summed it up: "The process of justice is a circus."

A third major controversy was debate on Argentina's tremendous international debt. It had increased from around $6 billion at the time of the coup in 1976 to $45 billion in 1983, a tremendous burden that hobbled democratic development. The left as well as many unions called upon the government to refrain from negotiating with the International Monetary Fund (IMF) because (1) any agreement would require an orthodox economic plan that would mean recession and greater privations for the working class, and (2) the debt should not be repaid because it was not invested into productive projects but corrupted away by authorities and the financial oligarchy. Street art targeted the IMF and financial elite as scapegoats. The two most common slogans were *Minga al FMI* (Screw the IMF) and "Let the national financiers pay." Other commentary consisted of "No to the economic plan of the IMF," "Popular consultation on the international debt," "Not one cent to the IMF," "Let the rich pay for the crisis—moratorium now," and "Neither Radical hunger, nor the IMF." One CGT poster graphically showed a starving child to illustrate the message, "Do not pay the international debt this way—only with social justice will democracy be consolidated." A quasi-mural in downtown Buenos Aires warned, "They will not pay the IMF with popular misery." The discourse began in 1983 and remained at an intense level up to 1987.

A fourth category concerned various union activities and elections aimed at restoring union democracy. Elections normalizing the unions did not occur all at once. They were spread over many months. For these elections, wallpaintings were the preferred medium as various factions fought for official control. The wallpaintings were colorful. Each faction adopted a color combination representing its voting list. For example, one faction's propaganda would be painted in green and white, "Vote for the green and white list," while another would solicit, "Vote for the brown and white list." The main thrust of other union activities reflected in the street art were announcements of events, rallies, May 1 celebrations, and strikes and general strikes. The CGT initiated thirteen general strikes against the Alfonsín regime, using them as a political tool against a government they did not support. Only once, July 1975, during the Isabel Perón government had a general strike been called against a Peronist government.[50] Posters, wallpaintings, and graffiti were utilized to mobilize workers and to announce to the public the general strikes and protest rallies. The CGT, for example, printed 30,000 posters to announce its May 1985 strike and demonstrations.[51]

A fifth issue, although short in duration and less controversial, was the two-month debate on the November 1984 referendum over ratification of the Beagle Channel treaty. This issue involved a historical dispute with Chile over sovereignty of three islands in Cape Horn. The Argentina junta had threatened war with Chile in 1978 over jurisdiction of the islands. The Vatican negotiated a treaty that was favorably ratified by the electorate in a referendum by a 4–1 margin. The referendum elicited emotional commentary by right-wing nationalists who viewed the treaty as a sellout of national interests. Their shibboleth, "No to treason" was profusely written in graffiti on the walls. The proponents used the peace dove as their symbol, "Vote for peace and solidarity." Other street graphics gave support, "Yes to the Vatican proposal—no to war with Chile."

The sixth set of issues was the government's economic policies, especially its premier package, the "Plan Austral." This initiative was announced in June 1985 as a "war economy" measure, the latest in a long series of economic plans over the decades aimed at curtailing Argentina's chronic hyperinflation. Wages and prices were frozen and a new currency, the austral, issued. Before the Plan Austral, there was much street art commentary pertaining to the economy in general, and to policies and prescribed solutions in particular. Along with human rights issues, economic questions constantly dominated the debate during the first three years of the restoration. The government's initiative forced a refocusing of the economic issue upon the narrower merits of the Plan Austral. Over this crucial policy, the government, through the Radical party, actively entered the public debate via street art, utilizing it to boast the merits of the initiative. The main slogans used by the governing UCR were "Development or dependency—together with Alfonsín we will enter history," and "Defend the future with Alfonsín." A UCR poster titled, "Now it's inflation's turn—UCR," went into an elaborate explanation on Radical accomplishments, "Resolving the great conflicts of the country was our motto, which we are now carrying out. First there was freedom, then human rights, then Beagle Channel resolution. Our social solidarity was expressed in . . . attention to forgotten groups. Now it's inflation's turn." Follow-up street art informed that "In a war economy it is necessary to wait—UCR," a referral to the economy package as a war against inflation. A UCR poster one year later proclaimed "If we had not initiated the Plan Austral a year ago, the country would have been paralyzed." The plan had many opponents, including unions and leftists. A Peronist poster sponsored by the left spelled it out in detail, "We're against the sellout—for the Fatherland, justice, freedom, and sovereignty—we oppose: the IMF and the payment of the international debt, the Plan Austral with its miserable salaries and economy recession, and the privatization of state enterprises which belong to the people." Other wallpaintings stated, "Workers without work—students without studies—no to the Plan of sellout and unemployment," and "Against Alfonsín's hunger and layoffs." Unions utilized street art to announce rallies, protests, and strikes designed to manifest opposition to these government economic plans.

The seventh theme was one of big political controversies of 1986–1987, the issue of divorce. The divorce controversy brought forth an array of street rhetoric by proponents and opponents alike. Divorce was not legal in Argentina. When a divorce bill was introduced, the Church which normally did not engage in using street art to lobby for its agenda, took to the streets in Argentine fashion and mounted an extensive campaign to halt it. The Church printed tens of thousands of posters, reported to be its greatest street propaganda effort ever, while partisans took to the streets to write graffiti slogans against divorce. Some street art announced a Church sponsored demonstration for July 5, 1986. Other posters portrayed a family happily strolling with a list of rhetorical questions stating the Church's basic position. "Why? We are saturated with pornography (the Church had called democracy under Alfonsín pornography democracy), we want the indissoluble unity of the family, we will defend life from conception." To oppose the Church's stance, prodivorce forces took to the streets. The result was an inundation of pro- and antidivorce messages and slogans. The most prolific graffiti were rhetorically simple, "Yes for divorce" or "No divorce," which allowed interesting alterations as each side easily crossed out the other's yes or no and inserted the opposite to reflect the opposite position. An elaborate prodivorce poster explained, "In order to defend the family what is necessary is more housing, better salaries, more jobs, more schools, more hospitals. You do not protect divorce by opposing a law but by improving the living conditions of the people." Other street graphic statements were "Divorce is better," "Divorce is not better, family yes, divorce no," "For God and country, no divorce," "Divorce for everyone except the Catholics," "Yes for the family, no to hypocrisy, yes for divorce," "For dignity, for liberty, and for love, yes for divorce," and a most amusing statement, "Why is it that *Primatesta* (the bishop) never married."[52]

Elections

A final topic is elections; these include the November 1985 congressional; the Buenos Aires gubernatorial elections of 1987; and the national presidential in 1989. For the November 1985 congressional, the electoral street art was of classic Argentine vintage. It proclaimed an emotional fight between the two major national parties, the Radicals and the Peronists and their union supporters, as well as by sundry smaller parties. The political campaigning for the gubernatorial elections in October 1987 extended over eighteen months. Much of the election propaganda was simple, "Vote for Cafiero (a Peronist) for governor," for example. The intensity for control of the Buenos Aires province was linked to national politics. Which ever party won the province would have the jump on presidential elections in 1989. The province was to Argentine politics what New York, California, and Texas combined are to presidential politics in the United States. To begin the gubernatorial campaign, much of the street art was for positioning and establishing name identification. Each Peronist faction used rhetorically simple maxims, "True to Perón," "Always with

Evita,'' or "Loyalty to Isabel,'' to connect itself in some way to one of the three Perón figures.

Not wanting the Peronists to steal the initiative, the UCR entered the pre-election fray with vigor by proposing its own candidates with qualifying identities. The party's messages stressed "continuation,'' trying to gain political mileage from the national and international issues that the party had worked to resolve since 1983. The Radicals considered it vital to the presidential campaign to retain Buenos Aires province. The party competed vigorously by inundating the province with wallpaintings, graffiti, and posters. The UCR missed, the elections of 1987 castigated the governing party, gave victory to the faction prone Peronists, and in so doing established a leader many thought would be the party's 1989 presidential candidate, Antonio Cafiero.

The 1989 presidentials had some surprising twists. Cafiero was a surprise loser to the La Rioja governor Menem in the Peronist presidential primary elections of November 1988. Menem, a firm believer in street art, immediately began his drive for the presidency the day after gubernatorial elections. To establish a visual presence in Buenos Aires province and get a psychological jump on Cafiero who was celebrating his victory, "Menem Now" posters and graffiti flooded metropolitan Buenos Aires the day after the gubernatorials. This onslaught by Menem did not cease until he was elected president of Argentina. Wallpaintings for Menem stated, "The people are now with Menem." A poster by the powerful SMATA union declared, "A productive revolution for social justice—Menem." Posters appealed to the cause of social justice, "Children do not vote, but they will become again the only privileged ones," "Children do not vote, but they need a better country." Menem's main poster themes were, "Follow me," "I am not going to defraud you—follow me," and "To change history." Each poster carried a simple photo profile of Menem.

UCR candidate Eduardo Angeloz countered with his own slogan, "A president for everybody." Radicals thought they had found an issue in the increasing street violence of the Peronists, an emotional reminder of the 1973–1976 Peronist era.[53] When street violence broke out during the CGT's twelfth general strike in September 1988, militant Radicals immediately provided the commentary and interpretation, painting the walls with "Radicalism or barbarism," synthesizing a theme they had employed a year earlier, "Us or chaos."[54] They attacked Menem's stature. Alfonsín had won international stature and the UCR played with that image. Radical posters depicted a miniature Menem dwarfed by the images of Bush and Gorbachev, with the caption, "Can you image him here?" The attacks on Menem did not cease following his inauguration. Sectors within his own Peronist movement blitzed him. Turning his back on Peronist populist traditions, Menem initiated an IMF-styled economic austerity package that caused many Peronists to cry foul. Graffiti accused him of betraying Peronist principals, "Cry Perón for little Carlos (Menem)." A more devastating blow was landed by his estranged wife. Menem, known as a womanizer, had reconciled his marriage with Zulema for the elections under the careful prodding of the Church. However, separation reoccurred several months after the inauguration. Zulema vented her rage by publicly siding with Peronists who accused Menem of betraying Peronist principals. She also jumped into the campaign charging the government with corruption. This heated up in May 1990 when a scandal linked Zulema to a poster campaign suggesting that Menem was surrounded by corrupt individuals, particularly his brother Eduardo.[55]

IDEOLOGICAL: LESS TIME-BOUND THEMES

The following section embraces less time-bound themes prevalent throughout the democratic period. First, the general conflict between the various ideological groups on the left and right as they struggled for turf and recognition, debating national issues and philosophizing about the merits of authoritarian and democratic systems. Both fascists and Marxists denounced the bankruptcy of the capitalist system. The left promoted their general theme of "power to the people." The right-wing fringe placed anti-Semitic graffiti and swastikas throughout Buenos Aires. Both had street art that was aggressive and antagonistic. They included symbols of heroes and martyrs, and their street art was enemy-driven. They divided the world between us versus them, good versus evil. Their overall tone was symbolic of a hostile society driven by emotional intergroup conflict. The presence of these groups was particularly felt in 1986 because they burst upon the scene with force and became prolific producers of street art, creating a feeling of social mobilization and causing dismay within certain circles. This visual mobilization produced the feeling that unstable polarization was reoccurring, adding to the fear that Argentina might not have the political maturity to break the vicious cycle. This feeling eased by 1992 through a firmer developing democratic consensus, a lessening of social tensions and polarization, a decline of antisystem radicals, and a control of hyperinflation.

The Right

The renewed and aggressive activity by the ultraright caused consternation, especially within the intellectual community, the human rights organizations, and the large Jewish community. For some, the ultraright symbolized blatant anti-Semitism and genocide. For others, they symbolized the worst of state terrorism and repression from the previous military regime. The aggressive street art campaign launched by the ultraright represented a mobilization of political forces, creating a feeling of an enemy within.

The ultraright, represented by fascists had definite views of who were the hostile enemies. For decades fascism enjoyed a strong following within certain important sectors of society. In 1986, there were six profascist groups and seven periodical publications with a readership around 6,000.[56] Taking advantage of the democratic climate, fascists sought to reach a broader audience than their periodicals did. In July 1985, the National Socialist party was officially launched. Fascist graffiti had been evident before the party's inauguration, but with its birth, the party launched a propaganda blitz to gain recognition and educate the citizenry that fascist ideology was yet relevant. Street art played a big role in this blitz. It entailed an incredible output of posters and distribution of fliers and made a big psychopolitical impact. The first fliers and posters listed the difference between fascism and Marxism. The propaganda stressed that fascism was pro-Christ while Marxism was atheistic. Marxism was touted as one of the symbolic enemies. The phenomenal volume of Nazi propaganda was demonstrated in August 1986 when the National Socialists pasted six different posters on the walls in key public spaces throughout Buenos Aires. The posters talked about the bankruptcy of the present democratic system. They especially made an appeal to the working class to join them in replacing the present worn-out system. Most posters were pasted in the downtown commercial and banking-financial district where major pedestrian traffic consisted of white-collar workers. In the industrial belt districts of Buenos Aires where the blue-collar workers congregated, the fascist posters were evident but at a reduced frequency. The importance of placing posters in the main commercial zone stemmed from consumer traffic and traditional fascist appeal directed toward recognition among the educated as well as the blue-collar workers.

The posters were directed at two main villains, the governing Radical party, and Marxism. Both were symbols of exhausted political systems. Propaganda stated, "Christ will come—religion or death; the Radical government permits the profanity of our Sacred Cross, we will not." The poster's message was accompanied with a skull and crossbones. Another more elaborate poster was titled, "Death to Marxism so socialism will live," embellished by a picture of a fascist crushing the tentacles of the Marxist octopus. A third poster made a direct appeal to the workers, "If the people govern, why are they dying of hunger?" The poster then showed a series of pictures comparing the standards of living of the workers and government officials: "The government officials drove a limousine, the workers rode in an old bus; the government officials feasted on a big chicken, the worker had an empty plate; the government officials lived in a big house, the workers, in shacks." Then there was a written commentary on each of these subjects. Additional posters paid homage to Hitler, "Adolf Hitler, the greatest man in history—Heil Hitler—Hitler is peace—Homage to Argentine National Socialism."

Common profascist graffiti consisted of swastikas painted on walls and buildings, mostly by profascist groups. Mostly is a qualifier because other groups also used swastikas. One was counterculture youth groups that sought identity by adopting swastikas as a status symbol to express their alienation. Additionally, leftist groups at times placed swastikas on buildings owned by groups and institutions considered reactionary. They placed swastikas on facades of Catholic cathedrals and churches. This gesture was meant to link and equate the conservative Argentine church with fascism, stemming from the Church's strong ties to ultraright elements within the military and its silence during the dirty war. The blatantly anti-Semitic graffiti made the Jewish community the villain. Graffiti proclaimed that "Hitler did not finish the job of genocide," but contradictory messages said, "The Holocaust never happened." There were graffiti that just said, "Yes to fascism," or "No to fascism" depending upon one's proclivity. Most anti-Semitic graffiti was anonymous, no group claimed responsibility.

The outburst of fascist street propaganda produced an alarm. At first, the appearance on the streets of an activist fascist movement was brushed aside as insignificant by the traditional media. They saw it as the work of a few individuals that occurred periodically. However, within a few months, the media began to take the movement seriously. This resulted in a series of articles and commentary in the major newspapers and magazines over how politically threatening this movement was.[57] Strong fascist and anti-Semitic sentiments have been in Argentina for decades. It was an interesting phenomenon to observe how quickly and effectively street art created an environment of psychological concern. As propaganda appeared, the questions arose: Will people be recruited by street art? Will it bring out hostile, supressed emotions? Are the fascists a growing movement? and How does society deal effectively with this undemocratic phenomenon? By the reaction to fascist propaganda, street art proved to be an effective symbolic tool of fascist psychological warfare given the appropriate political climate. Over the next two years fascism became a topic of public debate. When the prolific display of fascist street art subsided, so did public discussion and media attention.

In addition to concerns expressed in the press about fascist activity, Jewish groups reacted with their own stepped up street art and mobilization. In November 1987, supported by large numbers of social and political groups, the Jewish community organized its first big march against anti-Semitism in this period.[58] Zionist youth organized a counter street art campaign. Pro-Jewish graffiti have been evident for years, but in response to the fascist campaign it became more systematic, better placed, of greater quantity and wider distribution. In the Jewish district of Once, simple pro-Jewish graffiti said, "No to fascism," or "Jews are Argentines also," signed "Zionist Youth." This later slogan answered the longtime ultraright charge that Jews were not true nationalists nor did they fit the ethnic profile. The charge was based upon two factors: First, Jews were not true nationalists because they were pro-Zionist with primary international loyalties to Israel. Second, Jews did not fit into the parameters of the nation-state as defined by the Argentine fascist ideology. Only individuals with a Latin ethnic heritage could be considered legitimate citizens.[59] Anti-Semitic fascist messages were threatening because Argentina has one of the largest Jewish communities in the world. Other Jewish graffiti announced a "March against anti-Semitism." Some called for "Closing the magazine *Cabildo*," a publication known for its anti-Semitism and widely circulated within the military community. Anti-Semitism did not come only from organized fascist groups but also from mainstream groups. In 1986, when labor bosses affiliated with the Peronist party organized an anti-Alfonsín rally, they made Jews associated with the Radicals the point of attack. The walls of Buenos Aires were filled with Peronist posters disparaging the "Sinagoga Alfonsín," while graffiti declared, "Death to the Radical Sinagoga."[60] Anti-Semitic slogans were chanted at the rally.[61]

The Left

The psychological fears and reactions expressed about the ultraright also applied to the radical left. Street art, which marked the reemergence of certain radical leftist groups, created tensions and concerns. In 1986, the old Marxist guerrilla underground suppressed during the dirty war resurfaced, if graffiti were any indication of their presence. Both the Montoneros and ERP made their visual presence felt. ERP with their Red Star logo reappeared. Their graffiti were written on national monuments, public walls, and facades of buildings. The memory of their martyred leader, "Santucho," was kept alive with, "Remember Santucho," "Santucho lives," and "Homage on the 10th anniversary of Santucho's death." In keeping with the symbolic theme, the "Trelew" martyrdom was commemorated, "Homage to the fallen at Trelew."

The Montoneros were the larger and better financed of the two. Judging from the profuse graffiti and other street art in the mid-1980s, their partisans were better organized, more numerous and active than ERP. This outpouring of Montonero graffiti was related to the extradition from Brazil of their leader, Mario Firmenich, who was to stand trial for murder. Placed in prison, he became the focus for reorganizing the Montoneros and Revolutionary Peronist sector. Conservative anti-Montonero groups, especially the military, claimed the Montoneros were initiating a pro-Firmenich psychological campaign with their massive graffiti and other propaganda. It was designed to create a symbolic image of Firmenich as an Argentine patriot fighting military repression. The Montoneros portrayed him as a political prisoner who should be given his freedom. As a reflection of this campaign, pro-Montonero graffiti contained an array of messages, "Freedom for political prisoners," "Freedom for Firmenich" "Freedom for the patriot, Mario Firmenich," "Firmenich imprisoned for being a patriot," "Firmenich a prisoner—Alfonsín negotiates the life of Firmenich with the military assassins," and "Danger for democracy, Firmenich is a hostage of the oligarchy and military." After he was convicted and sentenced to a lengthy prison term, graffiti continued to demand his release. This was especially evident after Menem announced a partial pardon for security forces serving time for human rights violations. The sudden proliferation of leftist graffiti, which caused concern among the military and the more conservative political forces, did not come just from ERP and Montoneros.[62] Adding to this psychological milieu were the legalized leftist political parties of various ideologies, the Communist Party, Partido Obrero (PO), Partido Intransigente (PI), and Movimiento al Socialismo (MAS), all actively engaged in street art wars since the beginning of the democratic period.

Within military circles, a paranoia quickly surfaced over the perceived re-mobilization of left-wing subversives. Their reemergence symbolized for the conservatives an enemy penetration and the continued social and moral corruption of a system they thought had been neutralized by the heroic sacrifice of the armed forces during the dirty war. The military warned if the democratic forces could not deal with this social threat, the armed forces would.[63] The ultraright placed the blame upon the tolerance of the Alfonsín government and the democratic system. Because of this charge, the government responded by stating the country was now a democracy and as long as these groups remained nonviolent they had a right to organize and propagandize within the limits of a pluralist society. This justification was not consoling or convincing to the right. They communicated their discontent, dissatisfaction, and opposition in various ways. One was their own street art aimed against the government and Marxist elements. The fears of the ultraright were confirmed and given justification when a little-known leftist organization, the Movimiento Todos por la Patria (MPT) attacked La Tablada military garrison on January 23, 1989. The prior visibility of MPT came via some simple identification graffiti, "MPT," which began to appear on public walls.[64]

The Military

From 1987–1990 the military became the target of renewed pro and con focused street art commentary. This was inspired by four aborted coups headed by a faction known as the *carapintadas*. It was led by two renegade colonels, Aldo Rico and Alí Seineldín. They became the subject of blistering antimilitary street art. During the first coup attempt on Easter 1987, Alfonsín convoked a huge rally, April 1987, "In defense of democracy." The CGT declared a general strike in support. State-encouraged street art declared "For democracy— against coups." Both Rico and Seineldín became symbolic heroes to the ultra-right. Promilitary supporters kept their names in the public eye by filling the walls with simple graffiti, "Rico," "Seineldín," singularly or with added slogans, "Rico lives," or "heroes." They were touted as populist leaders through graffiti that declared, "Against hunger, injustice, corruption—Alí Seineldín— colonel of the fatherland and of the people." A group called the Unión Nacional Organizada pasted posters in 1989 with the pictures of Rico and Seineldín that proclaimed, "the Argentine people support the National Army and Seineldín and Rico—to assure the national project in democracy—to be against social-democracy and Marxism—let's rescue the spirit of the Malvinas for the national revolution." Veteran groups added support to the dignity campaign, "Argentina has heroes—for the dignity of the Army—he gave his life for God and for the fatherland." Their poster contained the name and photo of a fallen soldier in the Malvinas War. Menem fueled the dignity campaign when he honored early-nineteenth-century dictator Juan Manuel de Rosas who had died in exile in Great Britain. Menem arranged for the body to be exhumed and returned to Argentina for a hero's burial. National Sovereignty Day was declared. Posters paid homage to Rosas, wallpaintings by Peronists added to the visual celebration. A Peronist poster summed up the campaign, "Militarists are ours—San Martín—Rosas—Perón—we will recuperate history in order to consolidate hope." A Peronist poster portrayed Menem with his long sideburns of the caudillo tradition, placing him in a long historical line of caudillo figures, the inscription stated, "San Martin—Rosas—Perón, follow this line and triumph with the Fatherland." Any continuation of the dignity campaign ended when Seineldín led a insurrection against the Menem regime in December 1990. This was the final *carapintada* episode. Seineldín was apprehended, tried, and given a long prison sentence.

The Marginalized

Ethnic concerns were reflected in the street art. It came primarily from two groups, Jews and Armenians. As the Jews were discussed earlier, the focus here is on the Armenians. Periodically over the years, the Armenian community have been practitioners of street art. They were more visually prominent than were the Brazilian Armenians. In 1986, Armenian activists launched an extensive campaign with graffiti and posters placed strategically on public walls in Buenos Aires. The graffiti were sprayed in red paint to symbolize the genocidal suffering of the Armenian people and to claim blood revenge for those responsible, the Turks. The graffiti blitz campaign had seemingly two basic goals: to educate the Argentines on the tragic history of Armenians, and to warn Turks of retribution. The violent nature of Armenian graffiti was represented in the statements: "Justice for the Armenians—Turk assassins," "A free Armenia, for a free and sovereign Armenia," "Armenians reclaim justice for the Turkish massacre of 1915," "1,500,000 Armenians massacred by the barbaric Turks," and "Turkey will pay with blood for the genocide against the Armenians." An informative poster elaborated, the "Massacre in Turkey in 1915 was the first genocide of the twentieth century—yet despite international condemnation, still denied by the assassin state—survivors and their descendants are dispersed throughout the world, their land usurped, their rights denied—support the Armenian cause." The print media picked up the theme. As with the Jews, they ran a series of articles on ethnic minorities.[65]

By 1989, there was a shift in emphasis away from historical grievances to the conflict in the Soviet Union between Armenians and Azerbaijanis. An information poster began by attacking Mikhail Gorbachev and his decision to return the jurisdiction of the enclave (Karabagh) to the Azerbaijanis. The poster's headline, "Perestroika . . . ? Stalin—Gorbachev—history repeats itself." The poster then stated "That Stalin ceded the region of Karabagh to Azerbaijan in 1923, that in 1988 huge demonstrations of more than one million in Armenia and in the diaspora demanded the reunification of Karabagh with Armenia, in retaliation the Azerbaijanis organized a pogrom against the Armenians, and in 1989 the Soviet government in an arbitrary decision reaffirmed Azerbaijani sovereignty over the region.'' The poster ended with, ''Karabagh is Armenian.''

An additional theme with strong street art presence was imperialism and solidarity. Specifically, there was support for the Nicaraguan struggle against the United States, for the popular struggle in Central America, and for the Chilean efforts to overthrow the Pinochet dictatorship. Pro-Chilean solidarity groups were especially prominent because of the cadre of exile Chileans living in Argentina, a situation reflected in the street art until around 1987, when many exiles were allowed to return to Chile. They painted elaborate, stylistic murals reminiscent of the murals that characterized Chile during the Allende years. The murals and wallpaintings emphasized nationalism by using the national colors. Chilean slogans were rhetorically simple, ''Pinochet out,'' ''Out dictatorship,'' and ''Solidarity with Chile.'' Central American solidarity was less intense. The conflict more remote and less emotional than the Chileans'. Consequently, the street art did not seem as prolific. In the first years of Argentina's opening, the Central American question was reflected quite prolifically, ''Yankees out of Nicaragua'' was the most common of these graffiti. There were graffiti against president José Duarte of El Salvador, ''Duarte the assassin get out'' and ''Duarte was made by Reagan.'' There were anti-American graffiti related to David Rockefeller, the ultimate symbol of neocolonialism, who made a state visit to Argentina in 1986. Those who demonstrated against him, toasted him in their graffiti, ''Rockefeller get out, the south also exists.'' But overall, the solidarity Central American street art was greater than in Brazil, but not as great as in Spain and Euskadi.

Student politics generated fierce emotionalism and an incredible outpouring of graffiti and wallpaintings. Their struggles were more confined to locations appropriate to student activities like secondary schools and university facilities. However, student politics involved all the great national, international, and ideological issues, as well as factional identifications and student elections. Placement was located around educational facilities. Every inch of outdoor wall space was constantly covered. The institution's walls became rich historical depositories. The citizenry was not immune from student-sponsored graphics because the University of Buenos Aires facilities were spread throughout the metropolitan area just as secondary schools were. In no other case in this study was the level of student politicized street art as intense as at Argentine universities. As quickly as authorities repainted and cleaned the walls and plazas surrounding the educational facilities, they were vested with another round of street graphics.

NOTES

1. David Rock, *Argentina, 1516–1982* (Berkeley: University of California Press, 1985), p. 162.

2. Carlos Waisman, *Reversal of Development in Argentina* (Princeton, NJ: Princeton University Press, 1987), ch. I.

3. See Gino Germani, *Política y Sociedad en una Epoca de Transición* (Buenos Aires: Paidós, 1967).

4. Rock, *Argentina 1516–1982*, pp. 162–63.

5. Waisman, *Reversal of Development*, chs. 1–4.

6. See Robert A. Potash, *The Army and Politics in Argentina, 1928–1945* (Stanford, CA: Stanford University Press, 1969).

7. See Richard J. Walter, *The Socialist Party of Argentina 1890–1930* (Austin: University of Texas Press, 1977).

8. *Todo es Historia*, no. 183 (August 1982).

9. Walter, *The Socialist Party*, pp. 28–31.

10. Ibid., pp. 162–63.

11. See David Rock, *Politics in Argentina 1890–1930: The Rise and Fall of Radicalism* (Cambridge: Cambridge University Press, 1975), p. 101.

12. *Todo es Historia*, no. 170 (July 1981).

13. Sandra McGee Deutsch, *Counter Revolution in Argentina, 1900–1932: The Argentine Patriotic League* (Lincoln: University of Nebraska Press, 1986), pp. 112–13, 161, 203–4.

14. Quoted in Rock, *Politics in Argentina*, from Enrique Dickman, *Recuerdos de un Militante Socialista* (Buenos Aires: La Vanguardia, 1949), pp. 79–80.

15. See Potash, *The Army*.

16. Joseph A. Page, *Perón, a Biography* (New York: Random House, 1983), p. 125.

17. Daniel James, "October 17th, 1945: Approaches to the Study of Mass Protest in Argentina." Unpublished manuscript.

18. Page, *Perón*, pp. 101–2, 118.

19. Rock, *Argentina*, p. 261.

20. Page, *Perón*, p. 147.

21. *Todo es Historia*, no. 201 (January 1984).

22. See Rock, *Argentina*.

23. Samuel L. Bailey, *Labor, Nationalism and Politics in Argentina* (New Brunswick, NJ: Rutgers University Press, 1967), p. 119.

24. *Todo es Historia*, no. 183 (August 1982).

25. Page, *Perón*, p. 172.

26. Ibid., pp. 240–43.

27. Ibid., pp. 210–14.

28. Ibid., pp. 297–305.

29. See James, *Resistance and Integration*.

30. See Marcelo Cavarozzi, "Peronism and Radicalism: Argentina's Transitions in Perspective," in *Elections and Democratization in Latin America, 1980–85*, Paul W. Drake and Eduardo Silva, eds. (Center for Iberian and Latin American Studies, San Diego: University of California, 1986).

31. Rock, *Argentina*, p. 336.

32. Page, *Perón,* pp. 380–89.

33. See Daniel James, "The Peronist Left, 1955–1975," *Journal of Latin American Studies,* 8:2 (November 1976), pp. 275–96.

34. *Todo es Historia,* no. 75 (July 1973), p. 128.

35. The discussion of street art during the Onganía military period was taken from personal first-hand observation during stays in Argentina under this military government. These included a year residence 1967–68, and field research in 1971, 72 and 73.

36. See Guillermo O'Donnell, *El Estado Burocrática Autoritario* (Buenos Aires: Editorial Belgrano, 1982), and Rock, *Argentina,* pp. 348–49.

37. *Todo es Historia,* no. 75 (July 1973), p. 129.

38. Page, *Perón,* p. 351.

39. See Rock, *Argentina,* ch. 8.

40. Page, *Perón,* p. 422.

41. See Donald Clark Hodges, *Argentina: 1943–1987* (Albuquerque: University of New Mexico Press, 1988).

42. See Cavarozzi, "Peronism and Radicalism."

43. Marysa Navarro, "The Personal is Political: Las Madres de Plaza de Mayo," in *Power and Popular Protest: Latin American Social Movements,* Susan Eckstein, ed. (Berkeley: University of California Press, 1989), p. 253.

44. From personal observation in Argentina, 1975–76.

45. J. Laurence Day, "Patriotism and Pop Culture in the Falkland/Malvinas Conflict: A View from Buenos Aires," *Studies in Latin American Popular Culture* 2 (1983).

46. See *Nunca Mas* (Buenos Aires: EUDEBA: 1985).

47. Héctor Cámpora, respresenting the left-wing of the movement, was designated by Perón to be the presidential candidate in 1973, which he won. After several months in office he resigned, forcing new presidential elections which allowed Perón to run for the presidency.

48. See *Clarín,* August 23, 1985.

49. *Madres de Plaza de Mayo,* no. 60 (December 1989).

50. Hodges, *Argentina,* p. 186.

51. See *Clarín,* May 18–24, 1985.

52. Primatesta, a conservative bishop, was president of the Argentine Bishop's Council and outspoken critic of divorce.

53. See Cavarozzi, "Peronism and Radicalism."

54. *El País,* September 18, 1988.

55. *Los Angeles Times,* June 2, 1990, and *Latinamerica Press,* May 24, 1990.

56. *El País,* November 24, 1987.

57. See, for example, *El Periodista,* no. 101 (August 15, 1986); and *La Republica,* no. 34 (August 1986).

58. *El País,* November 24, 1987.

59. *Todo es Historia,* no. 179 (April 1982).

60. *El Periodista,* "Los Judíos," no. 101 (August 15, 1986).

61. Amos Elon, "Letter from Argentina," *The New Yorker,* July 21, 1986.

62. See, for example *Clarín,* December 3, 1989.

63. See *Clarín,* July–August 1986.

64. See *Clarín,* January 23–30, 1989.

65. See *El Periodista,* nos. 32 (April 19, 1985), 44 (July 12, 1985), 100 (August 8 1986), and 101 (August 15, 1986).

6

Brazil: Evolving Articulation

In evaluating the quantity and quality of street art in Brazil, this country rests at one end of the spectrum, Argentina and Euskadi at the other end, with Spain in the middle. Argentina and Euskadi have highly utilized systems and long traditions of street art as a medium for political expression. Argentine society is highly articulated and organized with polarized social conflict, and Euskadi society has some of the same characteristics. Historically, Brazil is much less politicized and articulated than Argentina, Spain, and Euskadi, with many interests remaining unexpressed.[1] The left and the working class, which accounts for much street art production worldwide, never attained the level of grass-roots development in Brazil that it did in Argentina, Spain, and Euskadi. The populism of the Getúlio Vargas period, 1930–1945, was more rhetorical than organizational. The democratic period that followed, 1945–1964, witnessed a rudimentary development of organized groups and increased social conflict, but was repressed by the military dictatorship of 1964–1985. In the late 1970s, a revival began of autonomous grass-roots associations and political parties. This was exemplified in the development of the Partido dos Trabalhadores (PT), trade unions, and various social movements. This led to greater representation of interests. However, collectives have remained weak, struggling to survive in the formal democratic opening that occurred in 1985. Comparatively speaking, Brazil had the least amount, and the least creative and sophisticated street art of the cases presented.

One problem in studying Brazilian street art is the country's immense size and dispersion of population. This made it difficult to collect primary data by observation from all the major urban centers, or observe its rural or small town manifestations. Brazil has, more so than any other case with the possible exception of Spain, various population centers. Spain's population dispersion though is easily accessible by road in a matter of hours from the country's central hub, Madrid. Brazil, with its multiple population centers, is larger than the continental United States. To compensate for Brazil's particular characteristics and its north-south cultural and socioeconomic differences, primary data collection was mostly confined to three urban sites—São Paulo, Rio de Janeiro, and the important northeast city of Recife.

HISTORICAL SETTING

In Brazil, political street art producers have included both antisystem and prosystem forces. The Vargas era of the 1930s had its corresponding street art. For the 1930 elections, posters were aesthetically more sophisticated than the mundane ones crafted today. Multicolored images were produced to engage emotions and attract the eye. Some posters contained extensive statements, others personalized the candidate through images, while others voiced issues of concern. The Liberal Alliance, which in the early 1930s supported Getúlio Vargas utilized posters, while graffiti and posters were popular tools employed by the opposition in the widespread 1932 mobilization against Vargas in São Paulo. A motto of the anti-Vargas movement read, "In defense of the Constitution." Students provided leadership in mobilizing the opposition; crowds up to 100,000 turned out. In this protest movement, citizens were called upon to actively participate, and posters called for sacrifices. One poster emotionally appealed to women to contribute financial resources for the "war" against Vargas; it showed a woman's hand with her wedding ring being carefully removed, her financial contribution to the resistance. The poster read, "For the good of São Paulo."[2]

The constitutional crisis and elections of 1945, which inaugurated a democratic opening following Vargas' authoritarian rule, stimulated a large amount of street art. As the political system opened, street art offered the citizenry alternative ideas. Pro and anti-Vargas forces competed. The Brazilian Communist Party (PCB), the labor movement, and the *Queremistas* (We want Vargas) entered the propaganda battle as pro-Vargas forces, in an effort to retain Vargas in power. They utilized street art to demonstrate their popular will. In 1945, the PCB emerged as a significant force, the fourth largest party. During its short three-year legal existence, the PCB became a prolific producer of street art until being declared illegal in 1948. The party's initial slogan, "Constitutionalism with Getúlio," was propagandized through street art. Street pavement painting became a common form of expression for the PCB in both the election of 1945 and 1947.[3] For example, in large lettering and with the hammer-and-sickle logo, the PCB painted propaganda on pavements and walls. In São Paulo, the party painted the hammer-and-sickle with the message, "Portinari, legitimate senator of the people—PCB for senator." This mode of street pavement painting was still utilized sporadically by the PCB in the 1980s. Some examples could be seen on pedestrian overpasses in Rio. Previously, the PCB had a significant cadre to carry out a systematic communication through street graphics.[4]

Pro-Vargas forces did not go unchallenged for the psychological control of the streets. In the 1945 transition period, anti-Vargas, prodemocratic sectors turned to demonstrations and placement of street art to lobby for two main causes—amnesty and constitutionalism. Students lead the pro-amnesty campaign. In Recife in a March 1945 demonstration broken up by the police, the president of the Student's Union of Pernambuco was killed. Following this, proamnesty week was proclaimed. Posters became a device for mobilization. One amnesty poster presented the simple message "Amnesty" over a background of a prison door opened leading out to blue skies. In addition to amnesty forces, the anti-Vargas União Democrática Nacional (UDN) party, which named old *tenente* leader General Eduardo Gómes as presidential candidate, made extensive use of street art in its election campaign. For example, in Belo Horizonte, the Gómes forces painted a huge liberty mural showing Gómes with a book in his hand. The poster read, "Constitutions," symbolizing Gómes as a democratic liberator with roots in the *tenente* reform movement of the 1920s. Posters carried simple messages, "Vote for Eduardo Gómes." They were personalized with his picture, followed by the statement, "For the people, for the republic and for the fatherland." Other pro-Gómes, UDN street slogans referred to the constitutional crisis of 1937 which Vargas manipulated to extend his rule. The poster was direct, "Remember 1937—Eduardo Gómes."[5]

Street art continued to be an electoral expression during the democratic period 1945–1964. Toward the end of this period, a prolonged political crisis terminated in the 1964 military coup. The crisis and the social conflict of the early 1960s brought a variety of new and old participants into the arena as purveyors of street art. The left became increasingly organized, although diverse in group composition and identity. Graffiti became a popular medium in the large cities. Acronyms for various groups and movements appeared on public walls. Marxist ideas and slogans were liberally scrawled on empty spaces throughout cities. In the Northeast, peasant leagues formed around the leadership of Francisco Julião. They employed graffiti to advance their visibility and cause. Circulating slogans and expressions of discontent were not confined to the left. Promilitary forces also took their campaigns to city walls. Names of military leaders supported by factions advocating a coup were liberally scrawled, giving a grass-roots aura to the movement. In Rio in 1961–1962, the name of Admiral Heck appeared prolifically written on walls with a simply "Heck," or "Admiral Heck." Other military names appeared. This set a psychological tone indicating an increasingly restless military. They were testing the political waters, jockeying among themselves, advancing one faction and leader over another, and heightening their profile to test public sentiments.[6]

The 1964 military coup had significant consequences for street art. The coup affected the form of street art utilized. During Brazil's twenty-one years of military rule, graffiti were a common mode for resistance. Graffiti, selectively placed, carried simple slogans such as, "Down with the dictatorship," "No to dictatorship," "No more torture," and the ubiquitous "Military out." It also conveyed commentary relating to repression, class struggle, economic issues, and special events. Examples might be announcements of strikes, as they began to appear in the São Paulo industrial belt in 1978. Communication about these special events would be selectively placed in the region where this activity took place.[7]

Street art discourse was not always antisystem. The armed forces fashioned a pseudo-democratic system by structuring regular elections whereby the electorate could chose between the only two designated political parties, the pro-system Aliança Renovadora Nacional (ARENA) and the opposition Movimiento Democrático Brasileiro (MDB). These elections generated a certain degree of street art that exploded with the open elections in 1982. The military itself produced street art. The regime's basic ideology rested upon developmental nationalism. Present gratification—consumerism and a higher standard of living for the masses—had to be sacrificed to long-term industrial development, which would propel Brazil into the ranks of the world's industrial powers. When Brazil won its third World Soccer Cup in 1970, the regime used the occasion to advance its ideological myths. Posters appeared with soccer star Pelé aloft scoring a goal, aside him the government slogan, "Nobody can stop this country now."[8]

TRANSITIONAL ERA: OVERVIEW

The direct elections of 1982, from city council to state governors but excepting the presidency, was a major step in the transition to democratic rule. National reform legislation of 1979 allowed new political parties to organize. Some parties worked to build grass-roots structures, others ignored it. For the left in general, grass-roots organization has always been central to their strategy.[9] Street art is a means to attract attention and build support. Not all party organizations agreed with this tactic. In a study by the research institute CEBRAP, conducted in a suburb of São Paulo, researchers found in 1982 that the Brazilian Labor Party (PTB) considered street art to be worthless. Campaign work should be directed toward talking to people.[10] The rationale reflected the nature of Brazilian politics. Voters were prone to think about politics in personalistic terms.[11] The newly formed PT, centered in São Paulo among industrial workers, built upon existing grass-roots groups as a means to expand into a national party, considered street art an important facet of its activism. They handpainted T-shirts with candidate names, placed their red star PT logo on available walls, and blanketed neighborhoods with PT identification and slogans.[12] Grass-roots politics with its activist emphasis was exemplified in mid-1989 when PT presidential candidate, Luís Inácio "Lula" da Silva suffered a decrease in support in his home state of São Paulo. An internal discussion flowed among nervous party officials. PT mayor of São Paulo, Luisa Erundina, opined the decline was due to excessive attention paid by the party to the countryside and the absence of militants on the streets. Lula promised the PT would take to the city streets.[13]

Murals

System changes generate changes in the types of street art medium. In Brazil the democratic transition stimulated the development of a nascent mural movement. Recife and its historical suburb, Orinda, became a point of significant interest when utilization of murals in the 1982 elections was perceived as an effective device for drawing electoral support. This process began when a group of artists organized *portinari brigades,* painting murals to support particular candidates. The murals were popular immediately and attracted national attention. A poll at the time reported indiscriminate use of graffiti was received negatively while murals were viewed as aesthetically pleasing and increased a candidate's appeal.[14] The practice became widespread during the 1986 elections but it then died rather quickly. No new murals were painted for the 1988 local elections nor for the 1989 presidential elections in Orinda although some murals were painted by party militants in and around Recife. These murals were simple. They did not have the color nor sophisticated themes of the Chilean and Basque murals. Themes depicted regional scenes, folklore figures and abstract designs. For example, a simple scene might have a woman's figure, a nature scene, or the face of a candidate. The name of the candidate in large letters would be written across the mural. For the gubernatorial candidacy of Miguel Arraes in Pernambuco state, murals had Arraes's portrait with the statement, "Miguel Arraes—Popular Front." The Arraes murals were but one example.

Periodically in Rio, murals for electoral purposes and issue-specific concerns appeared. Many of these murals were in the Gloria-Laranjeiras-Botafogo and Santa Teresa neighborhoods, especially along Rua Catete. Again, the murals did not have the artistic sophistication of the Chilean or Basque murals. In 1982, candidate Liszt Viera challenged neighbor groups to conceive of their ideal community and express this vision through wallpaintings. Santa Teresa area was home for several of these murals. A particularly large mural still visible in 1989 depicted an idyllic Santa Teresa with hills, stately mansions, and green belts, and the advocacy to "Vote PT." In 1986, Santa Teresa displayed five or six nationalistic murals celebrating Brazil's participation in World Soccer Cup championships in Mexico.

It was the walls along Rua Catete that became the site for many murals. A common theme was the environment. For the 1986 gubernatorial race, an antinuclear energy mural supported the candidacy of environmentalist Fernando Gabeira. It showed a "No nuclear energy" statement and a depiction of the nuclear power plant Angra, spelled with a large red S so it read, *Sangra* (bloody). The mural was scarred with counter-graffiti, "Viva Angra Viva." Other themes were anti-American—greed and speculation, linked to Uncle Sam's dollars. In 1986, two anonymous murals were placed side by side. One showed several individuals crawling on their hands and knees toward the almighty dollar colored in gold. It carried the comment, "Enough speculation." A second depicted the legs of a giant Uncle Sam with "$$$" signs adorning his pants about to crush a group of citizens trying to hold on to trees comprising the Amazon. In 1988–1989, the Organizacão da Juventud pela Liberdade (OJL), a youth group linked to Lula's Frente Brasil Popular, painted several murals along Rua Catete. One mural showed the map of the Amazon painted in green. President José Sarney was holding a bloody axe as was Uncle Sam. In the other hand was a bag of gold with the almighty $ logo. The two were making a deal. The written inscription was, "The Amazon, don't exchange, don't sell it—it is the Indians', it is the people's, it is ours." A second OJL mural implored, "Lift ourselves from this mud, Brazil." It showed two youth with a rope and pulley lifting Brazil, painted green, out of the mud and grasp of President Sarney and Uncle Sam. At each end of the mural was written, "Lula." A third mural by OJL showed a youth climbing over a wall. His multiple thoughts were given written expression: "I see a better future, I am dizzy on top of this wall because of the hypocrisy that surrounds us," then a written advocacy, "Better respect for young women—better level of education—better salaries for youth."

POLITICAL ISSUES

The Electoral System

During the first years, the primary focus of the democratic era was political. The period of transition to direct elections began in 1982 and terminated in 1989 with direct election of the president. During this time, street art revolved around political questions—party and candidate identification, electoral campaigning, the new constitution, and antiregime sentiments left over from military rule. Political parties had to be formed or rebuilt, their structures and organization reconstituted. Politics to a large extent in Brazil are structured around electoral contests, where personalism and clientelism dominate.[15] In 1979, a new multiparty system allowed for the dismantling of the military-mandated two party system.[16] Except for several minor parties, the political parties that became viable were new. They had few roots prior to the 1964 coup. Some formed around well-known politicians, others had to build visibility and recognition by advertising their identity. Starting with the 1982 elections, the abundance of street art revolved around candidate and party identification. Street art was valued as a direct inexpensive way to reach the public. This was important because of the financial limitations of these new parties and the weakness of associational organizations who support particular parties, such as labor unions. The first open elections were in 1982 and they generated a vast amount of street propaganda. Only two political parties the PMDB (MDB) and PDS (ARENA), the two legal entities from the military period who altered their names, were capable of mounting national campaigns. Between them, they won 86 percent of the aggregate vote.[17]

Complicating stable party formation was an electoral system that placed a premium on individual recognition, not on the party. The Brazilian electoral system allows voters to select among various candidates from the same party slate; a primary and general election process dovetailed into a single process. For the 1982 elections, the military-induced system required the electorate to write in a candidate's name. This process pressured candidates to promote themselves first, and the party secondarily, adding to the phenomenon of personalities overshadowing parties. In 1986, the common means of candidate enhancement was a small self-adhesive sticker. Supporters could spread them around a city quickly, placing them on lamp posts, telephone booths, buildings, walls, public transportation, street signs, and just about any place where they might be seen. They came in various sizes, colors, and shapes—round, square, and rectangle. The most common shape was round, about twice the size of an American silver dollar. Each candidate designed his or her own unique sticker. There was no conformity in style, shape, size, or even colors within the same party. Usually, the stickers were in bright contrasting colors, rather than black and white. Size and artistic design varied within the same party due to the financial resources of each candidate. For example in 1986 in Rio, the Partido Democrático Trabalhista (PDT) state deputy candidates had different stickers. Carlos Vignoli's was a crude sticker, the size of a long finger with no embellishments, Luiz Novaes had a larger well-printed sticker, while Jefferson Andrade's sticker was a larger one in well-blocked lettering with the party logo and the slogan, "The future is the PDT." For state and federal elections in 1986 most candidates, *(a)* individually advertised themselves and the party, *(b)* teamed with another candidate as a duad on the sticker, or *(c)* employed both *a* and *b*. An example of *b* was the sticker that promoted the candidate duad for state deputy and federal deputy, "For Federal Deputy Vicente Sobreira, for State Deputy Jefferson Andrade—PDT." Some federal deputy candidates identified their candidacy as representatives to the Constituent Assembly as the new Congress would rewrite the Constitution. Stickers varied considerably in image and message. Some were simple, "Antonio Pedregal 86" with no party label, campaigning as if the elections were nonpartisan. Others carried party identification and logo, "Cliveraldo Nunes, State Deputy—PT 86" with a red star logo. Further, some announced the candidate name(s) and party without designating an office, "Luiz Salomão, Luiz Henrique—PDT Socialista."

In addition, candidates elaborated and promoted themselves by utilizing a slogan, a special identity or image, or pushed an issue. Some examples were "Oscar Boechat—State Deputy 86" (no party label but logo) with a thumbs up, smiling face and the slogan, "We are going to work together"; Amaury de Souza (no party label but logo), the slogan, "Power to the people"; Fernando Gabeira, candidate for Rio governor, chose a butterfly logo for his symbol as an ecologist; Agnaldo Timoteo, PDS candidate for governor emphasized human rights and military rule, "Is it in your head? Never again"; Ribeiro (PDT) ran under the label Constituent Assembly representative with the slogan, "Plan a new Brazil"; Prestes (PDT) the logo of the white dove; Lysaneas (PDT) running as an incumbent, "For parliament again"; Lopes (Partido Democrático Cristão [PDC]) a youth image, "A new generation"; Salete (PT), "Fight and determination"; Sami Paskin promoted both youth and ethnicity (no party label) with star of David to dot the *i* and the phrase, "Our fight just began—power to youth," he joined in promoting a Jewish duad, "Paulo Goldrajch PSB [Partido Socialista Brasileiro]–Constituent and Sami Paskin state deputy"; Pinheiro (PDC) "Enough violence—the death penalty as punishment for cruel and bloodthirsty criminals"; Serpa (PMDB), "A force for education"; Alberto Brizola, "With love—for peace" with the peace dove logo; Silva (Partido Nacionalista Democrático », "Social Welfare, Education and Health"; de Mello (PMDB), "Better education for all"; Cunha, no party label and the image of truthfulness, "Our brother in truth" along with the appeal "Speak out for those who cannot speak, for the rights of everyone"; Dante (PTB), "In defense of human rights"; Jose Petronilho and Jose Maria Siviero, "New blood in 86" with no party identification; Azulay, "A youth force in the Constituent Assembly"; Dr. Jose Rocha (PDT), "A force of the Northeast vote" but running for federal deputy in São Paulo, "Quercia—PMDB 86" with no office identified; "Eudes and Rocha—socialist candidates—PDT 86"; and Eva Blay (PMDB), "A woman's voice in the Senate."

These examples illustrate how the system was structured toward individual promotion, images, and issues first, party promotion second. The secondary nature of party was evidenced by candidates unhappy with one party, bolting and promoting themselves on another party label. They were readily welcomed, especially if they were popular figures who could stand independently, thus serving party interests by garnering a larger aggregate vote that would determine the number of seats assigned to each party.[18]

Direct Presidential Election Campaign

One divisive issue of the transition, which generated a great deal of participatory street art, was the direct presidential elections. To maintain a modicum of democratic legitimacy following the 1964 coup, the military restructured the presidential system with a regular four-year, no-reelection rotation among military leaders. To maintain control, the president was elected indirectly by a Congress controlled by the military. The military agreed to terminate its rule with the election of a civilian president in 1985. However, the military was determined the president would be chosen through the existing system of indirect elections. The opposition lobbied for open direct elections.

To press its point, the opposition began a massive three-month mobilization campaign in January 1984 to pressure Congress into supporting an amendment for direct elections. The campaign became one of the largest political mobilizations in Brazilian history.[19] Several million citizens participated in public rallies held throughout the country.[20] The slogan was *Diretas já* (direct elections now). The direct election campaign enjoyed the support of a wide coalition of social forces discontented with the status quo. It was led by the anti-status quo parties, the PMDB, PT, PDT, PCB, and PSDB (Partido Social Democrático Brasileiro). They engraved the simple slogan "Diretas já," or "Diretas 84" in graffiti and wallpaintings on city walls, buildings, and roadside embankments. There were variations in the slogan, such as "Direct elections—the military out," or "Direct presidential now." While the direct elections amendment was defeated in April 1984, the campaign did have an impact. It awakened the electorate, realigned political forces, split progovernment forces in Congress, and led to the election of opposition candidate Tancredo Neves and the defeat of military candidate Paulo Maluf.[21] In May 1985, immediately following the official transition, Congress responded, amending the law to mandate direct elections. Many forces, either for principle or ambition, no longer accepted the legitimacy of a president elected by the old system. This was especially true when the more progressive Neves died prior to inauguration, and was replaced by his vice-president, Sarney, a collaborationist closely linked to the military. When Neves was elected, rumors circulated of a coup. The walls came alive with posters displaying Neves giving the victory sign. Profiled on the poster was the hammer-and-sickle and the PCB acronym, along with the words, "We'll get there." The poster's sponsor was Army Intelligence which attempted to utilize posters for disinformation practices to delegitimize Neves.[22]

With Neves's death, there were demands for Sarney to step aside and allow legitimate direct elections.[23] To delegitimize Sarney, certain political forces carried on a persistent, low-level campaign calling for immediate, direct presidential elections. This campaign found expression in the street graphic, "Diretas já." This slogan was particularly visible in Rio where Leonel Brizola, a presidential aspirant and personal leader of the PDT, was governor. The walls never ceased to have this message during Brizola's administration. Both the PT and the PDT were active in spreading the slogan, "Direct elections now— Sarney out." PT produced "Sarney Out" posters. The "Diretas já" campaign was revived with vigor in 1986–1987 when elections took place for the Constituent Assembly. This was to promulgate a new constitution and determine whether Sarney would be entitled to a four- or five-year term. Brizola followers campaigned hard for limiting Sarney to four years so direct elections could take place in 1988. "Direct elections—88" became the altered graffito slogan. Once the issue was resolved, which allowed Sarney five years, the campaign ceased and presidential aspirants geared up for the 1989 presidential elections. However, there were political communicators who wished the citizenry to reflect on the issue of indirect elections and an authoritarian system. They continued to express their sentiments in such graffiti as "Indirect elections—never again."

Sarney became a political issue and a liability. He never obtained credibility except for a short period in 1986 when his Cruzado Plan gained temporary favor. Furthermore, he garnered no popular adulation and in fact became the recipient of outright contempt. His ineptness resulted in an anti-Sarney street art campaign ridiculing him. The image of ineptness related to economic issues, especially hyperinflation which had traumatized Brazil for years. Sarney's attempts to deal with inflation were exemplified in his *pacotaos* (packages) discussed later in this chapter. Anti-Sarney feelings, which were universal, were reflected not only in the street art of the direct election campaign and opposition to his economic plans, but also in such graffiti as, "Fed up with Sarney," "Sarney should die," "Sarney's a crook," and "Death to Sarney—crook and traitor." Sarney became an important issue in the 1989 presidential campaign. Most candidates ran against him, including both second round finalists, Fernando Collor de Mello (Partido de Reconstrução Nacional—PRN) and Luis "Lula" da Silva. Collor took the lead. An unknown governor from a small northeast state, Collor, of conservative background, established credentials and gained national attention by conducting an anti-Sarney, antipolitics campaign. He attacked overpaid bureaucrats and aggressively made Sarney an issue.[24] This gave Collor the outsider image and removed the possibility of being tagged a Sarney surrogate or clone. As Collor rose in the polls to number one, candidates saw the advantage of tying Sarney's specter around their opponents' necks. For example, Partido Liberal (PL) presidential candidate Guilherme Afif became the recipient of an anti-Afif campaign when he began to rise in the polls to challenge for second place. Particularly visible were graffiti slogans that tied him to Sarney, "Sarney and Afif—they fight for injustice," "Sarney = Afif," "Sarney and Afif will drive us into the pit hole," "Sarney = Afif—together they will dig the pit hole for Brazil." Anti-Sarney sentiments did not cease with the elections. "Sarney out" graffiti appeared after elections, reflecting the popular wish he step aside.

Presidential Elections

The city and state of São Paulo consistently had the greatest quantity and broadest discussion of issues articulated through street art. In São Paulo graffiti, posters, and wallpaintings assaulted the visual space. São Paulo is economically and politically the most important city and state. In 1989, five out of seven major presidential candidates were from São Paulo: Mário Covas, Guilherme Afif, Lula da Silva, Paulo Maluf, and Ulysses Guimaraes. São Paulo became the center of intense political debate. Elections generated the greatest quantity of street art, both in São Paulo and nationally. The long 1989 presidential primary, which narrowed the field to two candidates, Lula and Collor, spawned the largest street mobilizations since the "Diretas já" campaign. Three million citizens attended 1,000 rallies in the last months of the first round.[25] The runoff, one month later between two ideological opposites, the upper-class conservative Collor and the working-class leftist Lula, generated intense interest and great display of street art, mostly in support of Lula. The PT, with its strong grass-roots organization, mobilized 100,000 volunteer militants and distributed more than one million posters.[26] It was the party that most utilized street art for disseminating issues.[27]

During the first round, the reformers split loyalties between several candidates, Lula, Covas, and Brizola. Once the choice was made, an avalanche of forces came together to support Lula. Brizola, who had dominated electorally the states of Rio de Janeiro (54 percent), and Rio Grande do Sul (61 percent), did not utilize street art to any great extent. In Rio, for example, there were only two distinct posters sparsely distributed. Brizola did not have to compete in Rio. Therefore, his PDT did not conduct a street art campaign.[28] There were more wallpaintings and murals supporting Brizola in Recife than in Rio. Some were sophisticated with an abstract touch. The Lula forces, rather weak in Rio (12 percent in first round), did not present a great challenge to Brizola in the street graphics. Everything changed in the runoff. Pro-Lula street art appeared overnight. The PT acronym and logo became widespread in graffiti, murals, and wallpaintings. Pro-Lula lapel buttons sold out in two days. This reflected the intensity of PT street graphics found in São Paulo. The issues Lula articulated, which found their way onto the walls of Recife and São Paulo during the first round, were duplicated in Rio and elsewhere for the runoff.

Lula not only articulated the most specific issues but also developed the most original slogans. The PT was closer to being a programmatic party than any other party in Brazil.[29] The two most widely used slogans were, "Lula-la," (inferring Lula there in the presidential office), and "Brazil is going to change its face," with a photo of Lula accompanying the slogan. There were extensive graffiti of the "Lula president," "Lula-la–PT" variety, some "good feeling" sayings, "Without fear of being happy—Lula lá," class-oriented slogans, "Candidate of the proletariat—Lula president," "Worker, you now have your party—PT," and multiple T-shirt themes and slogans. The most common T-shirt had an outline of Brazil with the red star and Lula bursting outward, or simply the red star logo with PT written inside the star and "Lula president." There were other street art motifs; "Lula president—you will see that your son will not flee from the fight," simple unsophisticated posters portraying Lula, and elaborate wallpaintings which were often utilized to articulate specific issues. These included: "PT—agrarian reform," "Lula—for free and public education," "Lula,—for a new university—employment for youth," "Lula—land and salary," "Lula—education and health," "Brazil—sovereignty," "Moratorium or 'suspend' the international debt."[30] General election themes included, "Lula president—permanent participation," "Urgent vote—Lula president," and "Brazil—democratic and popular—Lula."

The left in general and PT in particular emphasized corruption and violence. Corruption at the highest level and violent crime at the lowest characterized the system. Until Collor was impeached for corruption in September 1992, there was an ease with which white-collar crime and violence escaped the country's porous justice system. The issues the PT articulated during the 1989 presidential campaign had national significance. Only the PT with its national grassroots organization, and Collor, the candidate without a party, had national support.[31] The other candidates depended upon strong regional support to propel them into the runoff. The selection of two new faces, Collor and Lula, both in their forties, characterized the vacuum in national leadership and a general discontent with the status quo.

By 1988, the PT was the strongest party in organization and militancy. Its support reached from the middle classes in large cities to union laborers and *favela* (slum) dwellers, and into the most remote agricultural regions of the interior. Its limbs extended into all aspects and organization of society.[32] It was the first serious attempt to organize a genuine workers' party, although it was more than simply a workers' party.[33] The PT built on the leftist tradition of strong party organization and grass-roots development, Brizola did not.[34] Brizola recognized the PT's broad support, accusing it of being the creation of progressive Catholics and CUT (Central Unica dos Trabalhadores) unions.[35] Founded in 1979 to demand substantive social justice, the PT evolved from the grass-roots. It organized around a diversity of existing social movements and groups like CUT, the Church's 80,000-strong Ecclesial Base Communities (CEBs), rural workers' unions, ecologists, feminists, and shantytown associations.[36] Chico Mendes, assassinated rural leader of the rubber tappers' union, epitomized these crosscurrents of ecologist, union leader, landless workers' organizer, member of CUT, and PT militant.[37] To accommodate support, the internal organization of PT was composed of various blocs, Articulación, Nueva Izquierda, Vertiente Socialista, Corrientes Trotskistas, and PT a la Roja.[38] For the most part in street art, the PT was projected with a collective identity, and not as singular blocs supporting the PT. Singular identification came from other political parties that supported the PT in the national elections. In cases of bloc expression, the most visible was Vertiente Socialista, especially when it came to specific labor and economic issues not tied to elections. Articulación, the majority bloc within the PT, did not articulate its separate identity in street art.

Victorious candidate Collor, with no real party organization, relied on professionally designed profile posters and colored stickers to play on his name, each with COLLOR written across them. Collor was able to organize ten thousand electoral committees, distribute more than two million adhesive stickers, and organize sixteen convoys to carry his election propaganda of posters and self-adhesive stickers into the interior.[39] In Recife his committee pasted a massive number of posters in billboard style, utilizing three different posters. Collor was disdained by the left, and an anti-Collor street art campaign developed. Using a play on words, the propaganda stated, "Not color, but corrupt." This slogan came to life when Collor was impeached for corruption in 1992. The PT was most responsible for making the anti-Collor campaign visible. It produced the popular, "Collor—corruption" slogan, written in graffiti style on stickers. In the same vain, T-shirts proclaimed, "A new product of the dictatorship—Coca-Collor—for the people to continue taking it."

In addition to Collor, negative campaigning was directed at the conservative, military-tainted candidates, Afif and Maluf. Maluf, a presidential candidate again, garnered the simple "Maluf bad" graffiti. Maluf's campaign employed professionally produced posters with a Maluf profile. Anti-Afif graffiti from Recife found its way south as "Afif is Sarney," and, "Afif is against the vote for 16-year-olds." This referred to the 1988 Constitution giving 16-year-olds the right to vote. Guimaraes, candidate from PMDB, the largest political party, was ignored by his competitors. The antigovernment mood undermined his campaign, and party officials abandoned him. His campaign generated little street art activism. He was the invisible candidate, even though he received the largest amount of free TV time which was allocated based upon a party's previous electoral strength.

While the PT articulated issues via street art, Brizola relied more on generic slogans, "Brizola—savior of the country," "He is the people," or "Brizola—people." This motif was utilized by Lula and the left in general as well. For example, "Lula is the people." The concept of "the people" has an important image. It symbolizes the populist, mass democratic appeal.[40] In Rio, Brizola used a more general slogan, "Rio will carry Brazil—Brizola." Rio's strong support for Brizola was strategized to carry him into the run-off election and then on to the presidency. Although Brizola and Lula exchanged heated public charges, this was not reflected in street art. Brizola supported Lula in the run-off elections. Covas, a São Paulo regional candidate, produced the typical posters and stickers, and had nicely painted murals and wallpaintings in São Paulo. An especially artistically pleasing one was along the road leading into the University of São Paulo where Lula activists were particularly present with their street art.

The race for the runner-up spot was lively, especially given the hotly contested race between Lula and Brizola. This was reflected in graffiti commentary concerning polls, their importance, and the issue of corruption. With his substantial lead, it was a given that Collor would win the first round. The suspense was over the second candidate, where only a few percentage points separated the candidates. In Rio, where Brizola had his strong support, there was a constant reaction to polls that did not reflect his dream of coming in second. All candidates attacked the polls, conducted by Gallup and Ibope, the main polling institutes. In June 1989, when Collar rose in the polls and became the leading candidate, and when Lula began to challenge Brizola for the second spot, the question was raised about manipulation of the polls. An increase in a few percentage points, maybe artificially induced with a bribe to the pollsters, could help stimulate a swing in favor of the up-and-coming winner. In April 1989 when Collor rose in the polls, Brizola accused Ibope and *O Globo* media network, the country's largest, of creating the candidacy of Collor.[41] By implication, Ibope was paid to validate that Collor was a serious candidate. This same implied accusation occurred when Lula rose in the polls. Rio blossomed with graffiti, "Ibope—corrupt," or "Gallup and Ibope—corrupt."

In Recife, electoral street graphics were mainly a contest between Brizola, Lula, and Collar. Covas had practically no presence, nor did conservatives Afif, Ulysses, or Maluf. There was a large pro-Afif wallpainting in the Boa Viagam district, "Afif for president—faith in Brazil." Collor posters were the most prolific. However, in general, Lula dominated in street art. He had the greatest quantity, spread among posters, graffiti, and wallpaintings. However, there were far fewer political T-shirts in Recife than in the south. Collor's greatest support came from the interior of the state. Brizola's visual support was minimal, some posters, wallpaintings, and a mural or two. The PT had broad distribution of its street art in the favelas, and along side streets and alley ways. The PCB was active in Recife because its popular candidate Roberto Freire was from there. He won close to 7 percent of the city's vote.[42] Collor's propaganda articulated no issues. His profile posters were placed side by side billboard style with the simple statement, "Collor 20—vote for the president of Brazil," and graffiti, "Collor—n. 20." The number designated his position on the ballot. Only Lula discussed issues, although some propaganda simply stated, "Lula." Overall, the greatest quantity and most visible graffiti were the anti-Afif, anti-Sarney commentaries, and graffiti speaking to the problem of street children in Recife. This theme is discussed later in the chapter under "Social Issues." CUT was active with graffiti and posters, especially in the commercial center and near the harbor. Graffiti calling for strikes were plentiful and stressed such comments as "Down with repression—the strike continues." The newly formed Corriente Sindical Clasista (CSC) "classist" labor confederation, tied to the communists, advertised itself through graffiti and wallpaintings.[43]

Marginalized Parties

Marginal parties, particularly the established sectarian left, were major producers of street art in all cases presented in this study. In each, marginal organizations maintained a strong visual presence. In Brazil during the 1980s, the old left lagged far behind in their organizational and visual presence. They declined much more precipitously than in Spain, Euskadi, and Argentina. Of note in Brazil were the PCB, the PC do B (Communist Party of Brazil), the anarchists, the Convengencia Socialista, a Trotskyist group affiliated with the PT, and the Union of Socialist Youth (UJS). Each group produced some street graphics; however, they were minimal in comparison to leftist groups in other countries. Anarchists were marginally visible in Recife, São Paulo and Rio. Their main advocacy was, "Don't vote," and "Cast blank ballots (nulo)." Twelve people turned out for their "Cast blank ballots" rally in Rio during the 1989 presidential elections. "Vote Nulo" was not only an anarchist position.

It was used by other groups as a means to protest against the system. In addition, anarchist graffiti in São Paulo advocated "No to death penalty," and in Recife an antimilitary theme, "More arms—more hunger." The PCB, once a large producer, had a reduced militant base which eviscerated its ability to carry out sustained street art activity. With a revamped party image and new leadership, PCB ran a separate presidential candidate in 1989, Freire. It used the motif, "A new left—a new Brazil—Roberto Freire president." Its nonelection street art spoke to its historical roots, "67 years of struggle," its newly won legal status in 1985, "It's legal—join the party," and events, "Stroessner out," referring to former Paraguayan dictator Stroessner who was in exile in Brazil. Posters and graffiti listed their issues, "Moratorium on the external debt, agrarian reform, workers rights, no recession, direct elections for 1988," and support for strikes. They also periodically produced murals. The Stalinist-Maoist-oriented PC do B supported Lula in the presidential elections under the theme, "Long live socialism—the communists with Lula." They advocated, "Suspension of payments on external debt," "National sovereignty," and supported calls for general strikes with graffiti. They advertised their newly won legal status (1985), "The PC do B is for struggle and is legal." In 1986, their posters supported the PMDB in 1986, and others announced, "Regional Convention—Rio—July 13, 1986."

Both communist parties were recipients of counterattack graffiti for their conservative positions. They had resisted initial efforts to support and develop the PT and sided with the more conservative CGT confederation rather than the more militant CUT. Initially, they endorsed the PMDB instead of one of the working-class parties.[44] These positions subjected the communists to scathing scorn. During the 1986 elections in Rio, the PC do B supported the PMDB candidate for governor, the party of president Sarney. This resulted in anti-PC do B graffiti written over party election posters supporting the PMDB. Opponents aggressively accused the PC do B of being "Rightist and fascist." On some posters the hammer-and-sickle logo was redrawn into a swastika, on others large swastikas were drawn across the poster, or altered in such a way to make the PC do B look like it was confessing to being rightist, "We are with the right—we support the party of Sarney." Other posters were scrawled with graffiti that read, "We are supporting a governor of the '64 coup that was installed in power—we are of the right now."

São Paulo and Rio walls were the recipients of wallpaintings by the old radical MR-8 organization in support of PMDB candidates, "Quercia for president." It advocated issues such as, "Moratorium (debt) now." In Recife, there were some pro-Che graffiti, "Long live Che, JR8," and the anonymous "Death to imperialism—long live Che." UJS, the youth section of the Socialist party, was active in Rio and São Paulo with murals and graffiti. They took up the issue of the Constituent Assembly, "For the right of vote for 16-year-olds," spoke to their democratic credentials, "Youth for democracy," and announced their "2nd Meeting." In 1989, it was one group painting murals in

Rio. The Convergencia Socialista, which controlled the bank workers' union in Rio, sponsored posters with the CUT label, supporting protests and strikes.[45] In addition, in the mid-1980s there were occasional inter-American themes. The Uruguayan Committee for Democracy was active in 1983 and pasted posters to support its cause. Chilean solidarity commentary appeared with "Down with Pinochet." Occasionally, pro-Sandinista posters or graffiti materialized. While Uncle Sam was the point of reference on some political murals, generally there were not heavy anti-American themes expressed in the street art such as that found in other cases in this study.

SOCIAL ISSUES

Delayed Articulation

Up until the presidential elections of 1989, discussion of substantial social issues through street art was minimal. The agenda was primarily political restructuring, not debates on social issues. This was in contrast to the thematic tone present in Argentina, Euskadi, and Spain during their democratic openings.

Neglect of debate on social issues is due to the disarticulated nature of Brazilian society. Many groups remain unrepresented. Political pluralism is limited.[46] The military, through selective repression, demobilized and disarticulated a society already with a low level of articulation, neutralizing those sectors that posed the greatest threat: unions, autonomous parties, students, and leftists. An exception was the Church. Those neutralized had to rebuild their structures during the long democratic transition beginning in the mid-1970s. In Argentina and even in Spain the building process of political pluralism did not lag, a fairly articulated society was in place at the beginning of the transition. The political party structure emerged intact in Argentina, Euskadi, and somewhat in Spain. Labor unions remained potent in Argentina, and emerged with strength in Spain. Students were politicized in Argentina, Spain, and Euskadi. There was a core of strong organized groups on the left in Argentina, Spain, and Euskadi which quickly became advocates for issues based upon an agenda already defined by party and group elites. The organizational weakness of groups in Brazil accounted, in large part, for the differences in the quantity of street art as compared to Argentina, Euskadi, and Spain during the years surrounding the democratic openings.

In Brazil no strong political party emerged with the democratic opening. The entire process of reformulating parties, images, and ideology had to begin anew.[47] The post-military era party system that emerged was characterized by personalism and clientelism, weak party structure, lack of a defined ideological base, few ties to grass-roots movements, and self-serving to the state.[48] The exception was the PT. Illustrative was the widespread practice of individual politicians switching party affiliations, or founding new personalistic parties for the purpose of advancing careers or simply to be part of the party in power.[49] For example, the candidacy of Collor was personalistic. Six months before the elections he formed his own party. Brizola's party, the PDT, was also personalistic. PT's success was owed as much to the charisma, personalism, and organizing ability of Lula as to PT's program.

Accounting for the slow pace of social issues in the national discourse was the weakness of the left. In Argentina, Spain, and Euskadi, a plethora of leftist groups was in place which accounted for many pressing social issues being articulated through street art. In Brazil there was little in the way of the old sectarian left compared to the other cases in this study.[50] This had not always been the case. There was ideological articulation.[51] The late 1950s and early 1960s produced an array of organized groups on the left; however, most did not survive. The communist parties were also enfeebled. The PC do B lay impotent from leadership and cadre loss when its guerrilla foci was eliminated by the military in the mid-1970s.[52] The PCB garnered a mere 1 percent of the presidential vote in 1989. The PCB and PC do B did contribute some murals, graffiti, and posters to the political process; however, their contributions were minimal. Issues the left articulated in the other cases, such as solidarity, anti-Americanism, anticapitalism, human rights, commemoration of class struggle figures and martyrs, and repayment of the national debt (not relevant to Spain), did not receive the same attention in Brazil. For example, in August 1986 a rally for Central American solidarity, sponsored by PT and CUT in Rio, attracted fifty people.

One factor that may account for lack of a leftist articulation was the absence of politicized students. Students stirred the political cauldron in many Latin American countries and elsewhere. Highly politicized through the 1960s, the student movement in Brazil, which crested in 1968, was severely suppressed. It has yet to recover from this organizational decapitation. Brazilian university students have been characterized as apathetic and lacking politicization. Weeklies such as *Veja,* commented about their apathy during the presidential elections.[53] Their current nonpoliticized stance was exemplified in the street art. University campuses are a traditional arena for political expression and are normally inundated with layers of graffiti and posters. For the most part, the university campuses in Brazil were clean. There were few signs that university graffiti and posters had been painted over or removed. This contrasted with universities in the other cases presented where new street art quickly replaced any erased or removed. The Pontificia University in Rio had no indications of street art, neither did the Federal Fluminense University, nor the private Gama Filho University. There was minor activity at the State or Federal Universities of Rio. Only at the Federal University of São Paulo in the Humanities and Social Science schools was there evidence of any street art activism.

The Articulated Issues

The previous comments are not to imply social issues were entirely omitted from political discourse, or totally absent from street art. It was a matter of degree. The discussion of social issues slowly gained political space in the late 1970s when grass-roots associations began to evolve, providing a structure for the definition of social and economic issues by various groups. These included trade unionists, feminists, blacks, Indians, human rights activists, and ecologists groups.[54]

Ecology

By the early 1990s, the social issue with the greatest visibility in street art was ecology. Some ramifications were tied to agrarian reform. The ecology issue did not explode in Brazil until around 1988–1989. In a country with the great majority living in poverty, ecologists had a difficult time establishing political space.[55] Some individuals acquired fame for their ecological struggle and a Green party was formed. However, there were few visible signs of environmental awareness in the first several years following the democratic era. If field research for this project had terminated in 1986, it would have concluded that based upon street art, environmental concerns had not penetrated public consciousness in any substantial way. There were stirrings. In 1986 in Rio, antinuclear murals emerged around the gubernatorial candidacy of Gabeira. The murals attacked the nuclear power plant Angra, "Hiroshima never again—Angra, Aug. 6 & 7," the dates announcing days of protest. Gabeira ran on the Green party, but his main support came from the PT.[56] He utilized the star logo of the PT but colored it green to emphasize his ecological stance. Most street art supporting his candidacy contained the greening touch. The green star was embellished with the statements, "No violence—neither nuclear nor domestic." These beginnings gave way to a radical shift by 1988.

Prior to 1988, the prevailing rhetoric concerning the environment was based on an ideology of nationalistic jingoism prevalent during the military regime. Few questioned the rhetoric that environmentalists were part of an international plot to stifle Brazil's development. These views formed around the development of the Amazon and nuclear power. This view categorized environmentalists as subversive and unpatriotic, part of the international plot to keep Brazil a Third World peripheral country exploited by the industrial core. Development at any cost was the military's nationalistic ideology. The gaint Itaipú Dam which obliterated one of the world's great wonders, Sete Quedas Falls, was never questioned for its environmental impact until years after in the mid-1980s. Antienvironmental rhetoric was still powerful among developmentalists in the early 1990s. The military and cattle ranchers, led by the Rural Democratic Union (UDR), charged foreign interests and ecologists with backing the concept of Amazon reserves.[57] The developmentalist view was challenged by the countervailing opinion of ecologists who had gained political space. Serious questions were being raised about the dangers of nuclear energy. This was expressed in such wallpaintings as "Nuclear energy is bad" and "Get rid of the nuclear reactors." Antinuclear murals were painted in 1986 on the plaza walls of Rio's Botafogo and Largo do Machado subway stations. Other antinuclear murals appeared in Rio in 1989 along busy Rua Catete. In the city of Goiania, a mural was commissioned to commemorate a radioactive accident in 1987.[58] Visually, the antinuclear issue was the forerunner of the environmental movement before it reached widespread citizen consciousness in 1988–1989.

The evolution in ecology consciousness was stimulated by exiles returning from Europe. They developed an environmental consciousness and carried the ideas back to Brazil.[59] In all probability, this helped to influence the significant shift in thinking of Brazil's left. Sectors of the left moved from the rhetoric of an international plot to keep Brazil and the Amazon undeveloped, to the change in emphasis that multinational corporations were behind the scheme to develop and exploit the Amazon for their own greed. The new emphasis was stated in the slogan, "The Amazon is ours and we must protect it." The "Amazon is ours" was always part of the rhetoric, "protecting it" adds a different connotation and emphasis. A visual presence on the environmental issue, focused around saving the Amazon from wanton destruction emerged. This awareness was exemplified in the widespread national and international outcry over the December 1988 assassination of Chico Mendes—president of the National Council of Rubber Tappers, leader of the Workers Without Land movement, and ecologist—who organized to protect the Amazon from economic exploitation and ruin. He argued that certain activities such as rubber harvesting, which supported many families, was threatened by Amazon forest destruction caused primarily by clearing and burning land to create cattle ranches. The Mendes *seringueiros* (rubber-tappers) became the symbol for ecologists' argument that preserving the environment and making a living were compatible. However, these activists threatened big economic interests. The UDR, formed in 1985 by large landowners to stop agrarian reform, turned to violence, paying assassins to kill peasant leaders, church workers, and human rights advocates. The UDR was reputed to be behind the assassination of Mendes and other activists. Mendes was the sixth seringueiro killed in the town of Xapuri in 1988.[60]

As the ecology movement took hold, it penetrated official political structures. Several environmentalists were elected to the federal parliament, a national Green party was formed, local politicians became identified as ecologists, and more than 1,500 small environmental groups formed.[61] One significant development for the ecology movement was the quick evolution of the PT into a national party. By tapping into grass-roots organizations and through ties to the Green party, PT became an important conduit for national articulation on environmental concerns. Local PT politicians were involved as well since ecology tied into social and economic issues for certain local have-not groups. The PT, through its ties to the CUT, had supported the Mendes movement. Environmental concerns were reflected in street art since both the PT and the CUT employed it as a visible means to create public awareness and establish identity.

The attention placed on ecology was exemplified in the national media. Stimulus stemmed from media coverage of two events: pressure from United States' environmentalist groups that the country not support loans to Brazil unless reforms were taken to protect the Amazon and the assassination of Mendes who had links to the international environmental community. Thus, the international community had an impact on Brazilian consciousness. The pressure touched a national nerve, creating controversy, political discourse, and in the process a new awareness. The national weeklies *Senhor* and *Veja* began to regularly cover environmental issues. In 1989, there was a quantum leap from their 1988 coverage. *Veja,* for example, had a weekly section on ecology during 1989. The January 18, 1989, issue of *Senhor* featured as its cover story, "The Amazon of Chico Mendes" along with a cover page collage of various posters on agrarian reform and the Amazon. *Veja's* February 1, 1989, cover story focused on the overall ecological problems. Both *Senhor* and *Veja* covered various ecology demonstrations beginning with the 1986 demonstration billed as the first large ecology mobilization with 5,000 participants. The result in ecological consciousness was that President Collor appointed a leading environmentalist, José Lutzenberger to serve as secretary of environment. The goal was to stop Amazon burning. In addition, José Goldemberg, an outspoken critic of Brazil's nuclear program, was appointed secretary of science and technology.

In addition to graffiti, posters, and some murals, T-shirts and lapel buttons became visual supplements to popularize issues. T-shirts and lapel buttons not only identified the individual with the issue but also served as a means of generating revenues for groups and parties. Until 1987, most T-shirts supported a particular candidate. However, by 1988–1989 many were issue-oriented. In Rio, issue T-shirts were hawked by groups in Plaza Floriano (Cinelandia), a major pedestrian street in downtown Rio where political activists congregate and sponsor events. Various ecology T-shirts carried these messages: "Remember nature," "The Amazon is ours—those who hesitate, kill it," "The earth is our own—to defend it is to defend life," "Mineral exploitation can destroy the richest generating spring on the planet—preserve the Amazon," and "Progress with preservation—No devastation: the progress of extinction." This T-shirt pictured the devastation caused by burning. Lapel buttons were also popular and carried ecology messages, "For the defense of ecology," and "Green, I want you Green."

Human Rights and Violence

Another major social issue was human rights and violence which had a different intensity in Brazil than in neighboring countries. The results of state violence and human rights abuses in Brazil under the military never reached the same level nor conjured the emotional impact as in Chile, Uruguay, and Argentina. During the military regime, the São Paulo archdiocese became the country's consciousness. Members protested, chronicled abuses by the security forces, and published the results in a report titled *Nunca Mais*. It became a national best seller.[62] However, no strong, grass-roots human rights movement emerged to hold the military responsible as occurred in neighboring countries. Some street art, especially graffiti, reflected on the issue; for instance, "Torture—never again." For the most part, however, protests during the postmilitary era focused on the ongoing systemic repression and violence in society as a whole, not past military abuses. These concerns included violence in rural areas by organized landed elites carrying out selected assassinations against leaders and peasants pressing for agrarian reform; violence against organized labor pressing its demands; and urban violence by death squads and security forces against poor slum dwellers and street children. These immediate systemic problems touched the lives of millions. Grass-roots groups formed to channel these sentiments.

For example, the Movement of Rural Workers Without Land held sit-in demonstrations in public places to focus attention on rural violence and agrarian reform. Demands for reform accompanied the public sit-ins. Posters communicated their concerns. In 1986 in Rio, two posters with elaborate commentary spelled out the problem. Both posters had white backgrounds so written messages were clearly visible. The only adornment on the poster was the Christian cross, drawn diagonally and outlined in red. The poster stated that the Movement of Rural Workers Without Land, CUT, the Pastoral Commission, and other organizations wished to inform the public that "From March 15, 1985, to May 1986, since the installation of the new republic, the following people had been assassinated in rural areas: "two priests and two nuns, 13 rural unionists, 183 rural workers, and 17 Indians. The sacrifice of these martyrs was the result of latifundia and the decision by the government not to carry out true agrarian reform. Up to the present, there has been no prosecution of the assassins or the latifundist's bosses." The second poster sponsored by the Rural Workers Without Land listed the seven main objectives, and the ten specific points the movement wanted. These included, "legalizing land invasions, fixing the maximum size of acreage for rural estates, expropriating land from the latifundists, appropriating land from the multinationals, designating Indian reservations, prosecuting those responsible for violence against rural workers, ending government subsidies that help estate owners, and changing agricultural policy to give priority to the small producer."

The Confederação dos Trabalhadores de Agricultura (CONTAG), which organized agriculture workers, demanded agrarian reform. They pushed the issue with an aggressively designed poster. The poster showed a worker with his arms raised yelling out the message, "Agrarian reform now."[63] Some politicians took up the issue. In 1986, the PT candidate for state deputy in Rio, Sergio Murillo, campaigned charging that "Government police kill peasants." This was in reference to a widespread belief that police were linked to UDR landowners. However, the assassination of Chico Mendes touched the consciousness of Brazilians and the world and focused attention on rural violence perpetuated by the UDR. Posters and graffiti kept the issue visible. "Remember Mendes'' graffiti popped up, cries for "Agrarian reform" intensified, and the peace dove became a symbol recalling that Brazil was a country besieged by violence. To counter this image, the UDR held its own rallies in the interior. Horsemen paraded through the streets carrying hand-painted banners with information about what the latifundists produced each year.

One of the most visual, media-intense events on the question of military and police repression was the Volta Redondo martyrdom of three workers on November 9, 1988. This event generated a great deal of traditional media and street art commentary, especially in the Rio-São Paulo industrial belt. It exemplified the linkage between the military-industrial complex and the hostility of the military toward workers and strikes.[64] Volta Redondo, located one hundred miles southwest of Rio, is home of the National Steel Company. A strike, called by the union, was crushed when the military intervened, calling the steel mill a place of national security. The death of three young steel workers resulted and the labor movement had its martyrs. This helped to accentuate the workers' strong antigovernment, anti-Sarney sentiments, and underscore the continued policy of military repression against the working class.[65] The Community Group Against Violence placed a huge banner in the city that read, "We Will Not Construct Peace With Violence." It was featured in the *Senhor* article on Volta Redondo.[66] Graffiti was commonly invoked to honor the fallen workers. A November 9 Memorial was built in Volta Redondo to permanently commemorate the martyrdom; the memorial was designed by internationally acclaimed architect Oscar Neimeyer. Nine hours after the dedication, it was destroyed by a sophisticated bomb. The finger pointed to the military. *Senhor* highlighted its report on the destruction of the memorial in a cover page story that carried a photo of the destroyed monument with large-scale graffiti scrawled on the broken memorial base accusing the deed to the "Work of President Sarney."[67] The monument was rebuilt. On the first anniversary, CUT sponsored a poster that commemorated the event with the statement, "1st anniversary of Volta Redondo—a commitment to the struggle—the November 9 Memorial—William, Valmir, Barroso." This poster was distributed in Rio, São Paulo, and adjoining points.

In the late 1980s in Recife, human rights concerns expressed in street art addressed another topic, the problem of the street children and the systemic violence against them. Brazil has the most severe problem of abandoned children anywhere in the hemisphere. Some estimates reach 10 million, with millions of other children living in a state of critical need.[68] In Recife, according to Amnesty International, death squads are thought to have killed 1,000 street children over a five-year period. A campaign of awareness and compassion for the abandoned children was initiated in Recife and communicated through extensive graffiti. This prolific, inescapable graffiti cried out for public concern. Various themes informed the public, "Don't kill my children," or "Don't kill my children—who is responsible?" and "Don't kill my children our voice will not be muffled—we are those children you created and pushed out," or the rhetorical question, "Why do you smother our cry?—We are those children who spend 365 days a year, *Jogadas na Rua* (homeless)." Other graffiti reflected the dilemma of thousands of street girls pushed into prostitution, "Just in Recife alone there are 11,000 girl prostitutes between the ages of eleven and seventeen." Some statements were unsigned, other were signed *Jogadas na Rua*, (the street people or the homeless.) These graffiti reflected the grass-roots effort of street children with the organizing support of the Catholic Church.[69] In an attempt to protect themselves and their rights, the street children formed the National Movement of Street Children in 1985. They held national meetings and forums to advocate programs and rights for the street children. The movement, headquartered in Recife, held its second congress in Brasilia in 1989 with 1,000 delegates.[70]

The issue of the human rights problems besieging Brazil had various dimensions and cannot be limited to the martyrdom of Chico Mendes, Volta Redondo workers, or the violence surrounding the street children. The concern was often reflected in simple, unsigned graffiti, "Down with repression," or "End violence." Peace became a symbol for various politicians and groups. At times, it surfaced in street art. For instance, in Gabeira's gubernatorial campaign in Rio the graffito, "No to violence," referred to the worsening chronic violence and street crime in Rio. National weeklies, such as *Veja*, highlighted the problem in cover stories. Basically, Brazil was not at peace with itself; institutionalized violence was endemic.

Marginalized Groups

Other groups and issues tried to penetrate public consciousness. Some found direct expression through street art. The black movement, small, with limited financial resources, generated some street art. When South Africa gained international attention in the mid-1980s, it excited interest in Rio that found expression through murals. A series of ten to fifteen murals were placed along the walls of the entrance to the Botafogo subway station. The surrounding area was renamed Nelson Mandela Plaza. The stimulus came from the state of emergency declared by the South African government to put down the black rebellion. By 1989, these murals had weathered away and not been replaced, although there were large graffiti, "ANC—for a united and strong Africa," and "Free Nelson Mandela," signed by the ANC (African National Congress). Posters also advertised meetings and the commemorating of special events. Two particular events, November 20, Black Consciousness Day, and May 28, Abolition Day, generated posters to increase public awareness. Posters celebrated May 1988, the centennial of Brazilian abolition. For Black Consciousness Day in 1989, the black movement in Rio produced a simple black and white poster showing a pair of hands breaking a barbed-wire fence with the statement, "Zumbi—Quilombo is democracy—November 20, National Day of

Black Consciousness." There was an announcement of the time and place to commemorate the event.

In the state of Pernambuco, with more than twenty black organizations, many commemorative posters were produced over the years. Annually, posters announced the pilgrimage to Palmares and the Zumbi memorial in the Serra da Barriga mountains, a symbol of black resistance to slavery. Palmares was the most famous *Quilombo,* or black colony for run-away slaves. Other black movement posters advertised the "First State Meeting of Black Women" in Rio, the "1st national meeting of Black women," "Blacks in Portuguese Literature," "Black Art in Pernambuco," and the "Independent Black Movement—Debate Forum—August 1989—São Paulo."[71] In addition, there were ethnic buttons and T-shirts; one proclaimed, "Justice for the Black Race," while another read "Black Women."

In São Paulo, Armenians made their issues visible. Their street art was limited mainly to their particular neighborhood, designated by the subway stop, Armenia. One group was responsible, the Grupo Armenio Suicioa (GAS). This radical group painted the neighborhood with pro-Armenian graffiti proclaiming international recognition of Armenian grievances. In 1989, these graffiti read: "Armenia is for the Armenians," "Armenia is a Country," "Armenians in a struggle for a Free Armenia," "Armenia Lives," "GAS—Grupo Armenio Suicioa," and "Turks are Assassins." Gender issues had marginal visibility as well. In the southern city of Curitiba, gender murals planned by the municipal council on "The Condition of Women in 1986–87" focused on women in Brazilian society. They were designed to have a certain permanency. The stimulus came from the democratic era and the rewriting of the Brazilian constitution. The murals were commissioned to call attention to women's problems and to increase consciousness for debate about their rights under the new constitution. They depicted themes of violence, health, work, and education from the women's point of view.[72] Elections also generated gender visibility. The PT had a series of gender T-shirts. They were simple, "Much pleasure—women of PT" and a male version with almost the same wording, "The pleasure is ours—men of PT." Other gender T-shirts called "For a Brazil of free and equal men and women—PT women against discrimination" a more complex one, "Women, organize yourself and fight—with your new 'jeito' of becoming a WOMAN—you will generate a just and fraternal society." The T-shirt was embellished with painted figures of three women on a horizon, one holding a child, another stating, "Look how the dude eats, if you run away the dude will catch you; if you create a union, the dude will flee." Lastly, there was a general theme T-shirt under the heading, "From the clamor of the oppressed, a new hope is born," with women as one of the oppressed groups under the slogan, "Women are present in the fight." Presidential candidate Covas of the PSDB had a COVAS sticker with the O drawn into the international feminist logo, and there was the campaign sticker, a "Women's voice in the Senate."

ECONOMIC ISSUES

Economic issues were a contentious dimension of the national debate. Since the late 1960s, many spoke about the economic miracle. The country advanced from an economy based primarily on coffee exports to one balanced between heavy industry and agriculture. Brazil has the world's tenth largest economy, but an economic order burdened with the Third World's highest international debt, endemic inflation, inadequate educational and health care systems, and unequal distribution of wealth. More than 30 percent of the workers earn less than minimum wage, and millions more earn minimum wage. This distorted system made economics a volatile issue.[73]

Part of the normalization process was the reformulation of organized labor. During the military era, strikes by workers were illegal and repression made it difficult for workers to organize. Slowly, an independent trade union movement emerged. However, it took time to establish grass-roots organizations, enlist workers and establish funds. In general, labor unions, groups and political parties, which revolved around the working class, have been major producers of street art as a means of articulating their demands and raising issues. The labor movement was split between two large competing confederations, both recently formed. CUT founded in 1983 with some 5,000 unions, was linked to the PT; it was militant and confrontational. The Central Geral dos Trabalhadores (CGT), founded in 1986, contained Latin America's largest union, the São Paulo metalworkers; it was less militant, more prosystem, and tagged with being the collaboratist sector, or the *pelegos*. In 1989, CGT supported the presidential candidacy of Collor, while CUT backed Lula. CUT, in contrast to CGT, actively lobbied, demanded, informed, and presented their agenda via street art. The CGT was a marginal participant in street art communication.

As a relatively new organization, CUT did not have the infrastructure nor resources to communicate massively via street art like the powerful and financially secure Argentine CGT could. Given their organizational and financial limitations, CUT and the more militant unions were aggressive in placing posters and graffiti that articulated issues in defense of workers' economic rights. Artistically, their posters and wallpaintings were unsophisticated when compared to Argentine or Spanish labor. In Brazil, union posters and graffiti were selectively placed around the sites of strikes and areas where workers concentrate, and generally oriented toward the working-class clientele. They could not mount the massive distribution as in Argentina, where the unions through the Argentine CGT aimed to impact the general public. Only preceding general strikes when massive graffiti announced the strike, was there widespread national placement of street art.

In an attempt to stem endemic inflation, periodically President Sarney initiated a series of plans or *pacotes* (packages), these became known as the Cruzado Plan, Cruzado Plan II, the Bresser Plan, and the Summer Plan. Only the first, Cruzado Plan, was popular with the masses. It redistributed income to lower-income wage earners by raising minimum wages and freezing prices. With this plan, Sarney became popular overnight. The Cruzado Plan and Sarney received overwhelming positive support that found expression in street art. Under the Cruzado Plan, people became participants by enforcing the control of prices, anointing them *fiscales* (inspectors). Some businesses responded by placing posters in their windows saying people were welcome to check and compare prices. The most common graffiti and lapel buttons were, "I am a 'fiscal' for the government," or "I am a 'fiscal' of Sarney." Sarney's PMDB rode this popularity to a widespread victory in November 1986. There were opponents. Rio governor Brizola spoke out against the plan. Graffiti stated, "No to the Cruzado Plan."

A common sight were posters plastered across bank facades calling attention to the conflict between labor and management. As the Cruzado Plan adversely affected the banking industry, leading to layoffs, graffiti and CUT posters repudiated the action. CUT protested bank layoffs and requested shorter working hours to accommodate dismissed workers. One CUT poster read, "Terror at Itaú," so categorizing the layoffs at Itáu bank. Other posters had the slogan, "bank workers in struggle," some named the bank, listed the number of laid-off workers, and the bank's assets, and another announced a "National campaign against unjust layoffs." Graffiti were used to support the bank workers and to attack the Cruzado Plan. A common CUT graffito slogan was, *Abaixo* (down with) *o pacotão.*" There were anti-Sarney graffiti and CUT posters announcing, "Out with Sarney." After the November 1986 elections, when the Cruzado Plan was superceded by the extremely unpopular Cruzado II plan and followed by other noneffective and irritating packages, Sarney's popularity along with the PMDB plummeted. Each economic adjustment was greeted by attempts at a general strike called by the CUT. This generated much graffiti. Some graffiti referred to the particular plan by name, "Sarney out—down with the Cruzado Plan," "Out with Cruzado II," "No to the Summer 'Pacote,' " "The Summer Plan is cold—general strike—PC do B," or the slogans simply stating, "Down with the 'pacotao,' 'pacote,' or 'pacotes'," or "Everyone join against the 'pacotes'." Beginning with the Cruzado Plan II, CUT initiated general strikes as a way of protest and to reclaim salary adjustments. Graffiti announced each of the three general strikes: the December 12, 1986, strike against Cruzado II; the August 20, 1987, strike against the Plan Bresser; and the March 14–15, 1989, strike, the first general strike jointly sponsored by CUT and CGT. The first two general strikes were judged failures and seen as symptomatic of labor's weakness. The March 1989 strike was viewed as a success because greater numbers met the call.[74] Labor-sponsored graffiti that announced the general strikes, supported by the small communist parties, reached nationwide portions. Much was quite simple, "General Strike—12/12," "General Strike 12/12 in defense of salaries," "General Strike—CUT/CSC," "General Strike—

3/14 and 15," "General Strike—against Sarney, CUT," and "Day 12 the banks will stop—Bank workers Union of Rio."

In addition, graffiti and posters commonly accompanied the multitude of ordinary strikes and the variety of claims concerning inflation, salary increases, privatization, and protection of state enterprises. A 1983 poster sponsored by National Secretariat of State Employees Workers showed an outlined profile of Brazil formed from small Brazilian flags to emphasize a nationalistic sentiment with the statement, "Raise this flag for independence against the IMF, defend the state enterprises." Another poster on the same theme read, "Telecommunications are ours, join in the struggle, no to privatization." A strike poster in 1987 read, "Professors on strike—end low salaries"; these posters were selectively placed around the schools. An artistically drawn poster featured angry, militant bank workers with a list of demands, "Stability—end layoffs, a just reinstatement, real salary increases, end of free work." A poster depicting a crowd with the statement, "The bank workers express to the population their gratitude for your support." Stickers said, "Salary restoration—150 percent—ASFOC." And a poster, "An intransigent Banker—the strike will return." Generalized graffiti read, "Stop price increases," "Real salary increase—CUT," "Struggle against this abuse—40 percent increase," and "In struggle and in choice—worker against owner—Socialist Convergence—P1." Other examples of labor-economics clash were a 1986 Niteroi steelworker's poster supporting a particular voting *chapa* (list), "Vote Chapa 2—stability of work—1986," the poster pictured the boss giving a strong kick to a hard hat worker, symbolic of layoffs. A large poster in the form of an open letter informed the public about Gama Filho University's decision to close its hospital and lay off the staff. Thus, questions on privatization, layoffs, stability of employment, and salary increases to meet the high inflation were all areas of concern articulated in the political art.

NOTES

1. See Frances Hagopian, " 'Democracy by Undemocratic Means?' Elites, Political Pacts, and Regime Transition in Brazil," *Comparative Political Studies* 23:2 (July 1990).

2. *Nosso Século: Brazil 1900–1960* (São Paulo: Editorial Nova Cultural, 1980). The material for the historical section comes mainly from two sources. For the 1930s, 1940s, and 1950s the material comes from *Nosso Século: Brazil 1900–1960,* a historical series of archival materials and photos. The discussion of the early 1960s comes from primary observation during 1961–1962.

3. Ibid.

4. Ibid.

5. Ibid.

6. Notes from the author's primary observation in 1961–1962.

7. See *Brazil, The New Militancy: Trade Unions and Transnational Corporations.* Tie Report 17 (Amsterdam: Transnationals Informational Exchange, 1984).

8. Thomas Skidmore, *The Politics of Military Rule in Brazil, 1964–1985* (New York: Oxford University Press, 1988), pp. 111–12.

9. See Peter Evans, "Three Views of Regime Change and Party Organization in Brazil: An Introduction," *Politics and Society* 15:1 (Fall 1986).

10. See Teresa P. R. Caldeira, "Electoral Struggles in a Neighborhood on the Periphery of São Paulo," *Politics and Society* 15:1 (Fall 1986).

11. See Kurt von Mettenheim, "The Brazilian Voter in Democratic Transition, 1974–1982," *Comparative Politics* 23:1 (October 1990), p. 26.

12. See Caldeira, "Electoral Struggles."

13. *Latin America Weekly Report,* July 27, 1989.

14. *Jornal do Brasil,* July 20, 1986; and *Veja,* July 23, 1986.

15. See Evans, "Three Views."

16. Skidmore, *The Politics of Military Rule,* p. 219.

17. See David Fleischer, "Brazil at the Crossroads: The Elections of 1982 and 1985," in *Elections and Democratization in Latin America, 1980–85,* Paul W. Drake and Eduardo Silva, eds., (San Diego: University of California, Center for Iberian and Latin American Studies, 1986).

18. Hagopian, "Electoral Struggles," p. 159.

19. See Glaucio Ary Dillon Soares, "Elections and Redemocratization of Brazil," in *Elections and Democratization in Latin America, 1980–85,* Paul W. Drake and Eduardo Silva, ed., (San Diego: University of California, Center for Iberian and Latin American Studies, 1986).

20. *Veja,* November 11, 1989, puts the figure at 5.3 million.

21. See Soares, "Elections and Redemocratization."

22. Skidmore, *The Politics of Military Rule,* p. 251.

23. See Fleischer, "Brazil at the Crossroads."

24. *Veja,* November 15, 1989.

25. Ibid.

26. *Veja,* August 30, 1989.

27. *Veja,* November 15, 1989.

28. See *Jornal do Brasil,* November 18–20, 1989; and *Veja,* November 15, 1989.

29. See Hagopian, "Electoral Struggles."

30. *Latinamerica Press,* February 1, 1990.

31. *Jornal do Brasil,* November 20, 1989.

32. Ibid.

33. Skidmore, *The Politics of Military Rule,* pp. 220–21.

34. See Evans, "Three Views."

35. *Veja,* April 12, 1989, pp. 40–41.

36. See Margaret E. Keck, "Democratization and Dissension: The Formation of the Workers' Party," *Politics and Society* 15:1 (Fall 1986).

37. *Senhor,* January 4, 1989.

38. *Latinamerica Press,* June 28, 1990.

39. *Veja,* November 15, 1989.

40. von Mettenheim, *The Brazilian Voter,* p. 25.

41. *Latin America Weekly Report,* June 29, 1989.

42. *Jornal do Brasil,* November 21, 1989.

43. *Veja,* February 8, 1989.

44. Skidmore, *The Politics of Military Rule,* pp. 220–21.

45. *Latin America Weekly Report,* May 3, 1985.

46. See Hagopian, "Electoral Struggles."

47. Skidmore, *The Politics of Military Rule,* pp. 219–22.

48. See Hagopian, "Electoral Struggles."

49. See Scott Mainwaring, "Democratization in Brazil," *Comparative Politics,* 19:2 (July 1987).

50. See Markoff and Baretta, "Economic Crisis."

51. Hagopian, "Electoral Struggles," p. 162.

52. Skidmore, *The Politics of Military Rule,* pp. 117–23.

53. See Zuenir Ventura, *1968: O Ano Que Não Terminou* (Rio de Janeiro: Nova Fronteira, 1988); and *Veja,* October 19, 1988.

54. See Caldeira, "Electoral Struggles."

55. See Scott Mainwaring and Eduardo Viola, "New Social Movements, Political Culture, and Democracy: Brazil and Argentina in the 1980s," *Telos* (Fall 1984), and Hagopian, "Electoral Struggles."

56. See von Mettenheim, *The Brazilian Voter.*

57. See for example *Latinamerica Press,* June 14, 1990. The military's Superior War College issued a policy document in May 1990 attacking ecologists for stifling development and the economic potential of the Amazon basin.

58. *Veja,* February 10, 1988.

59. *Latinamerica Press,* September 28, 1989.

60. *Senhor,* January 18, 1989.

61. *Latinamerica Press,* September 28, 1989.

62. *Brasil: Nunca Mais* (Vozes: Petropolis, 1985).

63. *Jornal do Brasil,* June 12, 1987.

64. Skidmore, *The Politics of Military Rule,* p. 295.

65. *Veja,* December 7, 1988.

66. *Senhor,* June 14, 1989.

67. *Senhor,* May 10, 1989.

68. *El País,* September 7, 1988; the paper placed the figure at 35 million.

69. *Latinamerica Press,* April 5, 1990.

70. *Latinamerica Press,* November 23, 1989.

71. These posters were in a special exhibition in Recife, November 20, 1989.

72. *Jornal do Brasil,* June 3, 1987.

73. *Latinamerica Press,* February 1, 1990.

74. *Latin America Weekly Report,* March 9, 1989.

7

Conclusion: Explaining Street Art's Continued Utility

As we have seen in this study, despite today's emphasis on the high-technology electronic information revolution, in some countries individuals, collectives, and the state continue to preserve street art as a popular tool of communication. Why? What explains the tradition and culture of street art as political expression?

First, the cultural-historical factor. Street art is a time-honored form of expression. Societies have communicated their ideas visually in public places since the time of cave dwellers. In the Middle Ages, visual images were a vital means of expression. Painting played a part in public discourse, serving as a social conscience, recording history and customs, becoming a social commentator, generating symbols, telling people what to worship and fear, and touching on the full gamut of human emotions. In the late-1400s, bill posting was a common practice in Europe. Bill posters appeared in city squares, on the sides of churches and on public buildings. For example, Martin Luther nailed his protest to a church door, the accepted way to make a public statement. People began to air their grievances and protests publicly through bill posters in designated locations such as at St. Paul's Cathedral in London. The modern equivalent would be the famous, short-lived Democratic Walls in China in 1979.[1]

In the twentieth century, as society became more organized and politicized, and greater numbers of groups sought expressive outlets, people continued to turn to low-technology mass communication. In the Latin world, as seen in the case studies, politicized street art is a popular tool that varies in intensity from country to country. Widespread street art in the Middle East recorded the Intifada. In South Africa, symbols of street art—posters, banners, T-shirts, graffiti, and buttons—received international attention as a form of black resistance to white domination. Street art has been utilized in Mozambique, Angola, and

Eritrea, as well. In the Philippines and South Korea, the democratic "people's power" movement and antigovernment student protests had their public art component. Protest graffiti were employed by the Canucks in New Caledonia in their rebellion against French settlers during the mid-1980s.[2] The changes brought by glasnost and perestroika in the Eastern Bloc and Soviet Union were accompanied by new political expressions, actualized by an explosion of posters, banners, graffiti and wallpaintings produced by alternative grass-roots social movements to the dominant Communist powers. In Western Europe, street art has been widely employed in the Northern Ireland conflict, in the Basque resistance, and was institutionalized through the largest collective mural in the world on the renowned Berlin Wall, the detested symbol to a divided Europe. And in Greece, Italy, Portugal, and Spain, street art for protest, for electoral campaigning, for political space of new and old social groups, is a widely held communication form.

Second, the circumstantial factor. Street art as mass communication is influenced by the sociopolitical circumstances of each nation in any given period. This encompasses the nature of the political system, the level of social conflict, the degree of societal organization, the phenomenon of mobilization and political consciousness, and the type of political regime. Street art is particularly visual in countries and regions and in eras experiencing intense sociopolitical conflict for street art is linked to and reflects dissension.[3] Decreasing tensions and increasing consensus should lead to a reduction in street art. This seems to be the trend in three of the cases in this study, Spain, Euskadi, and Argentina. As the democratic transition process stabilizes and works itself through, tensions lessen as does street art.

Third, the credibility factor. In some nations low-technology modes of communication may enjoy a high level of respect and credibility. The high-techology system often lacks credibility because it is controlled by the state and dominant elite. This was seen in the former Socialist bloc. Low-techology media serves as a countervailing force, independent of state control.[4] It can be utilized to record a different historical memory than provided by the dominant elite, serving the resistance and various subcultures by imparting alternative visions.

Fourth, the inaccessibility factor. Closed, nonpluralistic societies are inaccessible to the nondominant elite. However, even in open societies, electronic and print media can be inaccessible, either for financial or political reasons. Politically, for example, groups with financial resources may not be able to present their views via purchased advertisements because of powerful interests that control access. In the United States, there is a long history of the networks refusing to accept certain advertisements for fear they will lose major advertisers. Major networks such as CBS and ABC do not accept "issue ads." The same is true with many print media empires. Thus, even issue groups that have finances face political obstacles.[5] Furthermore, in some countries, whether in democratic, authoritarian, or one-party states, growing media monopolies can effectively exclude opposition opinion.[6] The government often owns major newspapers, magazines, wire services, and radio and television networks. If marginal and mainstream political parties do not have access to electronic media, and if major newspapers refuse issue ads, it becomes extremely difficult to penetrate these media and gain exposure for messages. Therefore, alternative groups rely on their own limited publications—leaflets, street art, demonstrations, and other forms of communication and protest.

Fifth, the affordability factor. Street art, unlike other communication media, takes few financial resources, except with massive production of posters. Less financially able groups and parties can rely more on graffiti and wallpainting, while those more established and financially able can generate the more costly posters. Street art does not face the financial crisis of other media which may need a sound financial backing to maintain itself over a long period of time. Some alternative media die for financial reasons. Street art dies from lack of commitment and cadre. Generally speaking, volunteers provide the muscle for placing street art. In Euskadi where murals have been significant, and Argentina with wallpainting, organized brigades assume the responsibility for producing and placing the product. Poster placement has a well structured system. The placement of posters usually takes place in the late evening when the city is quiet, unencumbered by traffic or the vigilance of building managers and security forces. Posters are distributed to crews usually consisting of two or more individuals. It is their job to paste them before the city awakens at dawn. The crews travel by bicycle, pull a cart, walk, or carry the posters in trucks. With stacks of posters, a huge bucket of liquid paste, and a large round-shaped paint brush, one person quickly splashes the paste on the wall or building facade, another follows with the poster, pressing it against the moistened siding where it becomes a visual fixture. In many cases, when possible, ten to twenty posters are affixed side by side, one row over another, evoking the billboard effect. This visual layout proceeds block by block in the most heavily traveled avenues and targeted sections of the city. The visual impact the next morning is unavoidable. The multiple poster placement is designed to attract public attention through repetitiveness.

Sixth, the effects factor. Media in general and street art in particular, elicit certain emotions. Posters, murals, graffiti, or wallpaintings can be inflammatory just as speech, pamphlets, leaflets, or other visual symbols. Like music, cinema, and other media, street art can arouse base emotions in their audiences, and can increase the climate of tension. This is its appeal to the producer. As with any communication medium, response revolves around the question of selective perception and selective inattention, the way people see what they want to see, or do not see what they do not wish to see.

NOTES

1. Sally Henderson and Robert Landau, *Billboard Art* (San Francisco: Chronicle Books, 1980), p. 9.

2. *El País,* September 13, 1987, and June 13, 1989.

3. See Bill Rolston, *Politics and Painting: Murals and Conflict in Northern Ireland* (London: Associated University Presses, 1991).

4. See René Jean Ravault, "International Information: Bullet or Boomerang?" in *Political Communication Research: Approaches, Studies, Assessments,* ed. David L. Paletz (Norwood, NJ: Ablex Publishing Corporation, 1987).

5. See for example, *Los Angeles Times,* October 10, 1990. A paid commercial ad by the Committee in Solidarity with the People of El Salvador (CISPES) and other groups which took a stance against United States military aid to El Salvador was rejected by most networks.

6. See *Latinamerica Press,* October 18, 1990. Argentina is a case of a growing media monopoly, while in Brazil a glaring example is the domination of *O Globo* which is a multimedia network—radio, television, and print media.

Selected Bibliography

BOOKS AND ARTICLES

Ackelsberg, Martha. *Free Women of Spain: Anarchism and the Struggle for the Emancipation of Women*. Bloomington: Indiana University Press, 1991.

Barnett, Alan. *Community Murals: The People's Art*. New York: Cornwall Books, 1984.

Brooks, David. "More than Just a Mural: The Popular Memorial for Rodrigo Rojas de Negri and Carmen Gloria Quintana." *Studies in Latin American Popular Culture* 11 (1992).

Bushnell, John. *Moscow Graffiti: Language and Subculture*. Boston: Unwin Hyman, 1990.

Caldeira, Teresa P. R. "Electoral Struggles in a Neighborhood on the Periphery of São Paulo." *Politics and Society* 15:1 (1986–87).

Carr, Raymond. *The Spanish Civil War: A History in Pictures*. New York: W. W. Norton & Company, 1986.

Castleman, Craig. *Getting up: Subway Graffiti in New York*. Cambridge: MIT Press, 1982.

Chabalgoity, Ariel, Sengo Pérez, and Roger Rodríguez. *Chile: La Derrota del Miedo*. Buenos Aires: Puntosur Editores, 1988.

Chaffee, Lyman. "Political Graffiti and Wall Painting in Greater Buenos Aires: An Alternative Communication System." *Studies in Latin American Popular Culture* 8 (1989).

———. "The Popular Culture of Political Persuasion in Paraguay: Communication and Public Art." *Studies in Latin American Popular Culture* 9 (1990).

———. "Poster Art and Political Propaganda in Argentina." *Studies in Latin American Popular Culture* 5 (1986).

———. "Public Art and Political Propaganda: Argentine Protest, 1986." *Ibero Americana Nordic Journal of Latin American Studies* 18:2 (1988).

———. "Social Conflict and Alternative Mass Communication: Public Art and Politics in the Service of Spanish-Basque Nationalism.'' *European Journal of Political Research* 16 (1988).

Clark, Robert P. *The Basque Insurgents: ETA, 1952–1980.* Madison: University of Wisconsin Press, 1984.

Cockcroft, Eva, John Weber, and James Cockcroft. *Toward a People's Art: The Contemporary Mural Movement.* New York: E. P. Dutton and Co., 1977.

DeFleur, Melvin L., and Sandra Ball-Rokeach. *Theories of Mass Communication,* 5th ed. New York: Longman, 1989.

Departamento Cultural Vizcaina. *Expresion Mural.* Pais Vasco, Spain, 1986.

Deutsch, Sandra McGee. *Counter Revolution in Argentina, 1900–1932: The Argentine Patriotic League.* Lincoln: University of Nebraska Press, 1986.

Evans, Peter. ''Three Views of Regime Change and Party Organization in Brazil: An Introduction.'' *Politics and Society* 15:1 (1986–87).

Fleischer, David. ''Brazil at the Crossroads: The Elections of 1982 and 1985,'' in Paul W. Drake and Eduardo Silva, eds. *Elections and Democratization in Latin America, 1980–85.* Center for Iberian and Latin American Studies, San Diego: University of California, 1986.

Franco, Jean. *The Modern Culture of Latin America: Society and the Artist.* New York: Praeger, 1967.

Grieb, Kenneth. ''The Writing on the Walls: Graffiti as Government Propaganda in Mexico.'' *Journal of Popular Culture* 18 (1984).

Gunther, Richard, Giacomo Sani, and Goldie Shabad. *Spain After Franco: The Making of a Competitive Party System.* Berkeley: University of California Press, 1988.

Hagopian, Frances. '' 'Democracy by Undemocratic Means?' Elites, Political Pacts, and Regime Transition in Brazil.'' *Comparative Political Studies* 23 (July 1990).

Henderson, Sally, and Robert Landau. *Billboard Art.* San Francisco: Chronicle Books, 1980.

Jouet, Josiane. ''Review of Radical Communication Research: The Conceptual Limits,'' in Emile McAnany, et al., eds. *Communication and Social Structure.* New York: Praeger 1981.

Keen, Sam. *Faces of the Enemy: Reflections of the Hostile Imagination.* San Francisco: Harper & Row, 1986.

Kunzle, David. ''Art of the New Chile: Mural, Poster, and Comic Book in a Revolutionary Process,'' in H. Millon and L. Nochlin, eds. *Art and Architecture in the Service of Politics.* Cambridge: MIT Press, 1978.

———. ''Nationalist, Internationalist and Anti-Imperialist Themes in the Public Revolutionary Art of Cuba, Chile and Nicaragua.'' *Studies in Latin American Popular Culture* 3 (1984).

———. ''Public Graphics in Cuba.'' *Latin American Perspectives* 2 (1975).

LaDuke, Betty. *Companeras: Women, Art and Social Change in Latin America.* San Francisco: City Lights Books, 1985.

———. ''Nicaragua 1984: The Rifle and Paintbrush Coexist.'' *Journal of Popular Culture* 18 (Fall 1984).

Mainwaring, Scott, and Eduardo Viola. ''New Social Movements, Political Culture, and Democracy: Brazil and Argentina in the 1980s.'' *Telos* 61 (Fall 1984).

Mattelart, Armand, ed. *Communicating in Popular Nicaragua.* New York: International General, 1986.

Mattelart, Armand, and Seth Siegelaub, eds. *Communication and Class Struggle: Vol. 1, Capitalism, Imperialism*. New York: International General, 1979.
―――. *Communication and Class Struggle: Vol. 2, Liberation, Socialism*. New York: International General, 1983.
Navarro, Marysa. "The Personal Is Political: Las Madres de Plaza de Mayo," in Susan Eckstein, ed. *Power and Popular Protest: Latin American Social Movements*. Berkeley: University of California Press, 1989.
Payne, Stanley. *The Franco Regime, 1936–1975*. Madison: University of Wisconsin Press, 1987.
Philippe, Robert. *Political Graphics: Art as a Weapon*. New York: Abbeville Press, 1982.
Posener, Jill. *Spray It Loud*. London: Routledge & Kegan Paul, 1982.
Rock, David. *Argentina 1516–1982: From Spanish Colonization to the Falklands War*. Berkeley: University of California Press, 1985.
Rolston, Bill. *Politics and Painting: Murals and Conflict in Northern Ireland*. London: Associated University Presses, 1991.
―――. "Politics, Painting and Popular Culture: the Political Wall Murals of Northern Ireland." *Media, Culture and Society* 9 (1987).
Schrader, Bärbel, and Jürgen Schebera. *The "Golden" Twenties: Art and Literature in the Weimar Republic*. New Haven: Yale University Press, 1990.
Sheesley, Joel, and Wayne Bragg. *Sandino in the Streets*. Bloomington: Indiana University Press, 1991.
Simpson, Eve. "Chicano Street Murals: A Sociological Perspective." *Journal of Popular Culture* 13 (Winter 1979).
Skidmore, Thomas. *The Politics of Military Rule in Brazil, 1964–1985*. New York: Oxford University Press, 1988.
Smith, Anthony. "Mass Communication, Democracy at the Polls," in David Butler, et al., eds. *Democracy at the Polls*. Washington, D.C.: American Enterprise Institute, 1981.
Soares, Glaucio Ary Dillon, "Elections and Redemocratization of Brazil," in Paul W. Drake and Eduardo Silva, eds. *Elections and Democratization in Latin America, 1980–85*. San Diego: University of California, Center for Iberian and Latin American Studies, 1986.
Sommer, Robert. *Street Art*. New York: Links Books, 1975.
Sullivan, John. *El Nacionalismo Vasco Radical 1959–1986*. Madrid: Alianza Universidad, 1988.
Tillman, Terry. *The Writings on the Wall: Peace at the Berlin Wall*. Santa Monica, CA: 22/7 Publishing Company, 1990.
von Mettenheim, Kurt. "The Brazilian Voter in Democratic Transition, 1974–1982." *Comparative Politics* 23 (October 1990).
Weill, Alain. *The Poster: A Worldwide Survey and History*. Boston: G. K. Hall, 1985.
Zirakzadeh, Cyrus Ernesto. *A Rebellious People: Basques, Protests, and Politics*. Reno: University of Nevada, 1991.
Zulaika, Joseba. *Basque Violence: Metaphor and Sacrament*. Reno: University of Nevada Press, 1984.

ADDITIONAL SOURCE MATERIALS: INTERNATIONAL NEWSPAPERS AND NEWSMAGAZINES

ABC (Spain)
Boogie (Spain)
Buenos Aires Herald (Argentina)
Cambio 16 (Spain)
Clarín (Argentina)
Diario 16 (Spain)
La Epoca (Chile)
El Globo (Spain)
International Herald Tribune (Paris)
Jornal do Brasil (Brazil)
Latin American Weekly Report (London)
Latinamerica Press (Peru)
La Nación (Argentina)
Nuestro Tiempo Argentino (Argentina)
El País (Spain)
El Periodista (Argentina)
Senhor (Brazil)
Tiempo (Spain)
Todo es Historia (Argentina)
Veja (Brazil)

Index

About the Author

LYMAN G. CHAFFEE, Professor and Chair of the Department of Political Science, California State University at Dominguez Hills, specializes in comparative politics and popular culture. He has written at length on street art and political propaganda.